Contents

Acknowledgments

I would like to thank the many people who have helped in the preparation of this anthology, particularly the contributors who have consented to the appearance of edited versions of their articles, and those who have written specially commissioned pieces. Thanks also to Roma Gibson and to the staff of the British Film Institute Library.

Stills are courtesy of David A. Bailey, B B C Hulton Picture Library, Film and History Project, Filmverlag der Autoren (Munich) and New Yorker Films (New York), Lovable, M G M / U A Entertainment Company, National Film Archive, National Film Board of Canada, Nikor Film Industries, Salkind-Artistry Ltd. for Cantharus, Sheffield Film Co-op, Sigma Films, Warner Bros., Claudia Weill, Whiteway Publications Ltd., Winwood Company.

General Introduction

CHARLOTTE BRUNSDON

WITHIN commercial film production there have always been movies made specially for female audiences, often showcasing women's fashion and featuring 'women's stars'. While boys and men had action movies, thrillers, war films and westerns, women got romances, 'weepies' and melodramas. These films for women were usually stories of love, loss, longing and sacrifice. Since the revival of a Western feminist movement in the late 1960s, there have been important shifts and extensions in how films are made for women, who makes them, and where and how we see them. While the declining movie industry has increasingly 'targeted' specific audiences, and has located the commercial potential of a new female consumer, the Women's Movement itself has started to produce its own films. Often made in collectives, usually with unpaid labour, these films have rarely received theatrical exhibition outside subsidised venues, many remaining restricted to the community centres, halls and committee rooms where women meet. The extreme diversity of the films made for and by women reflects differing cultural and political priorities – and continuing debates.

This book brings together a range of articles on films made in Europe and North America since the emergence of the 'new feminism'. I was commissioned to edit a retrospective collection of articles which discussed films, rather than theories of women and representation. Although no criticism is without theoretical presuppositions, however obvious and natural they may appear, most of the articles in this book do concentrate on one or two films. The theoretical and political underpinnings to the film analyses differ, although all are broadly feminist.

As one way of limiting what has often seemed a rather overwhelmingly large field, I have chosen to focus on women as an audience *for*, rather than producers *of*, films. Thus, the articles focus on the representations of women that women have made, and which the film industry has offered us, rather than on the role of women as film-makers, in whatever capacity. There are no accounts of the difficulties of funding film production, nor of the economic constraints determining the final look of a film. Similarly, there are no reports by film-makers of the intentions behind a particular work. Instead, there is a series of 'readings' of films, sometimes overlapping, at times contradictory, which I have grouped in three parts: Documentary, Fictions and Hollywood, with a fourth section on Distribution and Exhibition.

While two of the films in the Documentary section – *Self Health* and *Not a Love Story* – would probably fit fairly easily into a commonsense category, 'documentary film', the other two films, *Daughter Rite* and *The Song of the Shirt*, are films which, through their formal organisation and reference, seek to assault the validity of this category. Grouped together, the analyses of these films illuminate some of what could be considered the proper concerns of documentary film-making: the attempt to provide filmic accounts and interpretations of existing social realities. The section is thus intended to raise questions about what documentary film, and particularly feminist documentary film, is and can be, as well as providing accounts of, and introductions to, specific films.

Part Two brings together a diverse range of films and critical approaches. The films discussed range from feature length 'art' movies such as *The German Sisters*, recent feminist 'hits' like *A Question of Silence* to more avant-garde shorts such as *An Epic Poem*. Although the production circumstances of these films vary, most have been produced in the grant-aided or state-subsidised sectors of film industries. It is this which at one level distinguishes the films discussed in this part from those in Part Three which were all produced within the Hollywood industry.

Part Four of the book collects together articles about the distribution and exhibition of feminist and women's film in Britain. The politics and practices discussed are not unified, and it is the range of ways in which different groups of women, with different concerns and aims, are mobilising as distributors, exhibitors and audiences which inflects a notion of films *for* women.

The collection is not offered as 'representative' – it is ordered according to my own sense of priorities, and it seems appropriate to outline some of the principles involved in selection. Firstly, I have tried to represent – sometimes in rather trace-like form – the important debates in what used to be called 'women and film': questions around realism and avant-garde form; the arguments for, and about, 'positive' images; the politics of the representation of the female body; attitudes to commercial cinema, and questions of audience. Running across these concerns, which are all concerns about the representation of women as a gender group, I have tried to pay attention to the differential experience and priorities of different groups of women. *Maeve*, for example, is a film which is centrally concerned with the relations between 'being' a feminist and 'being' Irish. *Burning an Illusion* was the first black feature film funded by the British Film Institute. Most of the articles commissioned for the collection were

2

commissioned to throw into relief the unmarked 'white heterosexual' which so often preceded the word 'women' in Film Studies. However, a little commissioning doesn't do much in terms of who gets their hands on the money and equipment to make films, and it was only in the latter stages of the preparation of this book that other relevant films, like *On Duty* (Cassie McFarlane, 1984) and *Majdhar* (Retake Collective, 1983/4), from the developing black independent sector in Britain, became available.[1]

I have tried to choose articles that are relatively accessible to the non-specialist. More extended, and differently emphasised, discussion of many of the issues raised can be found in Annette Kuhn's *Women's Pictures* (London: Routledge and Kegan Paul, 1982) and E. Ann Kaplan's *Women and Film: Both Sides of the Camera* (London and New York: Methuen, 1983).[2] Also, I should point out that the positions I take in my introductions, indeed the way in which I present and order the articles in the various sections, are not positions with which the authors included would necessarily agree.

Films for Women

I have generally chosen articles about films which have been made for female audiences, including several made by men (particularly in Part Three), if the films themselves, and the way in which they were marketed, seemed to address women. I have omitted consideration of certain films, like *Dressed to Kill*, which have been central to developing feminist debate about representation, because I understand them, in however threatened a manner, to be addressing their spectators as masculine.[3]

I use the notion of gendered address – films *for* women – quite loosely. Sometimes, particularly with documentary films with a voice-over or narrator, the designated audience is clear. The text will construct a 'we' or a 'you' which is clearly 'we women', or 'you women like us' – *Self Health* does this. Similarly, in commercial production, genres often have gender affiliations – westerns, sci-fi and gangster films being 'male', melodramas and weepies female. This doesn't mean that if you're the 'wrong' sex, you can't enjoy the film, but it does function to explain the genre conventions and pleasures with which most people are likely to be familiar. Marketing for commercial films will tend to reproduce these affiliations, but may also stress central identification figures. The fact that films such as *Julia* and *The Turning Point* are *about* women, with name female stars, was central in establishing them as films *for* women and – as I have argued elsewhere – films for new, modern women.

Outside documentary and campaign films, which often specify their address directly within the text, and commercially produced films which are marketed with clear target audiences in mind, questions of audience address are less clear cut. Many films address, or construct, their audience in different ways simultaneously. The use of subtitles to translate black English in *Babylon* obviously addresses a white audience, while the film was partly marketed for a black audience. Avant-garde films necessarily, I would argue, are made for small, self-conscious audiences, and the context of exhibition and modes of performance and distribution may here be more determining than any textual feature of the films. Similarly, the practice of women-only viewing sessions encourages women to read films as a gender group in ways which may be at odds with what might seem to be the 'obvious meaning' of the film. Feminists viewing pornography, often incorporating the address to a male spectator within their analyses, have read the films as symptomatic of the power relations between men and women rather than as erotic.

There has been considerable debate within feminist culture as to whether there are particular practices which are specifically or essentially feminine. In relation to film, as Pam Cook has pointed out, this might lead to the privileging of modes of expression that are traditionally associated with women: the personal, autobiographical modes of the diary and the letter, as in the work of Margaret Tait, Lis Rhodes, or Akerman's *News from Home*.[4] Or this could mean the validation of skills and practices that are thought of as feminine as in the narrative centrality of patchwork in *A Jury of Her Peers*, the imagery of the billowing washing in *Clotheslines* or Annabel Nicolson's use of a sewing machine in *Reel Time*.[5] These practices are historically feminine and lack prestige as art activities. Films using this type of imagery or expression will speak more directly to the experience of women than to that of men, and thus can be seen to address a female audience. Further, the use of this material raises the question of why it is culturally inferior.

The issue becomes more difficult when it moves from imagery, modes of expression and skill to more formal qualities such as rhythm and structure. The work of Judith Higginbottom, for example, partly uses cyclical rhythms to pose relationships between lunar and menstrual cycles.[6] There is a difference between what has been historically feminine, and what is considered essentially or biologically so. I am rather wary of the idea of this type of address to a female audience. It seems to invoke a transcultural, essential femininity which both denies the real differences between women, and seems to land women where we seem always to end up – outside language and culture, in some sort of ahistorical realm of the instinctual.

Finally, the use of humour can function as a way of speaking to a particular audience. There are not many funny feminist films about, but humorous moments that there are often directly address women as women, and particularly, as women who know – about men, about

4

women's lot, etc. It is this humour that is being invoked in the courtroom in *A Question of Silence*. Here, the women's laughter increases to the extent that the men can't understand what could possibly be funny. Similarly, the funny moment in *Thriller* is not when Mimi roars with laughter as she reads post-structuralist theory aloud (in French), which does not seem to me to be a gendered joke, but when the two male heroes climb out of the window without a word. This is funny because there really is no place else for them to go, but this inevitability is not tragic, as it is usually with heroes.

Films can be 'for' women in lots of different ways – and obviously women are not a unitary group. We may have biology in common, but the way in which we live out femininity is structured by class, ethnicity, sexual orientation, age, nationality, etc. – and our understanding of these factors. Many of the films discussed below were made for 'women', but turned out to be for white, 'educated' feminists.[7] Some incorporated an address to women within a more general address, perhaps to trade unionists and socialists.

The Song of the Shirt arguably addresses historians quite as much as feminists. *Burning an Illusion*, although mainly concerned with the experience of a young woman, is perhaps more focused on addressing its audience as black – women and men. Some films make a very specific address – the humour of *Comedy in Six Unnatural Acts* is primarily a humour for lesbian women, who share the represented sub-culture. Many of the more avant-garde films are inevitably, if unintentionally, only addressing viewers who already have cultural confidence about avant-garde art. Conversely, as several essays in the Hollywood section point out, many commercial films verge on incoherence in their eagerness to speak simultaneously to as many potential ticker-buyers as possible. The complexities and ambiguities of address often tell us more about the politics of a film than its more overt concerns. Jeanette Murphy's reading of *A Question of Silence* is, I think, validated by the way in which the film not only refuses to address a male audience, but repeatedly represents men within the film as people who cannot understand what is happening. This allows us to see that the film offers gender as the most important division between peoples, and works constantly to affirm this. These inflections in the ways in which the films discussed below construct their audiences – or the spaces for their audiences to occupy – are perhaps what has to be studied to open out the question of 'Films *for* Women'.

Ideally, apart from having lots more space and many more pictures, I would have chosen articles that condensed key debates through the analysis of widely shown films. However, the films which have attracted critical commentary haven't always attracted audiences, and vice versa. *The Life and Times of Rosie the Riveter*, for example, has been exhibited extensively in Britain, particularly by trade unions, but

5

there are no records of the discussions held, and no articles which document this type of exhibition. In fact, it has been very difficult to document innovative exhibition practices. This is mainly because the success or otherwise of a particular event is often immediate and experiential – it cannot be re-run on a Steenbeck by all the people involved. It is also because work of, say, the Birmingham Women's Film Consortium, is carried out by women who have other, full-time jobs.[8] Similarly, the workshops on Black Women and Representation held in London in early 1984 (see Part Four) were organised by a group of women with extensive other commitments.

The fact that there are so many omissions – of films, critics and issues – can, I hope, be taken positively to indicate the range and diversity of work being produced.

Notes

1. *On Duty* is set during the 1983 National Health Service dispute and based on the life of a black ward orderly. It was transmitted in the 'independent' (late Monday night) slot by Channel Four (16 April 1984). *Majdhar* (available from Retake Film & Video Collective, 25 Bayham Street, London NW1), which focuses on the experience of a young Asian woman, was shown in the same slot (18 March 1985). See also the tape slide, *Stepping Out of Frame,* by Laxmi Jamdagni and Amina Patel (available from the Resource Centre for Asian Studies, Robert Montefiore Building, Underwood Road, London E1.

2. See also Mary Ann Doane et al., eds., *Re-Vision: Essays in Feminist Film Criticism* (Los Angeles: American Film Institute, 1984), and Christine Gledhill, *Women and Melodrama* (London: British Film Institute, forthcoming).

3. See Tony Bryant and Griselda Pollock, 'Window Dressing . . . . A Poster Competition', *Framework* 15/16/17, 1981, pp. 96–8; Giovanna Asselle and Behroze Ghandy, '*Dressed to Kill*', *Screen* vol. 23 no. 3–4, 1982, pp. 137–143, and the discussion of *The Eyes of Laura Mars* by Lucy Fischer and Marcia Landy, pp. 4–19 of the same issue of *Screen*.

4. Pam Cook, 'The Point of Expression in Avant-Garde Film', in Elizabeth Cowie, ed., *Catalogue of British Film Institute Productions 1977–1978* (London: British Film Institute, 1978), pp. 53–6.

5. Margaret Tait's work is available from the London Film-makers Cooperative, 42 Gloucester Avenue, London NW1; *News From Home* is distributed by The Other Cinema; *A Jury of Her Peers* by Harris Films (Contemporary); all the other films and film-makers mentioned in this paragraph are distributed by Circles (see Part Four and Appendix).

6. Distributed by Circles.

7. For a sociology of the North American feminist film-makers, see Jan Rosenberg, *Women's Reflections* (Michigan: UMI Research Press, 1983).

8. There is an account of the work of the Birmingham Women's Film Consortium in Alison McKenzie, ed., *Handbook of Independent Film and Video in the West Midlands* (Birmingham: Birmingham Film and Video Workshop, 1985).

6

PART ONE
Documentary

Introduction

THE FIRST films made by the 'new' feminism of the late 60s and early 70s were documentaries and this type of film-making continued throughout the 70s giving us some of the better known feminist films such as *The Life and Times of Rosie the Riveter* and *Not a Love Story*. There have been many debates within feminism about the implications and politics of documentary film-making and this selection of articles is intended to indicate some of the major points at issue.

One of the most commonly held notions of documentary film is that it reveals the truth. Indeed, we can perhaps most usefully define documentaries as films which, through aspects of their presentation and the use of particular conventions (for example, the use of grainy, high-contrast film, or titles that give locations and dates), give the impression that the events and characters seen on screen have or had an independent existence apart from the film. The idea is that film simply records or reveals something that already exists – a documentary film is a film which indicates that this is what it is doing. Because film offers us a moving image with sound, it is often seen as the best medium for truth-telling, and it was this particular aspect of film which was so attractive to feminist film-makers in the early 70s. As Julia Lesage points out below, film was initially used by feminists to reveal women's experience – most particularly, the experience of oppression. As Gledhill puts it:

> . . . the first concern of the Movement was simply to put women recognisable to us as women, in the picture. The first independent women's film groups grabbed camera or video and went to talk to women about their lives and experiences.[1]

Gledhill's description participates in the political activity she describes – the construction of a new 'we', the 'we' or 'us' of women, bound together through our realisation that it is as women, as a gender group, that we are oppressed. So when Gledhill writes of the demand for images of women 'recognisable to us as women', the 'us' who do the recognising are feminists, women who have rejected the available images of women. Although the new 'we' sought to speak for all women, the common experience claimed (and sought) was frequently articulated by and for women who were privileged in terms of class and ethnicity.[2]

9

However, it was this initial excitement, and its political charge, which sustained the series of 'women-talking' documentaries which dominate early feminist film-making. Films such as *Janie's Janie* (Ashur, 1971) or *Women of the Rhondda* (London Women's Film Group, 1972) were centrally concerned with what it is to be a woman, and with bringing to visibility the female experience of familial networks – from 'a woman's point of view'. It is noticeable that quite a few of these 'women-talking' documentaries were made by middle-class women about working-class women, which could be understood to point in a different way to the fragility of the new feminist 'we' which so strongly stressed unity at the expense of difference.[3] As Julia Lesage argues, these early documentary films can best be understood in relation to the Women's Liberation Movement practice of consciousness-raising. Both are concerned to bring to visibility, and hence to share, experience that has previously been understood as personal, and thus to begin to understand individual predicaments as part of a wider social subordination of women as a group.

All the films discussed in this section can be understood in relation to this central 'women-talking' tradition of feminist film-making, although both *The Song of the Shirt* and *Daughter Rite* are concerned to disrupt and interrogate the tradition. *Self Health* and *Not a Love Story,* in very different ways, do make use of footage that could be described as 'women speaking the truth of experience', footage which is used to appeal to and consolidate the feminist 'we', which addresses its audience woman-to-woman. The article by Julia Lesage argues for the strength and political importance of this type of consciousness-raising film-making. Ruby Rich's analysis of *Not a Love Story* argues that a rather patronising moral opposition is set up by the film between feminist philanthropists and other, misguided women.[4]

The Song of the Shirt defines itself against this documentary tradition – a stance which, to a certain extent, it shares with *Daughter Rite*. Pam Cook, writing at a time when criticisms of this type of documentary were first being articulated, observed:

> Until recently, feminist film-making in this country has relied heavily on the techniques of direct realism in its attempt to establish an alternative feminist language of film. Interview material predominates, reinforced with synchronised sound which appears to emanate naturally from the image. The oppression of women appears as a self-evident 'truth' which the viewer can only accept or reject because he or she is not involved in the process of criticism and analysis at the point of consumption of the film.[5]

These early feminist documentaries were being made at a period when radical film work was dominated by hostility to 'realism'. The way in which cinema worked to reproduce dominant ideas (which it was often seen to do in a rather uncontradictory manner) was seen primarily to be at the level of form. It was not just a question of the stories told, the character types depicted, the sorts of ideas and recurrent themes that appear to be validated, but it was 'the reality effect' itself which was seen as the ideological culprit. It was precisely the way in which films seemed to effortlessly offer up their representations as 'real' which was seen to work against radical social and political change. Some of these arguments against the use of realist conventions are outlined by Sylvia Harvey and Jane Feuer below; the central point here is that it was precisely the elements of film which had first attracted feminist film-makers which were being seen as ideologically most complicit. The 'documentary idea', of revealing or telling a truth, was seen as most duplicitous, because what had in fact been arranged, set up, edited, was presented as if it 'just was', with nothing more than a neutral, recording camera intervening between audience and actuality. It is in this context that we can understand the tone of the article by Julia Lesage, because she is trying to argue *for* the use of realist forms in feminist documentary.[6]

Jane Feuer's discussion of *Daughter Rite* shows how this film too is informed by these same arguments about the politics of form, and particularly, documentary form. *Daughter Rite* looks, at least in part, like a 'women-talking' film – but was scripted and acted. Does this matter? Is it, as some commentators have seen it, a betrayal of the trust between film-makers, subjects and audience that has been seen as characteristic of feminist film? Or is it an exposé of the idea that there is such a thing as 'pure' documentary, and thus a film which marks the maturing of the 'women-talking' tradition?[7]

The Song of the Shirt, although sharing this concern to show itself to be constructed, and offering an interplay of film and refilmed video as one strategy towards this end, differs from the other films discussed in this section in several significant ways. *The Song of the Shirt* very directly tries to deconstruct some of the strategies associated with both feminist documentary and feminist history. It can most usefully be understood in comparison with feminist history films like *With Babies and Banners*, *Union Maids* and *The Life and Times of Rosie the Riveter*.[8] In these films, which are structured through an alternation between 'present day' interviews with women talking about the past, and historical material (archive footage, photographs, newspaper reports, etc.), the account given by the women speaking as witnesses is usually privileged as 'the truth', whereas the other material often functions illustratively in relation to what is said. *Rosie* was innovative in that the short propaganda films used as the historical material work in counterpoint to the account given by the women.[9] However, this too functions to give the women the status of truth-tellers. *The Song of the Shirt* not only refuses to privilege personal experience as truth, but also questions the idea that there is a 'truth' which can be revealed. The film collects together a whole range of materials – verbal, musical and visual, including novels, parliamentary reports, contemporary cartoons and ballads – concerning nineteenth-century needlewomen, and juxtaposes them. Thus there are various scenes in which actresses play seamstresses, and we have some sense of their experience, but these moments are not privileged above, for example, parliamentary reports. The film, through this formal organisation, challenges both ideas of documentary film and history. Film is shown to be a medium through which meanings are made, not something through which they shine. Similarly, history is argued to be something that is constructed in the present, not dug up from the past. There is not one simple, obvious account that can be constructed from all these diverse, juxtaposed materials. The difficulty of the film, perhaps, lies in the way in which these formal strategies make it rather impenetrable to audiences who are not already familiar with this type of idea about history and documentary film.[10]

The Song of the Shirt differs from the other films discussed in this section in that it rejects the feminist 'we', the construction of which, as I have suggested, has been central to the project of much feminist documentary. The movement in many feminist documentaries is that of a spiralling back and forth between the experience of an individual and the way in which that experience can be understood in relation to the subordination of women as a group. It is through this movement, which echoes the early feminist slogan 'the personal is political', that the feminist 'we' is constructed. *The Song of the Shirt* will have none of this, and to that extent is not an organising, political film.

However, if *The Song of the Shirt* doesn't achieve quite what is claimed for it in terms of a text without a 'meta-discourse' – which I would think is constructed in the editing and re-filming – it does ask a very different form of engagement from its audience to that demanded by *Not a Love Story*. This film has achieved notoriety by managing to offend nearly all interested groups in one way or another. Produced by the National Film Board of Canada, it has had only restricted release in Canada, but has been shown quite widely in the 'art circuit' in Britain. Evidently made as a feminist intervention in the 'pornography' debate, it has attracted a range of feminist criticism. Firstly, the film has been seen to use documentary format in a very naive way. The film has not been susceptible to the sort of defence mounted against these arguments by Lesage because of its particular use of pornographic material which, despite the intentions of the makers, arguably allows the film to function as a 'legit' pornographic film ('Porn film for Arts Centre'). The sequence of the Suze Randall/'pussy juice' photographic session has been seen as most offensive, although the general use of camera angles that adopt the position of the male spectator have also been criticised. Finally, and this is one of the main elements in Ruby Rich's critique of the film, it has been argued that the film offers a moral tale rather than an analysis of an enormously profitable business. These issues run across what has been a major area of debate within feminism, and which has been articulated in relation to films such as *Dressed to Kill* as well as pornography in general.[11] Rich's analysis is particularly useful because of the polemical way in which it focuses not only on the moral tone of *Not a Love Story*, but also on the terms of the debate within the Women's Movement.

Notes

1. Christine Gledhill, '*Whose Choice?*: Teaching Films About Abortion', *Screen Education* no. 24, 1977, p. 38.
2. See Hazel Carby, 'White woman listen! Black Feminism and the boundaries of Sisterhood' in Centre for Contemporary Cultural Studies, *The Empire Strikes Back* (London: Hutchinson and CCCS, 1982), pp. 212–23; and the articles in *Feminist Review* 17, 1984 for some of the critiques made in Britain of the racism and Eurocentrism of the Women's Liberation Movement.
3. See Jan Rosenberg, particularly on 'The Women's Film', in *Women's Reflections* (Michigan: UMI Research Press, 1983).
4. See also, Susan Barrowclough, '*Not a Love Story*': Screen vol. 23 no. 5, 1982, pp. 26–38; Jill McGreal, '*Not a Love Story*': Feminism and Pornography', *Undercut* no. 6, Winter 1982–3, pp. 1–5.
5. Pam Cook, 'Exploitation Films and Feminism', *Screen* vol. 17 no. 2, 1976, p. 123.
6. For an opposed position, see Stephen Grosz and Bruce McAuley, '*Self-Health* and *Healthcaring*', *Camera Obscura* 7, 1981, pp. 128–135.
7. See also, Jon Jost, '*Daughter Rite*', *Framework* no. 15/16/17, 1981, p. 37; Linda Williams and Ruby Rich, 'The right of re-vision: Michelle Citron's *Daughter Rite*', *Film Quarterly* vol. 35 no. 1, 1981, pp. 17–21.
8. See, particularly, E. Ann Kaplan's discussion of feminist documentary in *Women and Film: Both Sides of the Camera* (New York: Methuen, 1983); Patricia Erens, 'Women's Documentaries as Social History', *Film Library Quarterly* vol. 14 no. 1/2, 1981, pp. 4–9; Ruth McCormick '*Union Maids*', *Cineaste* vol. VIII no. 1, 1977, pp. 50–1; Sue Davenport, '*Rosie the Riveter*: Invisible Working Women', *Jump Cut* 28, 1983, pp. 42–3.
9. See Bill Nicholls, 'The Voice of Documentary', *Film Quarterly*, vol. 36 no. 3, Spring 1983, pp. 17–29 for an interesting discussion of who speaks in documentary film.
10. The film-makers explain some of their thinking in Susan Clayton and Jonathan Curling, 'Feminist History and *The Song of the Shirt*', *Camera Obscura* no. 7, 1981, pp. 111–127. See also Alison Beale, 'An analysis of *The Song of the Shirt*', *Cinetracts* vol. 3 no. 2, 1980, pp. 1–13.
11. Annette Kuhn, *Women's Pictures* (London: Routledge and Kegan Paul, 1982), discusses pornography, as does Rosalind Coward, 'Sexual Violence and Sexuality', *Feminist Review* 11, 1982, pp. 9–22. See also Angela Carter, *The Sadeian Woman* (London: Virago, 1979).

Political Aesthetics of the Feminist Documentary Film

JULIA LESAGE

The following is an extended excerpt from an article that appeared originally in *Quarterly Review of Film Studies* (Fall 1978). That article has been updated, combined with an extended analysis of an *experimental* feminist documentary, Joan Elam's *Rape*, and appears in *'Show Us Life': Toward a History and Aesthetic of the Committed Documentary*, ed. Thomas Waugh (Metuchen, NJ: Scarecrow Press, 1984).

FEMINIST documentary film-making is a cinematic genre congruent with a political movement, the contemporary women's movement. One of that movement's key forms of organisation is the affinity group. In the late 1960s and early 1970s in the United States, women's consciousness-raising groups, reading groups, and task-oriented groups were emerging from and often superseded the organisations of the antiwar New Left. Women who had learned film-making in the antiwar movement and previously 'uncommitted' women film-makers began to make self-consciously feminist films, and other women began to learn film-making specifically to contribute to the movement.[1] The films these people made came out of the same ethos as the consciousness-raising groups and had the same goals.

Clearly the cinematic sophistication and quality of political analysis vary from film to film, but aside from an in-depth discussion of *Self Health*, which I value both cinematically and politically, to explore such differences would be beyond the scope of this article. Here I shall describe the emergence of the feminist documentary as a genre, the aesthetics, use, and importance of this genre, and its relation to the movement from which it sprang – a discussion important to any consideration of the aesthetics of political films.

Many of the first feminist documentaries used a simple format to present to audiences (presumably composed primarily of women) a picture of the ordinary details of women's lives, their thoughts – told directly by the protagonists to the camera – and their frustrated but sometimes successful attempts to enter and deal with the public world of work and power. Among these films, which now have a wide circulation in libraries and schools, are *Growing Up Female* by Julia Reichert and Jim Klein, *Janie's Janie* by Geri Ashur, and *The Woman's Film* by the women of San Francisco Newsreel. Other films dealing with women talking about their lives include Kate Millet's

Three Lives, Joyce Chopra's *Joyce at 34*, Donna Deitch's *Woman to Woman*, and Deborah Schaffer and Bonnie Friedman's *Chris and Bernie*. Some films deal with pride in the acquisition of skills, such as Bonnie Friedman's film about a girls' track team, *The Flashettes*, or Michelle Citron's study of her sister learning the concert violin from a woman teacher, *Parthenogenesis*. Others have more political analysis and are often collective productions that provide a feminist analysis of women's experience with the following: (a) prison (*Like a Rose* by Tomato Productions, *We're Alive* by California Institute for Women Video and UCLA Women's Film Workshop); (b) the health care system (*Self Health* by San Francisco Women's Health Collective, *Taking Our Bodies Back* by Margaret Lazarus, Renner Wunderlich, and Joan Fink, *The Chicago Maternity Center Story* by Kartemquin Films, and *Healthcaring* by Denise Bostrom and Jane Warrenbrand); and (c) rape (*Rape* by JoAnn Elam).[2]

It is no coincidence that films about working-class women show their subjects as the most confident and militant about their rights in the public sector, and their willingness to fight for those rights. Yet even these films, from Madeline Anderson's *I am Somebody* to Barbara Kopple's *Harlan County, USA*, focus on problems of identity in the private sphere – how one strikeleader's husband views her union organising unenthusiastically, or how miners' wives reach a new solidarity only by overcoming sexual suspicions and jealousies. As feminist films explicitly demand that a new space be opened up for women in women's terms, the collective and social act of feminist film-making has often led to entirely new demands in the areas of health care, welfare, poverty programmes, work, and law (especially rape), and in the cultural sphere proper in the areas of art, education, and the mass media.

And if the feminist film-makers deliberately used a traditional 'realist' documentary structure, it is because they saw making these films as an urgent public act and wished to enter the 16mm circuit of educational films especially through libraries, schools, churches, unions, and YWCAs to bring feminist analysis to many women it might otherwise never reach.

Biography, simplicity, trust between woman film-maker and woman subject, a linear narrative structure, little self-consciousness about the flexibility of the cinematic medium – these are what characterise the feminist documentaries of the 1970s. The films' form and their wide-spread use raise certain questions. Why are they patterned in so similar a way? Why are these films the first ones thought of whenever a group of women decide they want to 'start learning something about women' and set up showings in churches, public libraries, high schools, Girl Scout meetings, union caucuses, or rallies for the ERA? Why do activists in the women's movement use the same films over and over again? What is the films' appeal?

These films often show women in the private sphere getting together to define/redefine their experiences and to elaborate a strategy for making inroads on the public sphere. Either the film-maker senses that it is socially necessary to name women's experience, or women together within the film do so, or a 'strong' woman is filmed who shares her stance with the film-maker and, by extension, with the women who see the film. Conversations in these films are not merely examples of female introspection; the film-makers choose not to explore the corners of women's psyches (as in Romantic art). Rather, the women's very redefining of experience is intended to challenge all the previously accepted indices of 'male superiority' and of women's supposedly 'natural' roles. Women's personal explorations establish a structure for social and psychological change and are filmed specifically to combat patriarchy. The film-maker's and her subjects' intent is political. Yet the film's very strength, the emphasis on the experiential, can sometimes be a political limitation, especially when the film limits itself to the individual and offers little or no analysis or sense of collective process leading to social change.[3]

Example: 'Self Health'

Among feminist documentaries, *Self Health* is an exemplary film in terms of its cinematic style, the knowledge it conveys, and the self-confidence and understanding it gives women about themselves. The film presents women in a group situation, collectively learning to do vaginal self-exams with a speculum, breast exams, and vaginal bimanual exams. Such groups have been conducted over the past five or six years by women who are part of an informal 'self-help' or 'self-health' movement in the United States; sometimes their work is connected with the home-birth movement and sometimes with pregnancy testing and abortion referral services. As the health care industry grows like a mushroom under capitalism, the general North American public has become more and more aware of the poor quality of the expensive services offered to them. The women in the self-health movement form part of a large, often informally constituted radical movement to improve health care delivery for the masses of people instead of for an elite.

The place where such a self-health session takes place is usually someone's home or a women's centre, rather than a medical clinic. In the film *Self Health*, the locale is a sunny apartment or informal women's meeting place. Although we see two women giving most of the explanations and demonstrations, no one is distinguished as nurse or doctor. As important to the film as the conveying of anatomical information is the fact that all the women discuss together their feelings about the experiences with their bodies and their sexuality, and that they very naturally look at and feel each others' bodies. To gain knowledge by looking at and feeling each other is acknowledged perhaps for the first time as woman's right.

Such a film attacks both the artistic and medical tradition of viewing women's bodies. These traditions, as well as the mass media's use of women's image to sell consumer goods, have robbed most women of a real knowledge of both their own and other women's bodies. Furthermore, many women have little personal sense of rightfully possessing their own bodies, little sense of what's 'normal' for themselves physically, and little sense of what sexuality on their terms or on women's terms in general might mean.

Toward the end of the film, one of the women puts on a rubber glove to demonstrate how to do a bimanual vaginal exam. The subject is a woman lying on a table in a sunny room with a flowered pillow under head and a green fern near her. The 'teacher' inserts two lubricated fingers into the vagina and pushes up underneath the cervix. First she shows the woman being examined and then the other women gathered around the table, how to press down hard on the abdomen to ascertain the size and location of the uterus and then the ovaries. 'Why does it always hurt when the doctor does it?' they ask. They also express surprise about the size and location of the uterus ('about the size of a walnut') and the ovaries ('feels like a Mexican jumping bean'). . . .

That so much of the basic physical information conveyed by the film is very new for women viewers (e.g., the film lets us see the cervix and the os, or the normal sebaceous secretion from the nipple) indicates just how colonised a space women's bodies still are. *Self Health* goes a long way toward reconquering that space.

Cinematically, the film is characterised by its presentation of women in a collective situation sharing new knowledge about their physical sexuality. About fifteen young women are gathered in a friendly, mundane environment rather than in a clinical white office where the woman patient is completely isolated from her ordinary social context. As the group does breast self-examinations together, they sit around in a circle in what might be a living room; hanging on the wall we see a Toulouse-Lautrec reproduction of a woman. Warm brown-red and pink tones predominate. As the women remove their tops, we notice them as individuals – some with rings and other jewels, some with glasses, many with different hair-styles. The group is young, they look like students or young working-women in flowered peasant blouses and dresses, shirts and jeans. In sum, the colours and the *mise en scène* create a sense of warmth, intimacy, and friendliness.

Even more important to the *mise en scène* is the women's collectivity. Women look at and touch each other; they all see their own sexual organs and those of others, probably for the first time. They learn the variety of physical types and the range of 'normality' in sexual organs

17

in look, colour, texture, and feel. The fact that almost any woman would feel shy and embarrassed about doing such an overt exploration is mitigated by these women's doing it in a group where everyone feels the same way. The women realise that their fears and doubts about their bodies do not originate from their individual situation as much as from women's physical and psychological 'colonisation' under patriarchy. Too often, women have experienced as degrading getting contraception information, having a gynaecological exam, and having a baby. Certainly at those moments, women's ignorance about their bodies was rarely dispelled. But this collective process gives them the self-confidence to demand answers from doctors face to face and to demand a different kind of health care overall. That such a film does not provide an institutional analysis of the health-care industry, as does *The Chicago Maternity Center Story*, limits how much this one film can achieve in directly promoting a different kind of health care for women; yet, because of the wide range of discussion and kinds of challenges to the established order it encourages women to formulate, it is useful in a wide range of women's struggles.

Visually and in terms of its overall structure, the film moves as far away as you can get from pornography, yet the cinematography also captures that kind of nervous tension and excitement of discovery which the women themselves undoubtedly felt. The film opens on a close-up of naked skin, the surface moving to the rhythm of a woman's breathing; there is a pan to a breast and a shot of either pubic or axillary hair in close up. As it starts out, the film could be porn. For most women audience members, the initial sequence provides a moment of tension – 'Do we dare to or want to look at this?' The voice-over assures us of what we want to hear: 'We're learning from our bodies, teaching ourselves and each other how each of us is unique . . . and the same . . . We see it as reclaiming lost territory that belonged to our doctors, our husbands, everyone but us.' As the title comes on, we hear the excited voices of women speaking all at once, a device also used at the end of the film over the credits. The voices of discovery, talking in a simultaneous outburst or sharing observations, needs and experiences – these are the tension-breaking devices, the part of the film that an audience unfamiliar with such a situation first identifies with. And these voices imply an outburst of discussion that cannot be contained, that begs to be continued after the film is seen.

In an early sequence, a woman lying on a table is surrounded by other women as she talks about and demonstrates the external genitalia, using her own body as a model. Various women talk here about their sense of being at a distance from their own sexual parts, of feeling squeamish about them. Alternating shots show close-ups of the demonstration of faces looking intently at what they are being shown. When the woman on the table demonstrates the use of the speculum and inserts it into her vagina, one woman's voice exclaims, 'Oh God!' which elicits nervous laughter in the audience and expresses the group's tension. As the women inserts the speculum and shines the light inside it, the camera cuts to another angle and zooms in to show her cervix and its opening, the os, that which the doctor always 'examines' but which we never see. Laughter and sounds of excitement are heard as the onlooking women comment and ask questions about what they see.

After this sequence, a high-angle long shot shows three women lying on the floor against pillows and sleeping bags propped up against the wall. Their legs are spread apart and they are all doing vaginal self-exams with speculum, flashlight, and mirror. A pan shot shows the whole group of women on the floor, lined up along the wall, doing the same thing with some women looking at or helping each other. A mixture of voices exclaim and comment on what they see, especially on the variety and uniqueness of the genitalia. This sequence is a first in narrative cinema. It decolonises women's sexuality. Women occupy the whole space of the frame as subjects in a collective art of mutual, tangible self-exploration. As one of my students said of this sequence, 'It has none of the "wow!" of *Candid Camera* and none of the distance of medical or so-called sex education films.' Particularly in this one section of *Self Health*, women film-makers have found a way to show and define women's sexuality on their terms – not with the thrill of possession and not with objectification, but with the excitement of coming to knowledge.

Later, as the film shows the women doing breast self-exams together, they and we notice and let ourselves deliberately look at the variety of women's breasts. The women themselves feel each others' breasts to learn what normal breast tissue is like. Although the Cancer Society promotes breast self-examination, women's breast tissue is fibrous and also varies with the menstrual cycle and the individual. As a result, women often do not know what is normal or what a 'lump' might be. A doctor can spot such phenomena from having had the opportunity to feel many women's breasts. Why should such knowledge not be made available to, or seized by, women themselves?

The anatomy lesson, the sharing of feelings, and the learning about others are all part of the self-health experience and all have equal importance in the film. Close-ups demonstrate specific examination techniques or show individuals talking and listening; long shots convey the sense of a communal experience in the self-health group. No woman is filmed as an object; everyone is a subject who combines and presents physical, emotional, intellectual, and political selves. The women filmed have an amazing spontaneity and lack of self-consciousness about the camera, particularly given the close range at which the filming was done.

19

Self-health groups and this film itself both function in an explicitly political way. Reclaiming 'the lost territory' of women's bodies and health care is a personal act that has a strong effect on women's identity, emotional life, and sense of control. This film also directly attacks the medical establishment. Women who see the film immediately want to talk about two things – sex education and health care – mainly in terms of what patriarchal society lacks.

In one sense, the film is utopian. It shows a new, collective form of women learning together. It would be an ideal film, for example, to show in high schools. But when I showed the film on the university level to women's studies classes and to film students, both sets of students agreed that the idea of such a collective form of learning about sexuality would have been viewed as 'pornography' in their high schools by the teachers, the school boards, and many of the parents. In cinematic terms, the film's vision of women's sexuality, of their being total subjects to one another and to the audience, is also utopian. Women's very physical presence is defined here in women's terms, collectively. And some might ask, in referring to documentary film alone, why haven't these images and these concepts of women's united physical and intellectual selves been presented by film-makers before?

Feminist Documentaries and the Consciousness-Raising Group

Cinéma vérité documentary film-making had features that made it an attractive and useful mode of artistic and political expression for women learning film-making in the late 1960s. It not only demanded less mastery of the medium than Hollywood or experimental film, but also the very documentary recording of women's real environments. Their stories immediately established and valorised a new order of cinematic iconography, connotations, and range of subject matter in the portrayal of women's lives. Furthermore, contemporary feminist film-makers, often making biographical or autobiographical films, have used *cinéma vérité* in a new and different way. They often identify personally with their subjects. Their relation to that subject while filming often is collaborative, with both subject and film-maker sharing the political goals of the project. The feminist documentarist uses the film medium to convey a new and heightened sense of what *woman* means or can mean in our society – this new sense of female identity being expressed both through the subject's story and through the tangible details of the subject's milieu.

Yet why do so many feminist film-makers choose to film the same thing? Film after film shows a woman telling her story to the camera. It is usually a woman struggling to deal with the public world. It seems that these feminist documentarists just plug in different speakers and show a certain variation in milieu – especially in class terms – from the aristocratic home of *Nana, Mom, and Me* by Amalie Rothschild to the union organisers' photos of their younger days in *Union Maids* by Julia Reichert and Jim Klein. In fact, the feminist documentaries have as a narrative structure a pattern that is as satisfying for activists in the contemporary women's movement to watch as it is for women just wanting to learn more about women. That is, these films evince a consistent organisation of narrative materials that functions much like a deep structure, the details of the individual women's lives providing the surface structure of these films.[4]

Such an organisation serves a specific social and psychological function at this juncture in history. It is the artistic analogue of the structure and function of the consciousness-raising group. Furthermore, it indicates to the film-maker a certain reason to be making the film, a certain relation to her subject matter and to the medium, and a certain sense of the function of the film once released. The narrative deep structure sets the film-maker in a mutual, nonhierarchical relation with her subject (such filming is not seen as the male artist's act of 'seizing' the subject and then presenting one's 'creation') and indicates what she hopes her relation to her audience will be.[5]

The major political tool of the contemporary women's movement has been the consciousness-raising group. Self-consciously, a group of about a dozen women would re-evaluate any and all areas of their past experiences in terms of how that experience defined or illuminated what it meant to be a woman in our culture. It was an act of naming previously unarticulated knowledge, of seeing that knowledge as political (i.e. as a way of beginning to change power relations), and of understanding that the power of this knowledge was that it was arrived at collectively. This collective process served to break down a sense of guilt for one's own united strength and potential for action. It was and is a political act carried out in the private sphere. . . .

Talking Heads/New Rules of the Game

The visual portrayal of the women in feminist documentaries is often criticised for its transparency (film's capturing reality) or for the visual dullness of talking heads. Yet the stories that the filmed women tell are not just 'slices of experience'. These stories serve a function aesthetically in reorganising women viewers' expectations derived from patriarchal narratives and in initiating a critique of those narratives. The female figures talking to us on the screen in *Janie's Janie*, *Joyce at 34*, *Union Maids*, *Three Lives*, *The Woman's Film*, and *We're Alive* are not just characters whom we encounter as real-life individuals. Rather, the film-makers have clearly valorised their subjects' words and edited their discourse. In all the feminist documentaries, the sound track, usually told in the subjects' own words, serves the function of rephrasing, criticising, or articulating for the first time the rules of the game as they have been and as they should be for women.

The sound track of the feminist documentary film often consists almost entirely of women's self-conscious, heightened, intellectual discussion of role and sexual politics. The film gives voice to that which had in the media been spoken for women by patriarchy. Received notions about women give way to an outpouring of real desires, contradictions, decisions, and social analyses. . . .

The feminist documentaries represent a use of, yet a shift in, the aesthetics of *cinéma vérité* due to the film-makers close identification with their subjects, participation in the women's movement, and sense of the films' intended effect. The structure of the consciousness-raising group becomes the deep structure repeated over and over in these films. Within such a narrative structure, either a single woman tells her story to the film-maker or a group of women are filmed sharing experiences in a politicised way. They are filmed in domestic space, and their words serve to redefine that space in a new, 'women-identified' way. Either the stance of the people filmed or the stance of the film as a whole reflects a commitment to changing the public sphere as well; and for this reason, these film-makers have used an accessible documentary form. In the 'surface structure' of the films, a new iconography of women's bodies and women's space emerges that implicitly challenges the general visual depiction of women in capitalist society, perhaps in many Socialist ones, too. The sound tracks have women's voices speaking continuously; and the films' appeal lies not only in having strong women tell about their lives but even more in our hearing and having demonstrated that some women have deliberately altered the rules of the game of sexual politics. All *cinéma vérité* is not the same, and much of the current discussion of and attack on cinematic realism dismisses the kind of documentary film style that most people are used to. If one looks closely at the relation of this politicised genre to the movement it is most intimately related to, we can see how both the exigencies and forms of organisation of an ongoing political movement can affect the aesthetics of documentary film.

Notes

1. Many of the feminist documentaries (I have given only a representative list of them) are described briefly in Linda Artel's and Susan Wengraf's *Positive Images: Non-Sexist Films for Young People* (San Francisco: Booklegger Press, 1976). Interviews with feminist film-makers often appear alongside reviews of their films in *Jump Cut*.
2. Experimental film-making techniques or an innovative 'stretching' of the *cinéma vérité* form are particularly well used in JoAnn Elam's *Rape*, Michelle Citron's *Parthenogenesis*, and the collectively produced *We're Alive*.

3. An activist in health care struggles criticises the political analyses offered in feminist health care films in Marcia Rothenberg's 'Good Vibes vs. Preventive Medicine: Healthcaring from our end of the speculum', *Jump Cut* no. 17, April 1978, p.3.
4. Such an idea loosely derives from the work of Claude Lévi-Strauss in *Structural Anthropology*, trans. C. Jacobson and B. G. Schoepf (Garden City, N.Y.: Doubleday Anchor, 1967).
5. *Cinéma vérité* films in the United States made by male film-makers are characterised precisely by the film's ironic distance from the subject and the film-maker's presentation of his vision of the subject as his 'creation'. Films by Frederick Wiseman, Richard Leacock, David Pennebaker, Tom Palazzolo, and the Maysles brothers fall in this category.

'Daughter Rite': Living with Our Pain and Love

JANE FEUER

From *Jump Cut* no. 23, October 1980, pp. 12–13.

MICHELLE CITRON's film *Daughter Rite* commences with the voice of a narrator, speaking in a dull tone as if reading from a diary. At the age of 28, the voice tells us, she began working out her conflicting feelings toward her mother. Now two years later, she is able to dedicate this film to her mother, 'a woman whom I am very much like and not like at all'. Presumably the 50-minute film we are about to see will detail this process. Under the voice, however, we receive a different message. In a blown-up home-movie image, slowed down to a crawl and printed over and over again, a little girl and her mother run toward each other, always missing each other's embrace. Finally, the mother grabs the daughter and the film's title comes up. A curious 'daughter rite', indeed. For the remainder of the film, similar narrated home-movie footage alternates with 'documentary' segments (described below) in which two grown sisters discuss their mother. Each 'story' expresses with visual and verbal force the schizophrenia every woman I know feels toward her mother: total hatred amidst total love. The diarist appears to move toward a resolution of this conflict; the sisters in the documentary do not.

Throughout the film, the diarist speaks directly of her ambivalence. As home movie images of the two little sisters carrying suit-cases appear to float slowly off to screen-left (as if trying to escape their mother's grasp), the voice intones: 'I hate my weaknesses ... my weaknesses are my mother'. The image switches to the little girls, dressed daintily and identically in blue dresses, leaving the house. The voice continues: 'I hate ... my bitchiness and my selfishness. That part, too, is my mother'. The little girls come toward the camera as the voice finishes: 'And in hating my mother, I hate myself'. Yet later in the film the diarist deals with that other side of mother-hating which is mother-loving. The home-movie footage is of a baby buggy race in which dozens of little girls in lace dresses are socialised into frilly feminine roles as their mothers cheer from the side-lines. And yet, over this scene which would appear the ultimate in indoctrination into passivity and weakness, the voice speaks of forgiveness: 'I am not the

24

angry one. I am filled with sadness and love for this woman'. In the final home-movie sequence of the film we see the mother as a young woman, laughing with her daughters, walking across a green field with her arm around the older daughter. The narrator tells of a dream in which her sister dies and the mother helps clean up the remains. The sequence ends with images of reconciliation and the words, 'She holds me in her arms and I start to cry'.

I have trouble finding the proper language with which to write about this film. Molly Haskell said she was a film critic first and a feminist second, but *Daughter Rite* does not allow for such dichotomising. I shall speak of Michelle Citron's film with the voice of the film critic, but I watched it as a daughter.

Already the film critic is dissatisfied with the daughter's description of the film. For in describing alternating 'documentary' and 'home-movie' segments, I have already imposed a questionable reading on the film. Although traditional viewing habits cause me to see only two segments, in fact, there are three separate 'channels', each seemingly belonging to the three major phyla of the film-making kingdom: fiction, documentary, and experimental. The first channel consists of a voice-over narration in the first person, a literary device associated with fiction film (but also a traditional documentary technique). The second channel, under the narration on the image track, consists of optionally reprinted scenes from home movies reminiscent of experimental technique. The third channel, presented separately, consists of 'documentary' footage of two sisters talking about their mother. It is both natural and tempting to interpret the narration as dominant and as the voice of the author due to a longstanding convention of 'voice of god' narration in documentary film. It is also tempting, because most films we see employ sound synchronously, to assume that the narration is describing the home movie footage under it. Finally, it is almost impossible on the first viewing not to try to create relationships among the narrative voice, the little girls in the home movie footage, and the adult women in the 'documentary' footage.

In trying to unify the three channels prematurely, one is tempted to call *Daughter Rite* a 'documentary'. This brings with it a set of expectations (which the film frustrates). If it is a documentary, then the home movie footage (which otherwise may seem staged due to the reprinting) must represent 'real' images of the relationship the narrator (who must be the film-maker) has with her mother (presumably the women in the home movie footage and the woman whom the sisters speak of obsessively but whom we never see). One student of mine even went so far as to assume that the older sister who narrates was the same as the older sister in the home movies and the older sister in the *cinéma vérité* footage. He deduced that the older sister must be played by the director herself. Years of watching films which demand such a unified reading make this a most sensible interpretation.

When we look at the film microscopically, however, the surface unity fissures. First of all, the 'reality' of the home movie footage is suspect, not because the raw material is not actually home movie footage (it is), but because that footage has already been subjected to a process of interpretation by the film-maker. Typical moments and movements are selected and printed over and over again: the mother grabs the little girls, pokes them; the girls wear 'party' dresses, hair curlers, wash dishes, learn feminine behaviour. Camera movements are added to provide new meanings; shots are taken from their original continuity and juxtaposed for effect. The original home movies no longer exist for us; the film-maker has revealed the 'reality' behind the façade of happy family celebration the father's camera recorded.

Moreover, this patchwork document of some woman's childhood is not necessarily there in subordination to that identical woman's narrative voice. The images not only possess their own ambiguity but also frequently contradict the voice. In the second segment of the film, the little girls ride with mother on the Swan boat at Boston's Public Garden. The mother sticks out her tongue at the camera, she waves at the camera. Is this not a joyous occasion? Yet the voice – always somewhat neutral and flat – speaks angry words: 'I hate her dishonesty.' Because the images do not pin down meaning to the extent that the words do, one's first temptation is to bind the words to that particular image. But might not the words apply equally well (in this case better) to other images, angrier images, not just those in the home movie footage but those in the *cinéma vérité* footage as well? Why not apply these words to the image of the older daughter in the home movies seeming to kiss the younger but also seemingly trying to strangle her? Or to a birthday party during which the mother's hand stabs repeatedly at her daughter's hair?

If we think of the information carried by the three channels as a kind of floating free play of associations, each viewer will be able to discover for herself a wealth of connections within the film without ever having to say, *this* is what the film means or *this* is the author speaking. Nor will there be a need to find a narrative progression in the film. The relationship among the channels and segments becomes thematic, not linear or chronological, and the voices that speak take on a more generalised identity. The voices speak not one neurotic woman who got messed up by her mother but rather the common experience of many daughters and many mothers caught up in cultural inevitabilities.

In this way the interaction among the channels becomes complex. Sometimes the voice-over is autonomous. At the end the voice speaks over black leader: 'I imagine my mother seeing this; feeling the pain, eroding the pleasure. "Why do you have to say all this?" she asks.'

26

Daughter Rite

Sometimes the voice seems to refer to the home movie footage, sometimes not. We see the little girls sitting at a table with mother. As the voices intones, 'We would never be close,' the camera flash pans down the mother's arm to the child, the mother reaching out for the child but not quite making it. A seeming synchrony. But in many other cases no such obvious connection exists.

Similarly, at times the *cinéma vérité* segments seem to relate to the home movie footage or to the voice or both – sometimes not. As in the home movie footage, we see two females ambivalent in relation to a mother figure. Both sets of sisters both hate and love the mother. In both, the mother is painted as devouring and yet nurturing. In both each sister in turn reveals a 'good' and a 'bad' relationship to the mother. And the voice could be describing either mother. How many mothers are there? How many daughters? The film forces us to ask such questions as we view.

This call for an ongoing intellectual as well as emotional involvement in the film seems to be issued by the *cinéma vérité* documentary segments as well. Those, too, like the 'reconstituted' home movies, are not what they seem. As the film progresses, the *cinéma vérité* footage challenges a whole film-making style. It's necessary to see *Daughter Rite* in a tradition of feminist film-making in order to comprehend just what is being deconstructed. *Cinéma vérité*, often referred to in America as 'direct cinema', evolved in the early sixties in reaction against heavily narrated documentaries which imposed a preconceived

27

point of view of the material. Direct cinema, in theory, represents an extreme 'realist' aesthetic in which the profilmic event is allowed to unfold before the camera, unscripted and without preconception on the part of the film-maker.[1] Julia Lesage has explained why feminist film-makers of the early seventies were attracted to this form of documentary, approximating as it did the structure of the consciousness raising group and of openness and trust among women. As Lesage explains it: 'Many of the first feminist documentaries used a simple format to present to the audience (presumably composed primarily of women) a picture of the ordinary details of women's lives, their thoughts – told directly by the protagonists to the camera'.[2]

Daughter Rite begins firmly within this tradition. Two sisters sit at their mother's kitchen table, and in one take, the younger sister describes her hostility at her mother's hovering over her at the birth of her child. The sister seems to be talking to the film-maker, presumably another woman, seated to one side of the camera. The sisters' interaction is natural and shows no camera awareness because they are addressing the camera/film-maker as women, simply and directly. In the second segment, the sisters sit side by side on a sofa, and their interaction (in direct address) is recorded with the full repertoire of *cinéma vérité* techniques. Out of respect for real space and time, there are no cuts. The camera pans to pick up each sister as she talks, coming to rest on the older sister for a monologue about her mother's invasion of her youthful privacy. As the older sister talks, we see the younger sister's hand come into the frame to brush back her sister's hair, again emphasising the presence of the younger in the offscreen space just to the left of the frame. Another *vérité* technique – zooming in for a closer shot and focusing up on screen (rack focus) – also avoids the necessity of cutting out any segment of the interaction as well as proving that the zoom was spontaneous, the lens not prefocused. The entire segment is 'coded' in *cinéma vérité* style. But we tend to interpret this stylistic coding as 'reality'. Both the 'naive' and the 'sophisticated' viewer are likely to assume that what they see is 'real'.

As the *cinéma vérité* segments progress, the mode of address shifts from one of direct address to the camera to one of objective observation of the sisters as they interact in increasingly intimate ways with one another. In a seemingly unmotivated segment, we watch them collaborating on a fruit salad with which neither winds up satisfied (echoes of the narrator's mother?). We watch them sitting on the floor hooting over their mother's phonograph records. An argument ensues over their mother's finances (again echoing the earlier narration). The camera pans the distance that has appeared between them. In the next segment, the younger sister returns to the mode of direct address as she narrates the story of a rape. Finally, we observe them again, going through the mother's bedroom drawers, making discoveries. In each

28

case, whether the address is direct or observational, the panoply of *vérité* techniques clues us that this footage is somehow 'true' or 'natural' or 'real'. Therefore many viewers are shocked to discover at the end of the film that these scenes have been played by actresses. A careful observer may have noticed that the camera work anticipated certain actions and that the sisters do things no one is likely to do in front of a camera, but in my experience even professional documentary film-makers have been 'deceived' by the footage of the sisters. Why is the film-maker trying to dupe us in this way? many have asked.

I believe this is a legitimate question and one whose answer opens up an inquiry into the appropriateness of the *cinéma vérité* mode for feminist film practice. It should also help us to question the meaning of terms such as 'truth', 'fiction', and 'documentary'.

Vérité means 'truth', but *cinéma vérité* never gives us a transcendent truth. The French school of *cinéma vérité* was far more honest than the Americans in acknowledging that the 'realist' style is merely another ideologically determined method of recording images on film.[3] Nonetheless, we tend to interpret footage shot in this 'realist' style as 'true'. *Daughter Rite* deconstructs such equations, substituting an enacted or 'fictional' version which grasps a number of contradictory truths about women's lives with mother, 'truths' which deny the easy resolution provided by narrative closure. Using actresses is arguably more 'true' in the philosophical sense than using 'real women' in such roles. This is because, in practice, *cinéma vérité* films become films about 'real' people dealing with the intrusion of a camera into their lives, a fact the French acknowledged from the beginning but that the Americans came to grips with much later or not at all (the Maysles' *Grey Gardens* takes the presence of the film-makers into account; the Raymonds' *An American Family* does not).

In slowly revealing to us the 'fictional' nature of her film, Citron is not deceiving us; rather, she is making us see that 'documentaries', in purporting to be 'truer' than fiction, may have been deceiving us all along. *Daughter Rite* in this sense interrogates traditional forms of film-making adapted by early feminist film-makers, asking us to consider what forms feminist 'documentaries' may take in the future.

The beauty of Citron's subject and of her treatment of it is that the more personal it becomes, the more political it becomes. The formal complexity of the film is necessitated by the complexity of the subject. Since even one woman's reaction to her mother is bound to be fraught with contradictions, and since Citron is broaching the long-taboo subject of sister-hating, it is necessary for the film to question its own roots as a feminist film. *Daughter Rite* has to avoid the easy Utopian solution that the *vérité* approach implies. Just as women can't suddenly love each other because it's politically correct, so also a film need not provide 'solutions' in order to be a valuable feminist document.

Ultimately, the value of the form *Daughter Rite* takes lies in the way it forces each woman to reflect upon her own daughter rites. *Daughter Rite* proves a sublimely painful experience not easily reduced to a message. In its emotive power, *Daughter Rite* might well teach a lesson to those avant-garde radical film-makers set upon sacrificing identification and emotional involvement on the altar of mere cognition. Every woman who has a mother ought to see this film.

Notes

1. See Stephen Mamber, *Cinéma vérité in America* (Cambridge: MIT Press, Mass., 1974), for a presentation of the philosophy animating early American direct cinema. See also Eileen McGarry, 'Documentary, Realism, and Women's Cinema', *Women and Film*, 2, Summer 1975, for a feminist critique of this notion of 'realism'. It should be noted that the French *cinéma vérité* tradition (Chris Marker, Jean Rouch) was far more interested in acknowledging the presence of the camera as part of the diegesis.
2. 'The Political Aesthetics of the Feminist Documentary Film', originally in *Quarterly Review of Film Studies*, 3, no. 4, Fall 1978. See pp. oo–oo above.
3. Eileen McGarry's article, cited above, as well as recent articles on documentary in *Screen* and *Jump Cut*, deconstruct the notion of *cinéma vérité* documentary as 'realist'.

Anti-Porn:
Soft Issue, Hard World

B. RUBY RICH

From *Village Voice*, 1983, pp. 56–67. Also in *Feminist Review* no. 13, February 1983.

WHY HAS the antiporn movement been so popular with the dominant media? My suspicions are not benign. For one thing, in a society that has failed to distinguish between sexuality and pornography, the antiporn movement is a perfect vehicle for lumping all feminists together into one posse, a bunch of sex cops out to handcuff the body politic's cock. The ensuing ridicule can always offset any serious statements. Second, the subject offers the chance to talk about sex – something the mainstream media are never loath to take up. Third, the antiporn movement is probably seen, and rightly so, as profoundly ineffectual, unlikely ever to make a dent in the massive commercial sex industry it would seek to topple. The porn companies don't have to worry about any consumer boycott by women; we're not their customers. It is even possible that the antiporn forces get press *because* they represent no threat. *Not a Love Story* – portentously subtitled 'a motion picture about pornography' – can open at the 57th Street Playhouse in a gala premiere, emblazon *Village Voice* and the *Times* as well with ads, boast a prestige distributor and a first-class PR firm, and even make it onto the evening news. Just in case there's any lingering doubt about its moral fibre, keep in mind that it's showing at the same theatre where *Genocide* just ran.

The Appeal

Documentary films, like fiction, have a script. The script may not be written before the shooting, as with fiction, but in that case it gets written in the editing room. *Not a Love Story* is no exception. Director Bonnie Klein, producer Dorothy Todd Henaut, and associate director and editor Anne Henderson seem to have scripted a religious parable.

In this moral tale, each character has a clearly prescribed role. Klein, who appears on-screen to supply an identification figure for the audience, plays the missionary in a heathen land. Seeking out the purveyors of porn, she is seen unearthing the sins of the world in order to combat them and save our souls. 'Blue Sky', 'Ravers', and other peep-show workers and strippers all play the collective role of victim.

31

Porn photographer Suze Randall, who photographs hard-core spreads in her studio, plays the classic madame; she who sells her own kind but probably, deep inside, is a true believer. The porn moguls interviewed are surely the forces of evil, whether represented by the sleezy panache of publisher David Wells or by the endearing just-like-your-Uncle-Henry spirit of one sex emporium manager. The male customers constitute the legions of rank sinners. A San Francisco-based group of men against male violence assumes the guise of *penitentes*; matching a 60s wire-rim style to an 80s sensitivity, they take the sins of their kind upon their shoulders and expiate them. There is, of course, a roster of saints: Susan Griffin, Kate Millett, Margaret Atwood, Kathleen Barry, and topping them all, Robin Morgan, who, with husband Kenneth Pitchford and young son, presents her own version of the Holy Family. Addressing the camera with a philosophical fervour (except for the more casual Millett), the saints embody the forces of righteousness arrayed against the sinful.

The pivotal figure in the parable is Linda Lee Tracey, a stripper with a comedic 'Little Red Riding Hood' act. She performs the role of the reformed sinner, without whom no religious faith could be complete. Her redemption seals the film's theme, binds the audience to it, and provides the necessary narrative closure. *Not a Love Story* opens with a series of valentines, ranging from soft-core 40s style to an up-to-date hard-core *Hustler* version, but clearly it is the Sacred Heart that takes over by the end.

Linda Lee is the real star of the film. A Montreal media personality famous for her annual 'Tits for Tots' charity-strips, she was a find for the film-makers. It is she who accompanied director Klein on all the interview sessions, frequently asking the questions herself, challenging the hucksters, haranguing customers from a soapbox on the street. If Klein empathises on screen, emoting outrage and concern, it is Tracey who acts, reacts, and takes the risks. Just how much of a risk is made clear toward the end of the film. The audience has already been buffeted by pornographic images and film clips, appalled by the attitudes of the porn kings, overwhelmed by the statistics, and alternately inspired and outraged by what has been shown and said. As the culmination of its guided tour, the audience gets to be present at a photo session set up between porn photographer Suze Randall and our by-now heroine, Linda Lee, who has decided 'to find out what it feels like to be an object'. In her willingness to embrace this risk, Linda Lee becomes the film's *dramatis persona,* the one character who is transformed, within the film, by the very experience of making the film. As if Christ had come back as a latter-day Mary Magdalene, she literally offers up her body for our, and her, salvation.

Halfway through the film, Linda Lee comments that 'it's starting to get to me at an emotional level'. She meant: that pornography. But I mean: the movie. *Not a Love Story* is, for me, more depressing than inspiring, more irritating than enlightening. The film hits its emotional stride early on and stays there, never straying into detours of social analysis, historical perspective, or questions of representation. Klein sets the tone with her pose of womanly empathy, polite outrage, and respectability. She recounts her decision to make the film after her eight-year-old daughter's exposure to porn magazines at the local bus counter. I suspect many viewers' response to the movie will rise or fall on the issue of identification with Klein. Mine fell. An aura of religiosity began to permeate the proceedings. Method and message began to blur as the film gained in momentum, upping the emotional ante into a cathartic finale.

Not a Love Story is no call to arms, but rather an exercise in show-and-tell. Gaze at the forbidden, react with your choice of anger or outrage or grief (or the male option: guilt), and leave a changed person. When Linda Lee undergoes her debasement at the lens of Suze Randall and subsequently emerges transformed and cleansed – running on the beach in the film's last frames – she is enacting a ceremony that the audience communally shares. A change in consciousness, a change of heart. Look here and weep. Post-screening goings-on, both at the New York premieres and in Canada, fortify the scenario. After-film discussions have turned the theatre into a secular confessional, eliciting testimonials, women's resolutions to confront their mates' porn collections, teenage boys swearing to forgo the porn culture that awaits them, male viewers alternately abashed or exploding in anger, etc. According to polls of the film's audiences, people are moved from seeing pornography as harmless to viewing it as harmful by the end of the film. Conversion cinema in action.

Is the appeal of the film, then, a religious one? A desire to pass through the flames, be washed in the blood of the lamb, and come out a new person? I think not. Instead, the antiporn film is an acceptable replacement for porn itself, a kind of snuff movie for an antisnuff crowd. In this version, outrage-against replaces pleasure-in, but the object of the preposition remains the same. Cries of outrage and averted eyes replace the former clientele's silent pleasure and inverted hats; the gaze of horror substitutes for the glaze of satiation. The question, though, is whether this outcry becomes itself a handmaiden to titillation, whether this alleged look of horror is not perhaps a most sophisticated form of voyeurism. The ad campaign reinforces the suspicion, with its prominent surgeon-general-style warning about the 'graphic subject matter' that viewers might want to avoid . . . if avoidance is indeed the desired goal.

The film's own methods compound the problem. While it would be unrealistic to ask *Not a Love Story* to solve problems the political movement it addresses has so far ignored, it's reasonable to expect the film to take up those problems relevant to its own medium. A host of issues raised by pornography are applicable to cinema, ranging from voyeurism or objectification to simple questions of point of view. Instead of facing these challenges, though, the film-makers seem unquestioningly to accept and deploy traditional cinematic practices. Given their subject matter, this decision creates a subtext of contradiction throughout the film.

For example, the early scenes of strippers performing their act are shot from the audience, a traditional enough technique for a rock concert movie, but problematic here. Doesn't such a shot turn the viewer into the male customer normally occupying that vantage point? Doesn't the camera's privileged gaze, able to zoom in and out at will, further objectify the woman on stage? Worse yet is the scene shot in a club equipped with isolation-masturbation booths, wherein the women on display communicate with the male customers via a glass window and telephone, with the duration determined by a descending black-out shutter timed to the deposit of money. The cinematographer lines the camera up with this same shutter, positioning us behind the shoulder of a male customer in the booth, protected by shadows even as the woman called 'Blue Sky' is exposed to our view. The cinematographer takes this alignment with the male customer one step further by zooming in for a close-up on 'Blue Sky' – thereby presenting us with an intimate view not even available to the real-life customer. (At such moments, Klein's use of a male cameraman becomes an issue.) Why visually exploit this woman to a greater degree than her

Not a Love Story

34

job already does? Why make the male customer our stand-in and then let him off the hook, without either visual exposure or verbal confrontation? Why not let us see what 'Blue Sky' sees? Instead, the film-maker proceeds to interview two of the women from within this same booth and from the customer's seat. Now the man has departed and we remain, sophisticated consumers, out for the show *and* the facts coyly paying money when the inevitable shutter descends.

The film-makers efface their own presence whenever the movie enters the sex emporiums. While Klein is prominent in the other interview sessions, she does not appear at all in the clubs. Furthermore, no second camera ever shows us the steady gaze of *this one* filming the scene for us, the performer's 'other' audience. True, we see the male audience – but only from the vantage point of another member of that audience. The camera is protected in its invisibility by the film-maker, just as the male customers are in turn protected in their anonymity by the camera.

This is a serious mistake, but it's a clue to the film's attitude. At no point does the camera offer a shot from the point of view of the women up on the stage. We're never permitted to share their experience while they're working – to inhabit their perspective when they're supposedly being most exploited and objectified. The result is a backfire: we remain voyeurs, and they remain objects – whether of our pity, lust, respect, or shock makes little difference.

Not all the problems arise out of shooting; others occur in the editing room, particularly in the choices of sound/image combination. The key scene is Linda Lee's porn photo session with Suze Randall, whose presence overwhelms us with frequent calls for such props as 'the pussy light', and 'the pussy juice'. Although the scene has Linda Lee speaking as she starts to pose, her voice gives way to a voice-over of Susan Griffin explaining eros. Only later do we get to hear Linda Lee's comments. Why use Griffin's words when the film could have reinforced Tracey's image with her own explanation? Instead, the considerable power she wields elsewhere in the film simply evaporates.

The power of the pornography included as exhibits throughout the movie does no such evaporation act. Why does the film present us with the porn materials intact? Any number of methods could have been used either to intensify their impact or to diminish it. Some kind of manipulation of the image is standard practice in films incorporating pre-existing footage. The film-makers chose not to, with two possible results: either we're made to undergo the degradation of porn, or we're offered its traditional turn-on. Klein wants the audience to eat its cake and have it, too.

In sum, *Not a Love Story* is very much a National Film Board of Canada product: concerned, engaged, up to the minute on social questions, but slick, manipulative, avoiding all the hard questions to capture the ready success of answering the easy ones. It may have a different subject from other NFB films, but its methods are inherited. These methods have been developed for decades, and they work. If *Not a Love Story* is successful, that will be because of its emphasis on emotion, the presence of Linda Lee Tracey as a genuinely appealing star, the shock of the porn characters, and the sympathy of Bonnie Klein as our Alice in Pornoland. Not incidentally, the film offers some of the porn its audience wants to see but wouldn't be caught dead seeking out in Times Square.

Most fundamentally, though, the film's fate will signal the prospects of the anti-pornography campaign itself. The basic questions are not, finally, about *Not a Love Story* at all. They concern the past and future of antiporn politics, the reasons for its appeal, and the questions of priority it raises.

Displacement, Confusion, and What's Left Out

There are many unanswered questions in *Not a Love Story*, the title itself not the least of them. Assuming that pornography is not about love, what is it? The film privileges the words of Susan Griffin, who defines one of the central tenets of the antiporn movement: pornography is different from eroticism. Kate Millett says the same thing, as have countless others. But, what is pornography and what is eroticism? One is bad, the other is good (guess which). Fixing the dividing line is rather like redlining a neighbourhood: the 'bad' neighbourhood is always the place where someone *else* lives. Porn is the same. If I like it, it's erotic; if you like it, it's pornographic. The rules don't seem much clearer than that, so the game gets murkier by the minute. Ready?

Two stories. Back in 1969, when I first started thinking about this distinction, my best friend worked as an artist's model; so, eventually, did I. She would model for painters but never for photographers, since with them you'd have no control over who saw your body. Once she broke the rule and modelled for a mutual friend, a photographer who did a series of nude photographs of her that we all loved. He had a show in a local gallery. One photograph of my friend was stolen out of the show. She went into a terrible depression. She was tormented by the image of an unknown man jerking off to her picture. Test: was that photograph erotic or pornographic?

Back in 1980, a woman I know went to spend the day with a friend's family. Looking around the house, what should she discover but the father's personal copy of the Tee Corrine cunt colouring book. Made for the women's community, the book usually was found only in feminist bookstores. Test: is the book erotic or pornographic?

I have other friends and other stories. Surely it is not merely an *image* which is one thing or the other, but equally (if not foremost) the *imagination* that employs the image in the service of its fantasy. It is time that antiporn activists stopped kidding themselves about the fine distinctions between eroticism and pornography. If any extra test is needed, the film offers us one in its final freeze-frame shot of a bikini-clad Linda Lee, snapped in midair, seaweed in hand. It is meant as an image of 'wholeness, sanity, life-loving-ness' according to the film-makers, but it comes out looking more like a soft-core Tampax ad. Is this image, perchance, pornographic as well?

There is no end of definitions as to what pornography is or isn't. For me, that's no longer the point. I have read the statistics, thank you, on whether porn causes violence or violence causes porn, taken part in the chicken-or-the-egg fights, steered clear of the currently chic analyses of porn in academic circles. I'm as fed up with pornography being identified as sexuality (in some circles) as with anti-pornography being identified as feminism (in other circles). The books, the articles, and now the films have been rolling out.[1] Such widespread acceptance is always a clue that the problem has moved elsewhere. Why is pornography so important, finally? Is it important enough to be consuming all our political energy as feminists? Certainly it is seductive. It offers no end of discourse, arguments, connotations, and denotations in which we can immerse ourselves, no end of soul searching and pavement pounding which we can enact if so moved. But whence comes its assumed political priority, and does the issue deserve it?

The film, like much Women Against Pornography campaign rhetoric, tends to identify porn both by what it is *not* (a love story) and by what it *is* at its most extreme (sadism, torture dramas). The film, like the antiporn movement lately, emphasises the extent to which sex-and-violence *is* the contemporary face of porn. But such a focus dodges the dilemma. If violence were the only problem, then why would the film include extensive footage of the strip shows and peep booths? If only violent sex were the object of wrath, then why would any Women Against Pornography group picket a non-violent live sex show, or girlie line-up? In fact, the reliance on violence-condemnation in the rhetoric is a clue to the appeal of the antiporn movement. Women today are terrified at the levels of violence being directed at us in society – and, to take it further, at powerless people everywhere. As one porn actress in the movie eloquently put it, we're 'the fucked'. Women are terrified at the crazy spiral of rape, assults on abortion rights, sterilisation expansion, domestic battering, and anonymous bashing.

Terror is not an effective emotion, though. It paralyses. The fear of escalating violence, accompanied by the larger social backlash, has resulted not in massive political action by feminists but rather in a reaction of denial, a will *not to see* the dangers . . . a desperate desire to see, instead, their disguises. Turning away from a phalanx of assaults too overwhelming to confront, the Women Against Pornography groups turn instead to its entertainment division, pornography. But whether symptom or cause, pornography presents an incomplete target for feminist attack. The campaign against pornography is a massive displacement of outrage that ought to be directed at a far wider sphere of oppression. Just as the film narrows the hunt down to sinners, villains, and victims so too does the anti-pornography movement leave out too much in its quasi-religious attack on the Antichrist.

The hunt for archetypes, darkly submerged drives, and other assorted ghouls of the pornography industry and the pornographic imagination has left livelier culprits out in the cold. So long as the conversion experience is the primary method, then the social, economic, historical, and political determinants get short shrift. As long as they continue, of course, it is unlikely that Dorothy Henaut will get her dream – announced opening night – of seeing the porn industry up and 'wither away'.

The emphasis on violence has masked the central issue of male/female power relations which we see reflected and accentuated in pornography. Any woman is still fair game for any man in our society. Without an understanding of these power relations, no analysis of porn will get very far. It certainly won't be able to account for the prevalence of fake lesbianism as a staple of pornographic imagery (without violence). It certainly won't be able to account for the difference between straight porn and gay male porn, which lacks any debasement of women and must raise complex issues regarding sexual objectification. If an analysis of porn were to confront its basic origin in the power relations between men and women, then it would have to drop the whole eroticism-versus-pornography debate and take on a far more complex and threatening target: the institution of heterosexuality. Here, again, is a clue to the antiporn movement's appeal for some battle-scarred feminists. Is it, perhaps, more tolerable for the woman who might attend *Not a Love Story* to come to terms with how her male lover's pornographic fantasy is oppressing her in bed than to confront, yet again, how his actual behaviour is oppressing her in the living room . . . or out in the world?

Also left out of the picture are all questions of class and race, subsumed under the religious halo of good versus evil. Does it do any good, however, to view the women employed in the porn empire as victims? Linda Lee herself, in the movie, describes having gone to a Women Against Pornography demonstration in New York and feeling the other women's condescension. Or, as 'Jane Jones' told Laura Lederer in the *Take Back the Night* anthology, 'I've never had anybody from a poor or working-class background give me the "How could you have done anything like that?" question, but middle-class feminists have no consciousness about what it is like out there.'[2] As long as the economic forces and social choices that move these women into the commercial-sex world remain invisible, they themselves will continue to be objectified, mystified, and misunderstood by the very feminist theorists who, wine glass in hand or flowers nearby, claim to have all the answers. The film equally ignores questions of race, even though the porn industry, in its immense codification, has always divided the female population up into racial segments keyed to specific fetishes.

Issues of race and class, here, are particularly troubling in that they divide so clearly the film-makers from their subjects. One friend of mine, herself a Puerto Rican activist, pinpointed the cause of her outrage at the film: 'All these years, she (Klein) was never bothered by my exploitation. Now, suddenly, *she* feels exploited by *my* exploitation, and it's this feeling that really upsets her.' The film never acknowledges that there might be a difference between the physical debasement of the women who earn their living in the sex industry and the ideological debasement of all women caused by the very existence of that industry. On the contrary, the anti-pornography movement has never taken up the issue of class. If it had addressed questions of class with attention or seriousness, then it might have avoided the seeming complicity with the State (like its notorious participation in the Times Square clean-up campaign, evidenced by its acceptance of office space by the forces advancing the street-sweep) that has made so many feminists wary of the anti-porn movement's real politics. Instead, the total and very apparent isolation of the film-makers from the women who populate the various sex establishments in their film cannot help but make the viewer uneasy. Empathy? Forget it. To put it bluntly, the anti-porn campaigners seem to view the women working in the commercial sex industry much the same way that the Moral Majority seems to view pregnant teenagers. The powerful sense of identification that has been such a keystone of feminist politics is absent; in its place is a self-righteous sense of otherness that condemns the sex workers eternally to the position of Bad Object (pending, of course, any Linda-Lee-like transubstantiation).

Also overlooked is the aboveground face of porn, its front-parlour guise as legitimate advertising. This was the first target of WAVAW (Women Against Violence Against Women) in such actions as the attack on the Rolling Stones' infamous Black and Blue billboard. The *Hustler* cover image that made the movie audience gasp (a woman churned into a meat grinder) made its feminist debut in the early WAVAW slide shows. Such actions have faded in recent years, as debate, theory, and red light district pressure tactics took over. *Not a Love Story* alludes to the intersection of pornography and advertising, even illustrates it at points, but never explicates the connections. The antiporn literature does the same, condemning the continuum without analysing the linkage. Hasn't anyone heard of capitalism lately? In order to use women to sell products, in order to use pornography to sell genital arousal, there has to be an economic system that makes the use profitable. Porn is just one product in the big social supermarket. Without an analysis of consumer culture, our understanding of pornography is pathetically limited, bogged down in the undifferentiated swamp of morality and womanly purity.

Significantly in these cold war times, the differing attitudes of Nazi and Communist societies are not cited equally. The historical usage of pornography by the Nazis (who flooded Poland with porn at the time of the invasion to render the population . . . impotent?) is mentioned by Robin Morgan in the film and has been cited by others in articles and talks. No one ever mentions (with whatever reservations) the contemporary abolition of pornography in Cuba or in Nicaragua. There, it is one part of an overall social programme; here it must be the same if it is ever to succeed in transforming our systems of sexual exchange.

The single-issue nature of the antiporn movement is one of its most disturbing aspects. Once the 'final solution' has been identified, there is no need to flail away at other social inequities. I'd guess that its avoidance of social context is another of antiporn's attractions. Racism, reproductive rights, homophobia, all pale beside the ultimate enemy, the pornographer. How politically convenient for a right-leaning decade. It is precisely this avoidance of context, this fetishising of one sector or one crime, that is the distinguishing feature of life under capitalism. It is also, of course, the same fetishism and fragmentation that characterise the pornographic imagination.

Retro Politics

How can it be that I, as a feminist, even one who objects to pornography and subscribes to many of the arguments against it, can at the same time object just as strenuously to the anti-pornography movement and to the method, style, perhaps even the goals, of *Not a Love Story*? Or that many other feminists share my objections? The answer, predictably enough, is political. It has to do with the conviction that, in the fight against pornography, what gets lost is as serious as what gets won.

Behind the banner of pornography is the displaced discourse on sexuality itself. Indeed, if the antiporn campaign offers a safety zone within which the larger anti-feminist forces abroad in 80s America need not be viewed, it also offers a corresponding zone that excludes personal sexuality. This depersonalising of sexuality is the common effect both of pornography and of the anti-pornography forces. It is a depersonalisation that is all too apparent in the film.

Only Kate Millett speaks with ease, in her own voice, and from her own experience, lounging on the floor with one of her 'erotic drawings'. It is impossible to connect the other spokeswomen personally to the texts that they talk at us. Both Susan Griffin (with, unfortunately, nature blowing in the wind behind her head) and Kathleen Barry (framed by drapes and flowers) speak abstractly, rely on the third person, and bask in an aura of solemnity that punches all of the film's religioso buttons. When Robin Morgan hits the screen, an even greater problem appears.

It is here that we realise just how much space the film has preserved for men. Not only has its debate been framed entirely in terms of heterosexuality; not only have we been forced to watch always from the seat of a male buyer; but now we are made to accept feminist wisdom from a woman in tears, reduced to crying by the contemplation of the great pain awaiting us all, and capable of consolation only by the constant massaging of a sensitive husband (in a supporting *penitente* role) and a prematurely supportive son, who flank her on the sofa as she tells of women's suffering, boyhood's innocence, and men's innate desire to do right. Isn't this going too far? Middle-class respectability, appeals to motherhood, and now, elaborate detours aimed at making men feel comfortable within the cosy sphere of the enlightened. Any minute, and the film will go all 'humanistic' before our very eyes. Men didn't used to play such a central role in the feminist movement. Nor used the women to put quite such a premium on respectability and sexual politesse.

What has happened here? It has been an unsettling evolution, this switch from a movement of self-determination, that trashed billboards and attacked the legitimacy of soft-core advertising, to a movement of social determination, that urges legal restrictions and social hygiene. When the anti-pornography movement traded in its guerrilla actions for the more recent route of petitioning a higher authority to enact moral codes, the political trajectory went haywire. I do not agree with those who go no further than a pious citing of the First Amendment in their pornography discussions; while the vision of free speech is a benevolent one, even at times a practicable ideal, I am cynically aware of its purchase power in this society, especially in a backlash era. While I do not, therefore, agree that WAP can simply be conflated with the Moral Majority, and that's that, I do think the notion that a feminist agenda can be legislated in our society is a naive, and ultimately dangerous, one.

Judith Walkowitz, in her essay on 'The Politics of Prostitution', traced the political ramifications of the British 19th century anti-prostitution campaigns, cautioning that 'the feminists lacked the cultural and political power to reshape the world according to their own image. Although they tried to set the standards for sexual

41

conduct, they did not control the instruments of state that would ultimately enforce these norms.'[3] Nor do we today. Nor are feminists likely to countenance any such movement to set let alone enforce, some notion of sexual 'norms'. This proscriptive tendency in the antiporn movement is not offset by any counterbalancing emphasis on an alternative sexual tradition (except for the elusive eroticism). Is it a coincidence that one of the film's anti-porn demonstrators could be a stand-in for Mercedes McCambridge in *Johnny Guitar*? The antiporn movement has a tendency to promote a premature codification of sexuality, and *Not a Love Story* may suffer for that emphasis.

Perhaps the film actually arrived just one season too late in New York. The questions of sexual norms and sexual codification exploded at the 1982 Barnard conference on 'the politics of sexuality' with a coalition of WAP and others pitted against women espousing 'politically incorrect sexualities'. The conference has trailed in its wake a series of attacks and counter-attacks, a sensationalising of the proceedings, and one of the worst movement splits of recent times. Again, my perennial question surfaces: Why pornography? Why this debate? It seems that after a long hiatus, following Ti-Grace Atkinson's polemical assertion that 'the women's movement is not a movement for sexual liberation', feminists have come back to sexuality as an issue to discuss, argue, and analyse. It is not, however, clear why this debate should focus either on pornography or on sadomasochism (the two extremes at the conference), why it should short-circuit its own momentum by immediate codification.

It's time that the women's movement got back on track. While Robin Morgan weeps on the sofa, there are worse things happening in the world. It's time to acknowledge the importance of analysing pornography, assign it a priority in the overall picture, and get on with the fight. Pornography *is* an issue of importance. It is becoming much too fashionable to 'study' pornography in academic circles to dubious effect. Unlike many of the theorists doing that work, I would agree instead with Monique Wittig in 'The Straight Mind'[4] when she stresses that, while pornography is indeed a 'discourse', it is also for women a real source of oppression. That said, however, I would suggest that women desist from putting ourselves through the study of it. Finally, here's a proper subject for the legions of feminist men: let them undertake the analysis that can tell us why men like porn (not, piously, why this or that exceptional man does *not*), why stroke books work, how oedipal formations feed the drive, and how any of it can be changed. Would that the film had included any information from average customers, instead of stressing always the exceptional figure (Linda Lee herself, Suze Randall, etc.). And the antiporn campaigners might begin to formulate what routes could be more effective than marching outside a porn emporium.

As for the rest of us, it is time to desist, stop indulging in false and harmful polarities, and look around. Outraged at the abuse of women in our society, there are any number of struggles that can be joined on a broad social front. Outraged at pornography's being the only available discourse on sexuality, there is a great amount of visionary and ground-breaking work to do in the creation of a multitude of alternative sexual discourses, a veritable alternative culture of sexuality, that people can turn to for sexual excitement instead of porn. It's about time we redefine our terms and move on, with the spirit of justice and visionary energy that always used to characterise feminism.

As the first mass-audience film to take up the subject of pornography, *Not a Love Story* is an important work. It opens up the issues, even if it closes them down again too soon. For the people whom the film makes think seriously, for the first time, about pornography, it is a landmark. It is fascinating to hear that the audience at a recent midweek daytime screening was all single men; is it encouraging that none of them walked out? or discouraging that they could stay? Perhaps the film sins, for all its righteousness, in being simply too little, too late, even though it's the first of its kind.

Because it can help move the political debate on to the next stage, *Not a Love Story* deserves attention. Because it shows all too clearly the stage the debate is now in, it deserves criticism.

This article owes its existence, in part, to the encouragement and fantastic editing of Karen Durbin, my *Village Voice* editor. In addition, the article benefited from extended conversations with Fina Bathrick, Lillian Jimenez and Sande Zeig.

Notes

1. See, for example, Irene Diamond, 'Pornography and Repression: A Reconsideration', *Women: Sex and Sexuality* (Chicago: University of Chicago Press, 1980), pp. 129–44; Bertha Harris, 'Sade Cases', *Village Voice*, 18 May 1982, p. 46; Gina Marchetti, 'Readings on Women and Pornography', *Jump Cut* no. 26, pp. 56–60; Lisa Steele, 'Pornography and Eroticism' (an interview with Varda Burstyn), *Fuse* magazine, May/June 1982, pp. 19–24; Ellen Willis, 'Feminism, Moralism, and Pornography', *Beginning to See the Light* (New York: Knopf, 1981), pp. 219–27.
2. Laura Lederer, 'An Interview with a Former Pornography Model', *Take Back the Night* (New York: Bantam, 1982), pp. 45–59.
3. Judith Walkowitz, 'The Politics of Prostitution', *Women: Sex and Sexuality*, pp. 145–57, or see the updated version, 'Male Vice and Feminist Virtue: Feminism and the Politics of Prostitution in Nineteenth-Century Britain', *History Workshop Journal* no. 13, pp. 77–93, with an introduction by Jane Caplan.
4. Monique Wittig, 'The Straight Mind', *Feminist Issues* vol. 1 no. 1, Summer 1980, pp. 103–12.

An Introduction to 'The Song of the Shirt'

SYLVIA HARVEY

First presented at a History Workshop Conference on Realism, in London, October 1979.
Published in *Undercut* no. 1, March–April 1981, pp. 46–7.

I WOULD like to begin by quoting Timothy Clark on the Paris Salon of 1851, as the statement offers us a framework for thinking about the film, *The Song of the Shirt*:

> Art is sometimes historically effective – the making of a work of art is one historical process among other acts, events and structures: it is a series of actions *in* but also *on* history. It may become intelligible only within the context of given and imposed structures of meaning, but in its turn it can alter and disrupt these structures.[1]

A work of art – in this case a film – must not simply be thought of in a general sense as a *part* of history but must be considered as part of its own particular history – the history of art. Each work of art must be seen as a productive act – part of the history of changing and shaping the language of the medium employed. It is most important to see this film as part of this process – of changing the language of the medium – and thus as an 'action in but also *on* history'. 'To reiterate Clark's last point – we may only be able to understand each work in terms of given, existing structures of meaning, but the interesting point is that the new work may also 'alter, and at times disrupt' these structures.

Clark goes on to talk about the way the work of art works its material, how it may take up certain ideologies but transform them as it organises them into particular forms of expression. Thus:

> A work of art may have ideology . . . as its material, but it *works* that material, it gives it a new form and at certain moments that new form is in itself a subversion of ideology.[2]

In the light of this quotation I'd like to look at particular strategies adopted by *The Song of the Shirt*, in the context of current film practice.

The Work of Construction
The Song of the Shirt takes various constructions of the world and re-works them into new relationships. Its apparent content is the

44

history of sewing women – sempstresses – in the mid-nineteenth century, a sort of animated version of the *Hidden from History*[3] project. But it is also an essay on the problems of delimiting your subject matter – a common problem for historians – and an essay in relating, correlating different sorts of material, different aspects and different versions of history, both visual and verbal.

Against Central Coherence

The film attempts to set in play a variety of different documents, different accounts of the position of the sewing women and of their historical context. The variety of sources used ranges from the writings of Adam Smith, of the Earl of Shaftesbury, of Carlyle, to Chartist documents, contemporary political speeches and popular fiction, information on the Co-operative movement, and so on. The film takes up the problem of records/evidence/sources common to many academic disciplines, and translates these into specifically cinematic concerns. So, for example, the film tries to make problematic its use of sources by contrasting different types of spoken 'evidence' and musical material: and by constant visual reference to graphics and historical texts. Moreover, the acted fictional scenes can be seen both to emphasise the partiality of the historical sources, and to raise questions about audience responses, readership and the social use of particular texts in a given historical period.

What may be found interesting or perhaps frustrating is that the film does not try to organise this wealth of material into a single coherent story: 'the' story of the sewing women, and the slop shops of the sweated clothes trade. It constantly moves off, following trails in a variety of directions; it does not have that narrative rounding that we have come to associate with various TV series and documentary re-constructions. It is not even quite certain that the film is 'about' the early nineteenth century, the period culminating in the passing of the Ten Hours Act and the opening of the Great Exhibition. For each of the three segments of the film begins in the present: a TV monitor set in a cafe, with women watching it. In addition the first section of the film begins with a woman (in the present) talking about how low her wage is, and how her unemployed husband can claim more than her own total wage for the whole family, through State benefits.

So the film seems to be suggesting connections on the position of women, across from past to present, but these are not neatly tied up, the connections are not exactly 'cashed'; we are rather left, if we are willing to do a little work, a little thinking ourselves about past and present, and the usefulness of historical parallels.

The Strategy of Not Presenting a Particular Version of the Past

There needs to be some discussion about the *desirability* and the *possibility* of this strategy in respect of other written or filmed histories.

45

We may argue that simply from the selection and arrangement of materials, a particular account of the past is offered, in fact, whatever the film-makers try to do, and however 'open' a story of history they seek to offer. Or we could argue that it is indeed the responsibility of the historians to offer their particular analysis and understanding of the past, not to avoid taking certain decisions about 'ways of seeing', i.e. that historians should not be content with a perpetual relativism that can certainly never come to terms with questions of causation or determination.[1] The problem with offering a multiplicity of accounts is that it leaves to one side the answering of the question – 'yes, but why did these things happen?' The question of whether *The Song of the Shirt* is about or a product of that kind of relativism is, it seems to me, an open one. Very positively, though, what the film tries to do is ask who gets to write history and how do they do it? And it leaves open to us, the audience, the task of doing our own history writing, making our own connections and conclusions.

The 'Leaving it Up to the Audience' Phenomenon

This kind of strategy will be familiar to those who keep up with contemporary independent film practice. However, it is a phenomenon which is still unclear, mysterious, to many people, in fact to a majority of people, so it's worth noting very briefly why certain film-makers have adopted this tack. The refusal to represent the world from a central and single point of view, and then to hand that over to the audience 'on a plate', is at a general level part of the massive crisis in twentieth-century art around the problem of representation. It asks the question – 'How do you begin to go about depicting or representing the world?' This area is a concern of writers like Mallarmé and Joyce, but develops as a particular problem for the visual arts. It's a crisis that the cubists tried to deal with in painting at the beginning of this century, by representing the world from a multiplicity of view-points, not the single point perspective of all western post-renaissance painting. It is in general an aspect of the crisis in representation which has come to be labelled 'modernism' – that is, a crisis around the recognition of the fact of a medium of communication as something which comes between or *mediates* between us and our world. Modernism understands that we cannot depict the world simply, directly, transparently, as though in a work of art we were looking simply and directly at reality, as through a window on the world. The language that we use, whether of words or images, mediates that world to us in particular ways: this is the cardinal recognition of modernism. This gives rise to the peculiar self-reflexivity of the modernist movement: a process of meditating on the practice of mediation, of calling attention to the means of representation employed.

It is this concern that causes the film-maker Godard, for instance, to show, at the beginning of his film *Contempt*, a camera tracking down the studio lot, following the actress who we then see repeat this exact movement (walking down the lot) later in the film, this time without the presence of the camera being shown. This kind of device is used in *The Song of the Shirt* when the camera weaves across and around a series of images of the nineteenth century, set up on various boards and TV monitors in a studio space. Thus the film sets up images within images, stories within stories, to call attention to the presence of the film medium itself. It also combines documentary and fictional modes, to emphasise that these forms themselves are representations, versions or accounts of reality and not reality itself.

Positive and Negative Aspects of Modernism

The concerns of modernism can be seen to have both positive and negative aspects in the context of any attempt at producing an historical account or analysis. On the negative side, there is the danger of falling into a total relativism – the idea that we can never know the world, that we are forever lost, and caught in the processes of representation which have become estranged forever from the world they seek to represent. On the positive side – the fact of representation is foregrounded, the fact that certain people claim the right to produce representations of the world and to have their particular representa-

The Song of the Shirt

47

tions or accounts of the world dominate – this is called into question. Thus, foregrounding the *means* of representation can help us to ask the question – *who* is representing, and *for whom*? This has important consequences for ideological and political struggle.

Modernism and Popular Culture

The problem for those concerned with the relationship between cultural production and social change has been that the concerns of modernism have been unavailable to a mass audience, not available in popular culture. Though we might find some exceptions to this general rule in the theatre of Brecht, and in our own context in the work of some theatre groups in Britain today. But the problem has been, historically, that despite the potentially politically progressive aspects of Modernism, these concerns have not been generally available. While a film like *The Song of the Shirt* is clearly not going to be a 'popular' film, I think it is going to raise, successfully, with a wider audience, this problem of depiction, of *who* represents *what* and *how*, which is, finally, a political question. This claim for the film can, of course, only be judged by the audience, but it seems to me that the film manages to hold in tension, or in some kind of relationship, both a concern with the problem of representation, the problem of depiction, and a concern for, an interest in, the social world that is being depicted. The final question must be: under what sort of conditions, in what sort of context, will audiences be able to grasp the political significance of this relationship?'

Notes

1. T. J. Clark, *Image of the People* (London: Thames and Hudson, 1973).
2. Ibid.
3. Sheila Rowbotham's *Hidden from History* (London: Pluto Press, 1974) is part of a feminist tradition of work which tries to recover 'lost' material that has relevance to women in history, and thus re-write the orthodox histories with new priorities.
4. Questions about the writing of an empirically grounded but not empiricist and non-relativist history are discussed by E. P. Thompson in his essay, 'The Poverty of Theory', in *The Poverty of Theory and Other Essays* (London: Merlin Press, 1978).

Further reading

'Special Dossier on the Radical Feminist Film, *The Song of the Shirt*', in *Cinetracts* vol. 3 no. 2, Spring 1980, includes: 'An Analysis of *The Song of the Shirt*' by Alison Beale, pp. 1–13; 'Interview with the film-makers Jonathan Curling and Sue Clayton', pp. 14–21; 'Editors' Debate on *The Song of the Shirt*', pp. 23–9.
'*The Song of the Shirt* (Susan Clayton and Jonathan Curling)', by Elizabeth Cowie, *Camera Obscura* no. 5, 1980.

PART TWO
Fictions

Introduction

THIS SECTION collects together articles on a mixture of feature-length and short films. All the films discussed either have central female protagonists or in some way address the difficulty of centring a film narrative on a female character. With one exception, all the films were directed by women, but in a range of production contexts, financed in different ways.

The films themselves, and the issues raised in the readings given below, are too diverse to allow for a unified introduction. Instead, I have chosen to provide comments on some of the structuring elements which have governed my choice.

The 1979 Edinburgh Feminism and Cinema Event

The Feminism and Cinema Event at the 1979 Edinburgh Film Festival had a dual focus on feminist film theory and practice. Unlike earlier 'women and film' events, the Edinburgh event did not have to concentrate on an 'archaeology' of women's involvement in film because a decade after the beginnings of the new feminism there was a great deal of contemporary film work to show and discuss. The papers on film criticism presented at the event have all been published and were seen by the organisers to be addressing the contemporary dilemma of feminist film theory and practice:[1]

> while attempting to build a new language of film, relevant and comprehensible, the very project of challenge and change restricts the audience reached.[2]

Many of the films shown at Edinburgh – *Taking a Part* (Worth), *Thriller* (Potter), *The Song of the Shirt* (Film and History Project), *Daughter Rite* (Citron) – have become quite well known through subsequent critical commentary and screenings. However, there were a great many other films shown at the event which cumulatively testified to the enormous diversity of feminist film practice, ranging from 8 mm avant-garde shorts to narrative accounts of life in a women's refuge.

It was quite extraordinary to see all these films in the same week. Suddenly, feminist film work was no longer dominated by campaigning and documentary films. Films were being made which took a feminist politics for granted, and built from there, rather than polemicising to establish that politics. It even became conceivable that there might be jokes in feminist films. Certainly, audience and film-makers had learnt some of the lessons posed by a film like *Jeanne Dielman, 23 Quai du Commerce, 1080 Bruxelles*, shown in Edinburgh in 1976 and again in 1979 as part of a Chantal Akerman retrospective. Chantal Akerman (see Angela Martin's piece in this section) had spoken of a desire to transform the hierarchy in images, whereby a car accident or a kiss is seen as more significant than washing up. The significant moments in *Jeanne Dielman* are shown through the heroine's relationship to everyday household tasks. There is a shot towards the end of *Often During the Day* (Davis) – a film concerned with the meaning of housework rituals – when an unidentified hand (not the hand of the houseworker) tears the just-neatly-folded butter paper when opening the packet – a narrative climax which met with a loud gasp from a previously silent audience. The hierarchy in images was shown to come from the way in which image and narrative are structured as well as from the social significance (outside the film) of what is represented.

Although the arrangement of this book separates out debates about documentary films, it is difficult to understand how some of the films discussed in both this section and in Part One look as they do without bearing in mind two related issues. Firstly, there is the debate about realism discussed in the introduction to the documentary section. Secondly, there is the way in which feminist critics approached and understood mainstream film production – particularly classical Holly-wood – during the 70s. Neither of these issues can be separated from the wider debates taking place within radical film theory and practice in the 70s, including the enthusiasm for 'Brechtian' and modernist ideas about film form.[3] The crop of films shown at the 1979 Edinburgh event had been influenced by these ideas and shared, if nothing else, an interrogation of conventional film forms and the way in which these forms construct and represent women. In retrospect, it is striking how difficult these films are – perhaps more so now that formal rigour has become less fashionable within radical film circles. The reasons for this difficulty are bound up with the debates mentioned above. Theoretically, the issues can perhaps be most clearly understood as an attempt to shift away from the idea that women are *misrepresented* in film. If women are misrepresented in classical cinema, the answer is a realist one – to represent women more truthfully, to show real women – as discussed in relation to some of the films in Part One. However, if the very way stories are told, the way in which the opposition 'man'/ 'woman' is produced as meaningful, the way in which cutting and *mise en scène* is organised, always functions to reassure and pleasure the masculine spectator, then it is impossible to use the same forms to effect different representations. It is not a question of real women misrepresented, but of the filmic representations of women contributing to, and constructing, our understanding of what a woman is. In these arguments, the film form cannot just be used to present positive or alternative representations because the forms themselves are complicit in producing women as subordinate.[4]

Many of these debates were conducted using a simple opposition, man/woman. This tends to construct 'women' as a unitary category in a way which reproduces the patterns of domination and subordination that exist within 'women' as a group. This can be particularly true at the very high level of abstraction at which much psychoanalytically-informed theorisation of the workings of cinema is conducted. For example, it seems clear that we cannot understand the excessive presence of white women as the sign of the desirable within classical Hollywood cinema without giving attention to the complex interplay of racist and sexist structures which produce the cinematic opposition between black and white women.[5] Black female characters generally either service the desirability of white women, or themselves function as the ultimate, but illegitimate, site of sexual desire.[6]

The analysis of the workings of classical cinema referred to above demanded that feminists make films which, if they did not invent a whole new film language, at least interrogated and refused the old conventions.[7] This creates a problem of articulation, a question of how, and from where, to speak. This problem of articulation – whether there is an 'I' that is not masculine, or somehow patriarchal – sometimes emerges as the direct concern of women's film-making, almost as if it consumes too much effort to find a possible place to speak from, and consequently the film can only be 'about' this effort. Thus Lis Rhodes' film, *Light Reading*, which is almost impenetrably dense on first viewing, circulates around the (im)possibility of the fragmentary narrator 'perceiving herself as the subject of the sentence'. The multi-layered structure, and images, of the film, the excess of language with no unambiguous meanings, is precisely the evocation of language as alien, with no place for a non-patriarchal 'I'.

It is of course not only in relation to film that feminists have argued that existing conventions systematically exclude non-patriarchal representations of women, just as it is not only women who are structured out of dominant modes of representation. In relation to women the argument has most evidently been conducted about language itself.[8] There have been attempts to re-write history as herstory, to challenge a language which appears only to allow camera*men*, and a culture which specifies the marital status of women, not men. More abstractly, and using a rather different theoretical framework, it has been argued that the language through which we order our perception of the world is founded on the repression of the feminine, or the construction of the Feminine as Other. In this understanding, the traces of this repression/construction are neces-

53

sarily found only in disruption, the irrational – and the avant-garde. This is because the 'feminine' becomes, in this theorisation, *by definition*, outside, or in the margins of language. So one analysis leads more to a 'corrective' or 're-ordering' filmic strategy, while the other necessarily embraces difficult and avant-gardist strategies.[9]

Thus, as the theoretical papers read at Edinburgh indicate, the later 1970s brought a co-incidence of specifically feminist interest in new film forms with the dominance, certainly within British radical film culture, of the political authority of rather austere, deconstructive film-making. The Berwick Street Collective (*Nightcleaners*, 1975), the Film Work Group (*Justine*, 1976), Mulvey and Wollen (*Penthesilea*, 1974; *Riddles of the Sphinx*, 1978), the Film and History Project (*The Song of the Shirt*, 1979) and, to an extent, the London Women's Film Group, were all working in the shadow of Godard/Gorin, Straub/Huillet, and the particular 1970s re-appropriation of the work of Bertolt Brecht and Dziga Vertov.[10]

It is in this context that we can understand the earlier critical enthusiasm for the cool, modernist aesthetic of Yvonne Rainer and Chantal Akerman, and the heralding in 1979 of work such as *The Song of the Shirt, Daughter Rite, Taking a Part* and *Thriller*. The textual difficulty of these films, the way in which they can only be successfully approached with some acceptance of the political necessity for interrogating film form, was seen positively – at least at Edinburgh.[11] I can remember introducing screenings and discussions to a less specialised audience at the Birmingham Arts Lab later in the year, where there was rather less enthusiasm.

This modernist, or avant-gardist, 'canon' of 1979 (which has been very formative for me) has, arguably, very precise institutional and academic supports. To concentrate on this aspect of feminist film-making is to ignore the traditions of agitational and propagandist work which continued throughout the 1970s and which produced the more directly campaigning films such as those of the Sheffield Film Co-operative – *That's No Lady* (1977) and *Jobs For the Girls* (1979) – which are often of more use 'on the ground'. However, the theoretical point remains important – what was being investigated was not just film form, but the way in which the conventions and traditions of film-making produce particular constructions of 'the feminine'. All these avant-garde films, in one way or another, reject the strategy of presenting more 'realistic' images of women. Instead they demand that the audience sees film as one way, among others, in which the idea of woman is produced in this culture, and that filmic and narrative conventions are not neutral.

Daughter Rite and *Song of the Shirt* are discussed in Part One; *Often During the Day* and *Light Reading* in Part Four. Pam Cook's discussion of *An Epic Poem* in this section traces some of these issues in an analysis of a more recent short film. Similarly, Claire Johnston's article on *Maeve* touches on questions of experimental film form.

Coming to Terms with Art Cinema

Much feminist criticism has addressed mainstream Hollywood cinema. Hollywood, as the world dominant cinema, exports ideals of white femininity world-wide. British critics in particular have tended to avoid discussion of European art cinema – partly out of a commitment to what is regarded as a non-elitist popular cinema (Hollywood), partly in recognition of Hollywood's greater power and influence, and partly out of a distrust of the greater ostensible realism of art cinema.[12] European art cinema has been seen as duplicitous in relation to women whereas it has been argued that Hollywood films at least are obviously constructed and stereotypical. This critical avoidance of art cinema as a genre produces rather curious effects, given that it is within this genre that nearly all the feature-length films directed by women are produced. Thus, although there may be discussion of individual films directed by Mai Zetterling, Vera Chytilova, Agnès Varda, Liliana Cavani and Lina Wertmuller, or even of a directorial oeuvre, the terms of these discussions usually rely unproblematically on the traditional critical vocabulary of authorial expressivity and vision.[13] Angela Martin raises some of these issues in the extracts from her Akerman dossier.

We need to pay more attention to generic textual determinants, and be wary of attributing generic code to gender expressivity. Chantal Akerman's monosyllabic, restless heroines are partly pleasurable because they offer a feminine figure starring in the familiar 'what is the meaning of life?' art cinema story. And, crucially, their lack of speech is within the best art cinema traditions of refusing to remove ambiguity about possible answers. Similarly, although the work of Yvonne Rainer is most usefully approached in terms of the New York art world – with a focus on minimalism and modernist dance – her films do also display many of the generic characteristics of art cinema: subjective voice, interior realism, unresolved narrative, marked formal self-consciousness, etc.[14]

The situation is different in relation to women directors in West Germany, where the complex of state funding and subsidy introduced since 1964 has been organised around the concept of the 'Autorenfilm', and where there is an historically identifiable art cinema.[15] It is noticeable, though, that the New German Cinema has been thought of as a 'Cinema of the Sons'. It was not until the mid-70s – incidentally when the funding system begins to break down – that the sisters, daughters, wives and mothers noticeably got their hands on the camera.[16] But for British and American audiences, films such as those directed by Margarethe von Trotta, Helke Sander and Helma

Sanders-Brahms occupy both an art cinema and a women's film space. Ellen Seiter's article in this section looks at different critical receptions given to the films of Margarethe von Trotta in Germany and the United States, pointing to the way in which knowledge of cultural and political contexts can affect the reading of a film.[17]

For British directors such as Sally Potter and Jan Worth, who both have completed first features in the 80s (respectively *The Gold Diggers*, 1984, and *Doll's Eye*, 1983), the relative absence of an indigenous art cinema raises different problems. The main contenders for a British art tradition have been seen as either (or both) the Documentary movement of the 1930s or the 'kitchen sink' realist films of the late 50s and early 60s.[18] Neither of these groups of films possesses the qualities of attention to interiority, subjective vision, etc. which produce the co-incidence between the emerging women's cinema and the traditional (male) art cinema with which I am concerned at this point. Geoffrey Nowell-Smith, reviewing the British art film, *Radio On* (1979), observed that there was very little in the way of a British art cinema for this film to be associated with – and hence it would be very difficult for audiences to make informed choices to see it.[19] Although contemporary feminist directors might not wish to be associated with 'art cinema', the absence of this type of cinematic (as opposed to theatrical) tradition, despite the current 'revival' of tales of provincial and imperial life, creates particular problems in relation to film exhibition. It is difficult to programme films that don't fit into recognisable categories, and will be equally difficult for these films to break out of a feminist ghetto. And within film culture, as happened with *Riddles of the Sphinx*, films become isolated and have to bear an excessive exemplary, even missionary status.[20]

Changing Consciousness

Two of the films discussed in this section, *Burning an Illusion* and *A Question of Silence*, have the classic 'odyssey of consciousness' structure that has frequently been popular in 'tendency' fiction.[21] In cinema, the classic examples are films like *The Mother* (V. I. Pudovkin, USSR, 1926), where the initially apolitical and symbolically nameless (i.e. typical) mother gradually takes on the politics of her revolutionary son through confrontation on his behalf with the repressive Tsarist police and State apparatus. At the end of the film the mother dies, heroically and defiantly holding the red flag in a demonstration. The journey from false to true consciousness is the motivating narrative drive of this type of fiction and the audience is intended to make this journey with the central protagonist.

As Annette Kuhn has usefully pointed out, the heroine of this kind of odyssey can either be shown to be typical, and thus representative, as in (to use her examples) *Salt of the Earth* (H. Biberman, USA, 1953), or remain a unique individual, as in *Norma Rae* (Martin Ritt, USA, 1979),[22] However, in both cases the tendency is towards the use of realist conventions to render the film form transparent and facilitate identification by the viewers.

Both *Burning an Illusion* and *A Question of Silence* offer a heroine for identification in this manner, and rely mainly on realist film conventions. The heroine of *Burning*, however, is constructed as 'ordinary' through the provision of both realist family detail and young women friends. It is partly Pat's friends who function to reveal how her own consciousness changes. She is thus, in the sense outlined above, presented as a typical or representative character. The heroine of *Question*, a professional middle-class woman, is not shown with women friends or peers, and if she is in any sense representative, it is in her isolation in her job and her marriage.

Pat's journey, in *Burning an Illusion*, is from aspirations expressed within the terms of white culture to a designation of this culture as racist, and a re-claiming of her Afro-Caribbean heritage. The transformation is marked physically in her appearance and dress, and the audience is shown the books, such as *The Autobiography of Malcolm X*, which replace the Mills and Boon romances she burns. Pat's changing consciousness is intimately connected with the victimisation, imprisonment and increasing militancy of her boyfriend Del. As with *The Mother*, the woman's politicisation is sparked off through love. The film articulates gender construction through an analysis of racism which, in the second half of the film, is shown to be the structuring force in all the (sympathetic) characters' lives. The film ends with a freeze frame, identifying Pat as part of a resistant black culture.

A Question of Silence has a simpler project in that is deals only with a white world, and thus does not have to take on the interface of feminist and anti-racist struggle. There is, however, a similar narrative of changing consciousness although the journey here is from non-feminist heterosexuality to woman-identification. At a schematic level, the film offers a utopian bonding of its female characters crossing the boundaries of class, occupation and age. The middle-class psychiatrist becomes increasingly involved with her clients: a secretary, a café-worker and a housewife/mother, while the silent witnesses are an older, bourgeois woman and two teenage girls. It is the unspoken allegiance of all these women that is established against the uncomprehending state apparatus of a male world. Jeanette Murphy's reading of the film argues for the film as a radical feminist or separatist text.

Within two 'change-of-consciousness' narratives we thus have different inflections of the representative. Pat's typicality comes from her representational grounding in south London black culture. The psychiatrist is only constructed as typical to the extent that she is representative of a particular class position in a film which tries to offer a spectrum of representative white women.

Although *Maeve* (Pat Murphy and John Davies, 1981) does not have this change-of-consciousness narrative, its use of memory functions partly to allow the audience to understand how the contemporary political positions of the characters – particularly Maeve – have been arrived at. These positions are narratively significant because the film offers formal set-piece debates between the voices of Irish republicanism and (?)British feminism. So feminist politics, and, as Claire Johnston observes, different cultural constructions of femininity, are opened up for debate in relation to other political ideologies.[23]

Women's Genres and Female Audiences

One of the noticeable features of the developing feminist criticism of the 1970s and 1980s has been the love/hate relationship with traditional women's genres such as melodrama and soap opera. Jane Feuer has usefully traced the way in which criticism of these genres has moved from dismissal to a positive celebration of the contradictions they embody, while Pam Cook has argued for the necessity for an historical approach in feminist analyses of the genre.[24] The fascination and pleasure for many women of these often very masochistic texts offer a very precise moment for analysis – is it a pleasure *despite* or a pleasure *because*? Also, because these are genres that have historically always been aimed at – for – women, it can be argued that attention to these genres, and particularly at the way in which they address their audience, gives us further understanding of how the position of 'being a woman' is constructed at particular historical moments. A good deal of critical work on the cinema has been concerned with the question of whether the cinema spectator is constructed as masculine.[25] These films for women require an analysis of how cinema works which accommodates real, diverse female audiences.

Alongside the critical re-evaluation of women's genres, there has been a good deal of feminist film work which has situated itself on this representational terrain of personal life, families, illicit love, etc. Nearly all the films discussed in this section bear generic traces of melodrama and women's pictures, while some – such as *The German Sisters* (*Marianne and Juliane*) – have been understood to be directly re-working this type of material. It is this romantic/melodramatic tradition which Pat rejects as illusory in *Burning*.

Female audiences are not unitary, and this issue is raised by Michelle Citron in her discussion of Jan Oxenberg's film, *A Comedy in Six Unnatural Acts*. Because the film plays with cultural stereotypes of lesbianism, it has been read as homophobic; Citron, however, suggests that lesbian audiences usually find the film funny, sharing its subcultural references and jokes. So, once again, we return to the importance of the culture and social context of the audience to determine how a film text is read – for further discussion in Part Four.

Notes

1. Some of these papers had been published before the Edinburgh event, and some were published subsequently: Pam Cook, 'The Point of Expression in Avant-garde Film', in Elizabeth Cowie, ed., *Catalogue of British Film Institute Productions 1977–1978* (London: British Film Institute, 1978), pp. 53–6; Claire Johnston, 'The Subject of Feminist Film Theory/ Practice', *Screen* vol. 21 no. 2, 1980, pp. 27–34; Laura Mulvey, 'Feminism, Film and the Avant-garde', *Framework* no. 10, 1979, pp. 3–10; B. Ruby Rich, 'The Crisis of Naming in Feminist Film Criticism', *Jump Cut* 19, December 1978, pp. 9–12; Christine Gledhill, 'Recent developments in Feminist Film Criticism', *Quarterly Review of Film Studies* vol. 3 no. 4, Fall 1978, pp. 457–93. There were also papers presented by the editors of magazines such as *Camera Obscura, Jump Cut, Frauen und Film* and *m/f*.
2. Programme, Edinburgh International Film Festival 1979, p. 8.
3. Laura Mulvey's paper, 'Feminism, Film and the Avant-garde', gives a clear exposition of this conjunction of interests. The influence of Brechtian ideas on radical film culture is discussed by Sylvia Harvey, *May '68 and Film Culture* (London: British Film Institute, 1978), while *Screen* vol. 16 no. 4, 1975/6, documents the *Brecht and Cinema* event at the 1975 Edinburgh Festival.
4. 'Representation vs. Communication' by Elizabeth Cowie, Claire Johnston, Cora Kaplan, Mary Kelly, Jacqueline Rose and Marie Yates, which was presented at the 1979 Socialist Feminist Conference in London, provides one example of this argument. Reprinted in *No Turning Back*, ed. Feminist Anthology Collective (London: The Women's Press, 1981).
5. Some theorists primarily concerned with the construction of racial difference have used related psychoanalytic theorisation – see, for example, Homi K. Bhabha, 'The Other Question', *Screen* vol. 24 no. 6, November–December 1983, pp. 18–36.
6. The 'classic' instance of the former is Hattie McDaniel's (oscar-winning) performance in *Gone with the Wind*. See also Sybil DelGaudio, 'The Mammy in Hollywood Film', *Jump Cut* no. 28, 1983, pp. 23–5. It is frequently a 'tragic mulatta' figure who functions as the latter – a British example would be Sapphire in the 1959 film of the same name.
7. Sayer and Jayamanne (in this section) raise a similar point in relation to black film-making. See also Jim Pines' interview with Isaac Julien in *Framework* 26–27, 1985, pp. 2–9.
8. A summary of some of the issues at stake can be found in the review by Maria Black and Rosalind Coward of Dale Spender's *Man Made Language*, entitled 'Linguistic, Social and Sexual Relations', *Screen Education* no. 39, 1981, pp. 69–85.
9. The validation of the avant garde that this generalised and condensed account suggests is most commonly associated with French structuralist

and semiotic work. The collection by Elaine Marks and Isabelle de Courtivron, *New French Feminisms* (Brighton: The Harvester Press, 1981), makes associated positions available to the English-language reader.

10. Alan Lovell, 'Epic Theatre and Counter Cinema', *Jump Cut* no. 27, 1982, pp. 64–8, and no. 28, 1983, pp. 49–51; and Sylvia Harvey, 'Whose Brecht? Memories for the Eighties', *Screen* vol. 23, no. 1., 1982, pp. 45–59, provide retrospectives on '70s Brecht'. Annette Michelson's 'From Magician to Epistemologist', in P. Adams Sitney, ed., *The Essential Cinema* (New York: Anthology Film Archives, 1975), and Stephen Crofts and Olivia Rose, 'An Essay Towards *Man with a Movie Camera*', *Screen* vol. 18 no. 1, 1977, pp. 9–60, provide 70s accounts of the work of Dziga Vertov. See also Martin Walsh, *The Brechtian Aspect of Radical Cinema* (London: British Film Institute, 1981), particularly for discussion of Straub/Huillet.

11. See Lesley Stern, 'Feminism and Cinema – Exchanges', *Screen* vol. 20 no. 3/4, 1979/80, pp. 89–105; Helen MacKintosh and Mandy Merck, 'Rendezvous d'Edinburgh', *Time Out* no. 490, 7–13 September 1979, pp. 22–3.

12. Claire Johnston, 'Women's Cinema as Counter-Cinema' in C. Johnston, ed., *Notes on Women's Cinema* (London: Society for Education in Film and Television, 1973).

13. See, for example, the relevant essays in the following: Joan Mellen, *Women and their Sexuality in the New Film* (New York: Dell Publishing Co., 1973); Kay and Peary, eds., *Women and the Cinema* (New York: Dutton, 1977); Patricia Erens, ed., *Sexual Stratagems* (New York: Horizon, 1979).

14. Art cinema as genre is discussed by David Bordwell, 'The Art Cinema as a mode of Film Practice', *Film Criticism* vol. 4 no. 1, Fall 1979, pp. 56–64; Steve Neale, 'Art Cinema as Institution', *Screen* vol. 22 no. 1, pp. 11–39; Tom Ryall, 'Art House, Smart House', *The Movie* no. 90, 1981, pp. 1798–1800. See also essays by Mandy Merck and Jane Root in this volume.

15. See Neale, 'Art Cinema as Institution'; Sheila Johnston, 'The Author as Public Institution', *Screen Education* no. 32/33, Autumn/Winter 1979/80, pp. 67–78; Thomas Elsaesser, 'The Post-War German Cinema' in Tony Rayns, ed., *Fassbinder* (London: British Film Institute, 1976), pp. 1–16.

16. This is not to imply that *no* German women were involved in film-making in the 1960s. See Marc Silberman, 'Cine-Feminists in West Berlin', *Quarterly Review of Film Studies* vol. 5 no. 2, Spring 1980, pp. 217–232; 'Film and Feminism in Germany Today', Special Section, *Jump Cut* no. 27, 1982, pp. 41–53, and no. 29, 1984, pp. 49–64.

17. Eric Rentschler discusses the American critical reception of West German cinema in *West German Film in the Course of Time* (New York: Redgrave Publishing Company, 1984).

18. Alan Lovell, 'The British Cinema: The Unknown Cinema', BFI Education Department Seminar Paper, 1969; John Hill, 'Working-class Realism and Sexual Reaction: Some Theses on the British "New Wave" ', ch. 18 in James Curran and Vincent Porter, eds., *British Cinema History* (London: Weidenfeld and Nicolson, 1983), pp. 303–11. See also, John

Ellis, 'Art, Culture and Quality – Terms for a Cinema in the Forties and Seventies', *Screen* vol. 19 no. 3, 1978, pp. 9–49.

19. Geoffrey Nowell-Smith, '*Radio On*', *Screen* vol. 20 no. 3/4, 1979, pp. 29–39. See also Thomas Elsaesser, 'Images for England (and Scotland, Ireland, Wales . . .)', *Monthly Film Bulletin* vol. 51 no. 608, September 1984, pp. 267–269.

20. *Riddles of the Sphinx* (Laura Mulvey and Peter Wollen, 1977) was perhaps *the* feminist film event of its time in Britain. I'm aware that it makes a rather odd history to omit discussion of both this and the other Mulvey/Wollen films but they have received extensive documentation elsewhere; see: Script, '*Riddles of the Sphinx*', *Screen* vol. 18 no. 2, Summer 1977, pp. 61–78; Ann Kaplan, *Women and Film* (New York: Methuen, 1983), pp. 171–181.

21. By 'tendency' fiction, I mean fictional works in which the moral universe of the fictional world – which is generally presented through realist conventions – is constructed through and made meaningful in relation to explicit political affiliations.

22. See Kuhn, *Women's Pictures, Feminism and Cinema* (London: Routledge and Kegan Paul, 1982), pp. 140–146.

23. See also Janet Hawken, 'Maeve', *Undercut* no. 6, Winter 1982–3, pp. 8–10.

24. Jane Feuer, 'Melodrama, Serial Form and Television Today', *Screen* vol. 25 no. 1, 1984, pp. 4–16; Pam Cook, 'Melodrama and the Women's Picture', in Sue Aspinall and Robert Murphy, eds., *Gainsborough Melodrama*, BFI Dossier 18, (London: British Film Institute, 1983), pp. 14–28; Tania Modleski, *Loving with a Vengeance* (London and New York: Methuen 1984; first published Hamden, Connecticut: The Shoestring Press, 1982).

25. Annette Kuhn, 'Women's Genres', *Screen* vol. 25 no. 1, 1984, pp. 18–29. See also Janice Winship's work on the pleasures of women's magazines: Janice Winship, *Inside Women's Magazines* (London: Pandora Press, 1986).

Chantal Akerman's Films: Notes on the Issues Raised for Feminism

ANGELA MARTIN

Extracts from 'Chantal Akerman's films: a dossier', *Feminist Review* no. 3, 1979, pp. 24–47.

> I won't say I'm a feminist film-maker . . . I'm not making women's films, I'm making Chantal Akerman's films (Interview, 1979).[1]

> I *do* think [*Jeanne Dielman* . . .] is a feminist film because I give space to things which were never, almost never, shown in that way, like the daily gestures of a woman (Interview, 1977).[2]

> This film perpetuates the out-dated attitude that a woman's sexuality is not indigenous but bestowed by a man (Virginia Dignam, *Morning Star*, 1 June 1979).

> The film's time-span covers a Tuesday (stew and potatoes), Wednesday (wiener schnitzel) and heady Thursday (meat loaf . . .) . . . Relatively speaking, the schnitzel was rather skimped, but I now know how to make a meat loaf (John Coleman, *New Statesman*, 1 June 1979).

THIS YEAR [1979], three films by Chantal Akerman (including *Jeanne Dielman, 23 Quai du Commerce, 1080 Bruxelles*, referred to in the above quotations), have come into distribution in Britain. Since the films are feature-length (or more) and in French, the cost of making English-language prints is enormous, but offset by their commercial potential. On the other hand, they are not actually commercial-type films, or even 'art cinema' films. It's clear, for example, that the critics quoted above are entirely antipathetic, yet this is perhaps because they were viewing the films in a commercial film or art cinema context.

The films therefore raise interesting questions *vis-à-vis* the women's movement – we also like to go the movies; why not? (especially to see films by women). Akerman points out, however, that two women critics who could have interviewed her declined the offer, one of them saying that her films were marginal to the interests of the women's movement. But surely a film (*Jeanne Dielman* . . .) dealing with 'the daily gestures of a woman' cannot be so lightly dismissed? Is it the way these gestures are filmed, or is it that because some of us find housework boring we don't want to watch someone else doing it for some three hours? Whatever the response, the fact that housework is shown on the screen is already important, and for this reason our response to it is important too. [. . .]

Can a film-maker who claims not to be a feminist make feminist films?

Should we expect a feminist film to speak to us directly and immediately? Or is it acceptable to suggest that films which require work on our part (as audience) are not necessarily elitist, and can be equally rewarding?

Are we looking for images of real women or films which are really about women?

Is a new women's language possible? How would it relate to visual imagery? Is a new language necessary, if indeed positive images do exist now (see responses to *Julia*, and so on)? Or, as Laura Mulvey[3] points out, does the new only grow 'out of the work of confrontation that is done' *vis-à-vis* traditional forms of expression and communication?

Should we attempt to understand better the forms through which images are produced? Is it important to distinguish between 'reality and its representation'? Or is the image (the representation) all we need to talk about?

Chantal Akerman began working in a way marginal to the film production system, but is now in the position of having to take on that system, which includes having her films screened at festivals to get recognition; distribution on a commercial (or at least financially viable) basis; and the press. This has a number of implications, since none of those institutions is in the main touched by feminism. Eventually, however, it does also have to do with the way we respond to the films, since we read the press, go to cinemas and so on. But to what extent?

How do we cope with the individualism inherent in the notion of 'the artist' in relation to the preference in sexual politics for a notion of collectivity? Is it a problem?

A number of questions arise about the specific films, but there is a more general one relating directly to all the films: the question of voyeurism. The lesbian love-making scene in *Je Tu Il Elle* is discussed in terms of whether it meets the requirements, as it were – the conventions – of pornography, or whether in fact certain formal elements prohibit this response on the part of the audience. In *Jeanne Dielman . . .*, John Coleman feels: 'This orgasm-bit is bound to strike the serious-minded as an unfortunate bow to crass commercialism . . .', while Marsha Kinder, in *Film Quarterly*, says of the

bathroom sequence that 'the graphic details destroy the eroticism . . .'.[4] Thus the question of looking is very important. Who looks
at whom; whose look does the camera represent; how are we as the
audience placed in relation to that point of view and what it shows?
And this question of voyeurism is no less important in terms of *News
from Home* and its long, static-camera shots of people in the streets and
on the subway.

From this question arises the further one of desire and its fulfilment
or the pleasure of potential fulfilment, or the discomfort of its denial.
Not only in terms of the pleasure of looking (sexually), but also in
terms of the pleasure we derive from a film narrative – reaching the end
of a story (the resolution of an enigma set up at the beginning of a film).
What kind of pleasure do we derive from Akerman's films, if we do,
and if we don't, where does the displeasure lie?

There are film-makers who prefer not to talk about their work
because film is their way of speaking; if you need to ask them questions
about it, either you aren't sensitive enough or it hasn't been successful.
Others have made a policy decision always – or as often (or for as long)
as is practicable – to accompany their films and engage in discussion
with an audience. Both these situations imply, in a way, that the source
of meaning of a film lies in its director. This is reinforced by what
sometimes happens when film-makers appear with their films. In a
sense, the meaning of the film is often immediately anchored by
whatever the film-maker says about it. But obviously the usefulness of
such a dialogue depends on how the film-maker views her or his work
in the cinema. John Ford, for example, used the cinema to tell stories;
Chantal Akerman, on the other hand, is working on how cinema
constructs stories.

The suggestion of a relationship between the film-maker's intentions and the look of the film therefore implies that everything that has
gone into producing that surface appearance is due solely to her or his
creativity. It ignores other factors like the script, the production
situation (for example, major studio or small crew and small budget),
the technical skills and the professional codes that operate them (for
example, soft lighting on women's faces and harder lighting on men's).
It also assumes that we won't have our own interpretations (readings)
of a film when we see it. For example, it was really only when black film
critics began to be more widely read that the racism of John Ford's
films was shown to have been overlooked by white critics; similarly,
the position of women in Ford's films when women critics started
writing from a feminist perspective.

The Director as Creator
The importance accorded a film director (over and above other people
working on a film) comes from a notion of 'the artist and his creativity':

64

'. . . an intuitive, mystical rapport is proposed between spectator and creator, at best a matter of hit and miss' (Mulvey, 1979)[5], which is very much part of the European cinema context in which Chantal Akerman works.

A great many people working throughout the cinema would like to (or do) see themselves as artists, but the European cinemas have the idea more firmly built into them than the mainstream American cinema, which has until recently had the general notion that a film should only entertain and make money. (Of course, it still has that idea, but in recent years has discovered that 'artistic' movies can make money too: for example, *Julia*, *Taxi Driver*, *Alice Doesn't Live Here Any More*.)

But it is quite within the European art cinema tradition that a film-maker with Akerman's concerns (see Godard, Straub/Huillet, Fass-binder) is able to make *feature*-length films which are not such immediately obvious commercial certainties. (Though it is, of course, also partly a result of the existence of the women's movement that Akerman, a *woman* film-maker, is equally now given that oppor-tunity.) And it is in line with this European tradition that we – and Akerman too – talk about 'Chantal Akerman's films'.

The notion of 'a Chantal Akerman film' may appear to contradict the concern of the women's movement to break down the elevation of the individual by asserting the notion of collectivity. It could be argued, though, that given the enormity of the framework of cinema production, it is necessary for women to assert their right, equal to that of any male director, to make films at every level. Additionally, however, I would suggest that there are two ways in which Akerman breaks with traditional cinema: her work in the avant-garde, and her work on images of women; and that this is in itself an important intervention. [. . .]

The Spectator and the Critic
The women's movement has insisted on the importance of the personal, and personal response to films is very important and totally valid. I personally find Chantal Akerman's films pleasurable, but I'm not sure I should assume anyone other than my close friends would find it interesting to know that.

But in a sense, this is what many journalist-critics believe, or at least it seems it is what they are paid for – to expound from their personal point of view. And although such critics would probably acknowledge that this is *their* point of view, which you are entitled to disagree with, they do tend to assume that theirs is more valid since it is more refined. It may well be that a critic's comments are insightful, but in this respect insight is relative. Sometimes they say more about the critic than about the object under review. John Coleman, in the *New*

Statesman, is obviously unable to situate *Jeanne Dielman* anywhere other than in relation to his attitude that what is important in the world does not have to do with whether or how you show housework.

The audience Coleman addressed himself to is perhaps – in general – assumed to be one that is always looking for sensitive portrayals of its own concerns, as in films like *The Deer Hunter*, *An Unmarried Woman* and *Hard Core* as much as *Claire's Knee* and *The Man Who Loved Women*, to which he will guide them. But this throws up a problem. If someone suggested going to watch a movie lasting three hours about housework, would you be enticed? Well, obviously some people are and some aren't. The real question here is what one goes to watch films for. Do we want entertainment, gentle persuasion of an argument, or active engagement with a film (either about its form or its content or both)? It makes a difference, but the whole viewing situation suggests that it doesn't. Given that Akerman's films don't so easily fit into the viewing pattern, how do we view them?

Akerman's Films, Exhibition and the Press
Akerman's films compound many of these problems of exhibition and audience response. The three now [1979] in distribution are feature-length or longer and made with relatively big budgets. The cost of putting them into distribution is high and requires not just new prints but English-language sub-titled prints. If they are to be successfully distributed they need to be known about. This requires them to be opened in London on a commercial basis. And in order for films to be commercially successful (so neither the film-maker, the cinema owners or the distribution company lose money – not to mention other people further back down the line), they have to be written about in the national press. This is a fact of life if we want to see more films by women at the cinema (that is, the commercial film circuit).

Previously Akerman could talk about not caring if anyone saw her films; now she is more widely known; her budgets are getting bigger; and the press is an inevitable part of this.

But the terms in which the press talks about films are not the terms in which Akerman's films are made. In other words, the press does not just talk about whether films are realistic or not, but also about the subject matter – what is the narrative, and is there some 'universal' truth here?

Akerman's Films and Feminism
The important question for feminism, as Christine Gledhill points out[6], is not – is it a film about real women? – but, is it *really* about women? What does it tell us about the position of women in the world and in art? *Jeanne Dielman*, for example, could in this sense be crudely compared to *Alice Doesn't Live Here Any More*. They are both women

alone with teenage sons. In *Alice* . . . we have a story about a woman in this situation which is entertaining, we can identify with it. But if the question of 'real women' and their relationship to *our* lives is really important, where is our relationship to this story of Alice? Unless we are really in a similar situation there are certain limitations on what the film can say directly to each of us. *Jeanne Dielman*, on the other hand, is about a female situation which is much more fundamental to the position of women in society. We are not, in this film, pulled along on a wave of (classic Hollywood) realism and emotion, but are impelled to watch and reflect on the process, the gestures of the daily lives of the majority of women.

Obviously the project in each film is different. *Alice* . . . offered us a kind of 'positive heroine', something we had been looking for; perhaps Janet Maslin did not feel she had found one.[7] Another difference between the two films is their relationship to us as spectator. *Alice* . . . invites us to sit back and enjoy; *Jeanne Dielman* expects us to sit up and pay attention. One is entertainment; the other engagement. For this reason, Akerman's films require, if not a different viewing situation, at least a different viewing attitude. When friends have asked me if going to see one of the Akerman films at the weekend is a good idea, I find it difficult to answer simply, yes, without saying, well, it's not a normal Saturday night type of movie.

Akerman's Films, Feminism and the Avant-Garde

In the sense of narrative we are used to, Akerman's films do not have a beginning, middle and end. In *News from Home* there is no character to identify with, and in the other two identification is not a concern in the conventional sense. The form/language of film is not hidden as it is in mainstream: there is often a minimal use of sound or an excess of it; there is often either no dialogue, or there is a voice-over, or it is difficult to hear what is said; the camera is often static and the shots of such length that their duration and the non-movement of the camera become 'apparent', particularly in relation to their content and its conventional representation.

Laura Mulvey's excellent article, 'Feminism, Film and the Avant-Garde' (*Framework* no. 10, Spring 1979), discusses how:

> . . . feminists have recently come to see that the arguments developed by the modernist avant-garde are relevant to their own struggle to develop a radical aesthetic . . . The questions posed by the avant-garde, consciously confronting traditional practice, often with a political motivation, working on ways in which aesthetic challenges alter relations both with modes of representation and with expectations in consumption – all these questions arise similarly for women . . . (p. 4).

67

particularly in view of the desire to find a new language for women, or at least to find out if one is possible. As Mulvey points out:

> . . . the crucial problem has to be faced: whether the new can be discovered, like a gold-mine in a garden; or whether the new grows only out of the work of confrontation that is done (ibid.).

Much avant-garde work is concerned only with confrontation at the level of form (that is, with the formal means of re-presenting the world without narrative or fiction):

> But women cannot be satisfied with an aesthetic that restricts counter-cinema to work on form alone. Feminism is bound to its politics; its experimentation cannot exclude work on content (p. 9).

The importance of Akerman's work is that it is on both these levels at the same time. And, to come back to the original question, the importance of her comments on her own work and cinema in general is that she contributes through her work to the debate about representation and women.

Extracts on 'Jeanne Dielman'
Synopsis: *Jeanne Dielman, 23 Quai de Commerce, 1080 Bruxelles* (1975) – in colour (3 hours 20 minutes). This is one of the most difficult films to synopsise. Jeanne Dielman (Delphine Seyrig) is a Belgian widow with a teenage son. There is little communication between them, and what there is is functional; the same is true with other people she comes into contact with. Much of the film-time is concerned with the minutiae of her daily routine. The film covers three days, and elements of the routine are repeated with precision so that even objects not in use express and emphasise the ritual. But this routine makes space for prostitution as well, which eventually disrupts the order of her daily life. [. . .]

> Above all I wanted to work on language by taking images which tend to be elided in the cinema in general and are the most devalued. [. . .] Because there is a hierarchy in images. For example, a car accident or a kiss in close-up, that's higher in the hierarchy than washing up. Washing up is the lowest, especially from behind. And it's not accidental but relates to the place of woman in the social hierarchy. Moreover, if I had shown Jeanne Dielman making love with the two clients, a close-up of her mouth and the perspiration when she washes, her curved back, etc. – I could have made the audience cry, but I would have been working with traditional cinema. With the same subject I could have made a commercial film: not showing what generally develops within the ellipsis. Whereas I work with images which are between the images (Interview, 1976).[8]

Jeanne Dielman

Chantal Akerman's *Jeanne Dielman*, all 198 minutes of it, is an example of what is frequently referred to as 'minimal' cinema. So far as one can make out from previous experience (e.g. the works of Straub), this means that the camera rests for the maximum amount of time on something boring before there is a cut to a new static set-up and a prolonged stare at something even more boring . . . Jeanne Dielman is stoically embodied by the elegant Delphine Seyrig, here looking drab . . . The film's time-span covers a Tuesday (stew and potatoes), Wednesday (wiener schnitzel) and heady Thursday (meat loaf and Jeanne has an orgasm and kills her client with a pair of scissors). This orgasm-bit is bound to strike the serious-minded as an unfortunate bow to crass commercialism on Ms. Akerman's part: it kept me hanging in. After the murder, Jeanne sits at a table, for five minutes by my colleague Nicholas Wapshott's watch. Relatively speaking, the schnitzel was rather skimped, but I now know how to make a meat loaf (Coleman, 1979).

This film perpetuates the out-dated attitude that a woman's sexuality is not indigenous but bestowed by a man. An attitude which runs counter to the radical belief of sexual politics which states that a woman is responsible for and acknowledges her own sexuality. [. . .] At a time when women's role in society is being increasingly challenged, it is reactionary to return to such demoralising myths. The Victorian 'sexualisation' of marriage has contributed to many of the ills of the enclosed nuclear family which still demands sexual role-playing (Dignam, 1979).

The central problem in feminist film and literary works now is this: is it possible for the woman to express her own desires? Who speaks when she speaks? In Rainer's *Film About a Woman Who* . . . , for example, the woman's thoughts are spoken by a male voice-over narration. The woman is separated from her own language. She is quite literally spoken by men. In *Jeanne Dielman* the problem is expressed through diegetic[9] silence. Although the repression of the woman's voice is naturalised by the fiction – most of Jeanne's time is spent alone, and she and her son need few words to sustain their relationship – the duration, both of the shots and of the fiction, and the lack of variation in the enunciation of images work to denaturalise this repression [. . .]

The controlling discourse is constructed of looks, not voices. A dialectic operates between the one looking (camera/director) and what is being looked at (characters' actions, characters' space). Unlike the network of looks in most films, which is mediated predominantly by eye-line matches and other kinds of match-cutting, the logic of viewer/viewed in this film bypasses the fiction. The system of subjective shots is eliminated and with it a logic of spatial matches rationalised by the interest of various characters. The logic of the organisation of shots reverts to the camera and its marked controller, a feminist film-maker [. . .]

Jeanne Dielman brings us into a discourse of women's looks, through a woman's viewpoint. It is the quality and interest of the controlling look that makes *Jeanne Dielman* stand out formally as feminist, and not any particular formal feature such as the absence of the reverse shot or the duration, alone. That this discourse is realised in silence adds to its eloquence. Who knows yet what an unalienated feminine language would sound like? We know that *Jeanne Dielman* was made in a feminine environment: the director, the main actor, the camera-person, the crew, were all women. The look of camera/director is permissive in that it allows Jeanne her space and the time it takes to complete her actions. Akerman said: 'It was the only way to shoot that film – to avoid cutting the woman into a hundred pieces, to avoid cutting the action in a hundred places, to look carefully and to be respectful. The framing was meant to respect her space, her, and her gestures within it.' Yet it is a look as obsessive in its interest as Jeanne is in her movements. *Jeanne Dielman* is the image of the old viewed actively, with fascination. *La jouissance du voir* is not denied (Bergstrom, 1977).[10]

Notes

1. Interview with Chantal Akerman, London 1979. See *Feminist Review* no. 3, 1979, pp. 28–31.
2. Interview with Chantal Akerman, *Camera Obscura* no. 2, Fall 1977, p. 118.
3. Laura Mulvey, 'Feminism, Film and the Avant-Garde', *Framework* no. 10, Spring 1979.
4. Marsha Kinder, 'Reflections on *Jeanne Dielman*', *Film Quarterly* vol. 30 no. 4, Summer 1977.
5. Laura Mulvey, 'Guest Appearances', interview with Chantal Akerman, *Time Out* no. 475, 25–31 May 1979, p. 7.
6. Christine Gledhill, '*Klute*: Part 1 – A Contemporary Film Noir and Feminist Criticism', in E. Ann Kaplan, ed., *Women and Film Noir* (London: British Film Institute, 1978).
7. Janet Maslin, 'Hollywood Heroines Under the Influence: Alice Still Lives Here', in Karyn Kay and Gerald Peary, eds., *Women and the Cinema: A Critical Anthology* (New York: Dutton, 1977).
8. Marie-Claude Treilhou's interview with Chantal Akerman, *Cinema 76* no. 206, February 1976, pp. 90–92.
9. Diegesis is a term used to indicate everything in the film-story, the fiction.
10. Janet Bergstrom, '*Jeanne Dielman, 23 Quai du Commerce, 1080 Bruxelles*', *Camera Obscura* no. 2, Fall 1977, pp. 116–18.

Films of Jan Oxenberg: Comic Critique

MICHELLE CITRON

From an article in *Jump Cut* no. 24/25, 1981, pp. 31–2.

> *He*: Have you heard the women's movement has no sense of humour?
> *She*: No. How does it go?

JAN OXENBERG makes politically important, humorous films. They are important not only because they are part of a small group of films that describe the lesbian experience in America but also because they have a lot to say about the ideology of film and about feminist film-makers' expanding search for appropriate film aesthetics.

Oxenberg's films have always been controversial. Depending on the biases of who's doing the judging, they are usually accused of being apolitical, sentimental, or technically unrefined. Suffering from the negative criticism levelled at many feminist films, Oxenberg's films are additionally ghettoised by people who cannot relate to the films' lesbian subject matter.

In spite of such criticism, Oxenberg's films have had an enthusiastic reception by lesbian and feminist audiences. The films have been programmed over and over again and have achieved a feminist and lesbian cult reputation. In turn critics have dismissed this pheno-menon, saying that lesbian audiences are myopic in their acceptance of these films, misguided by their enthusiasm for the subject matter into ignoring other, and by implication, more important filmic qualities. Frequently feminist films, independently made on very low budgets, are accused by critics of poor technical or 'cinematic' quality.

Admittedly, sections of Oxenberg's films do suffer from technical problems arising from the economics of independent film-making, especially serious for the openly lesbian film-maker. But technical roughness is rarely a barrier for sympathetic audiences' understanding the films although people who want to sidestep the real issues often use this as the excuse to dismiss a film.[1] There are those who find films too threatening that critique our heterosexist culture, including film's function in perpetuating that ideology, especially when the films simultaneously take the lesbian experience seriously and validate it.

Rather than argue about politics, it is much easier to attack the form.

A less obvious explanation, and one that I'd like to explore further in this article, is that Oxenberg's films are using a cinematic aesthetic not perceived by most critics.[2] A lot of political analysis in these films, especially in *Comedy in Six Unnatural Acts*, occurs through manipulating the form, and it is lesbians and feminists who have no need to evade the politics of *Comedy's* formal analysis and jokes and who are receptive to its lessons. Oxenberg's films present, celebrate, and validate the lesbian experience. They provide a way of looking at what images do to us as well as at our own attitudes. The films use humour to begin to analyse politically and critique homosexual and heterosexual cultural stereotypes as well as to explore the complex relationship between film and ideology. At the same time they confront the audience with its own prejudices. [. . .]

Comedy in Six Unnatural Acts (1975, 26 minutes) is divided into six separate sections: 'Wallflower', 'Role-Playing', 'Seduction', 'Non-Monogamy', 'Child Molester', and 'Stompin' Dykes'. Each section critiques pervading myths about lesbian culture. The film works by playing in a comic way on our expectations. It presents icons and behaviours we are accustomed to seeing, seducing us into feeling comfortable about predicting each section's outcome, but then each section ends with a totally different explanation from the traditional one. An example is 'Role-Playing'. Shot in soft light with diffusion filters, the sequence shows us a culturally conventionally beautiful woman preparing to go out on a date. Instead of the traditional image of her putting on make-up, we see her dressing 'butch': knotting her tie, slapping on cologne, greasing back her hair. This last action is shown in excruciating close-up, the woman's fingers scooping up handfuls of slimy goop. At one point the gel slips out of her fingers onto her nose. The audience laughs and cringes. The image is powerful, resonating with memories of teasing, curling, spraying, plucking, and, yes, slicking back hair. The image reinforces our sense of how women twist and contort themselves to fit some cultural notion of beauty and acceptability, whether heterosexual or lesbian. It also suggests male grooming routed through female actions – a strong lesbian stereotype. The woman puts on her suit jacket, gives herself one last look in the mirror, picks up a bouquet of flowers, and walks off to meet her date. When she rings the doorbell, our expectation is that it will be answered by the 'femme' counterpart to this 'butch'. However, a woman answers dressed in exactly the same way with suit, tie, and slicked-back hair, and she is also holding flowers. The women exchange bouquets, wink at each other, and go off holding hands.

In 'Wallflower', we see a high school dance with the inevitable woman on the sidelines pathetically isolated from the dancing couples on the floor. After an excruciatingly long time, her date walks in but stays just off screen. We see the 'Wallflower' turn and look up smiling. As the camera pulls back, we see not a handsome male date but a tall, blonde woman whom the Wallflower adores.

This device, though simple, is much more than just a joke with a visual punchline. It is a set-up. Oxenberg carefully codes sequences in particular ways to ensure a predictable cultural reading of the codes by the audience. For example, in 'Role-Playing' she relies on our reading that the woman wearing a suit and tie is a 'butch' who, we think, will of course date a 'femme' in order for Oxenberg to make her joke. 'Wallflower' is much more complex because the codes can be read in a number of different ways. It offers a game of fill-in-the-blanks within the context of the patriarchal ideology of dating. Here, as at the end of each sequence, we realise that we have been led to misread the signs. And these one-line jokes become political precisely because they reveal the cultural construction of the codes themselves.

The sequence leading up to the visual punch line in 'Wallflower' is a textbook of teenage, heterosexual game-playing. Men and women dance in bear-hug embraces, the women lost in the physical massiveness of their male partners, the male hands trying to 'feel-up' their dates while the women continually push the men's hands away. In the background, visually isolated and looking very uncomfortable, is the Wallflower (a woman without a man is alone). At one point a prospective partner approaches the Wallflower. He gives her the once-over, she sneers at him, and he decides she's not worth it and walks away – to her visible relief. We adjust our reading of the sequence in keeping with our knowledge of the film as a lesbian film (a woman alone is a dyke). At this point, the record on the turntable skips and the couples turn and look expectantly at the Wallflower, who is obviously supposed to fix it, yet she is too lost in her own world of discomfort to realise what's going on (a dyke alone is pathetic). When the sequence finally ends happily, we have been led through the complexity of our ideological assumptions, the film revealing in each twist and turn yet another level of erroneous assumptions. This woman may be without a man, but her discomfort does not come from loneliness.

These sequences critique not only homophobic assumptions, but heterosexuality itself and the misappropriation of some heterosexual ideology in lesbian culture. These levels have their clearest articulation in 'Seduction', where we see two women tentatively approaching each other in the initial stages of romantic acquaintance using all the ploys associated with heterosexual courting: there's, 'Maybe some day you can come over and see my maps?', candlelight, a gypsy violinist, and the accidentally spilled glass of wine that gives an excuse for touching. The sequence slips into a satire of lesbian courtship (camping trips and sweetly oversupportive dyke friends helping out a 'new' one). But there is an absurd edge to the women's behaviour which is emphasised by the acting: we are not watching real people but actors very obviously playing roles. Beyond the fact that the behaviour is 'not natural', it also doesn't fit. Despite attempts, lesbians do not fit into the model of romantic love. The film emphasises this by having the scene played not in a public restaurant as it would be with a heterosexual couple, but in the privacy of someone's living room. The lesbian as an outsider is a theme that runs throughout the film. In 'Wallflower' the last shot shows the lesbian couple walking through the parted teenage crowd who throw rice at them. Such a tactic emphasises once again their 'other' status and the impossibility of such a fantasy ending.

Oxenberg is not just criticising heterosexual romanticism; she is critical of lesbian romanticism as well. In 'Non-Monogamy', we see a woman (played by Oxenberg herself) juggling fruits and balls. As the narrator reads from a political tract about the lesbian nation as an army of lovers and about the positive side of non-monogamy, the juggler offers her own critique of that militant platform by increasingly losing control over her balancing act. Oxenberg is saying in this metaphoric act that living within patriarchal culture is difficult and that lesbians should not just imitate heterosexual behaviour nor should they try to just do the reverse of the dominant norm. For Oxenberg, lesbians must always be questioning and critical of their actions. The 'lesbian nation' is still learning and developing its alternatives.

Except in 'Non-Monogamy', the models of romantic love seen in *Comedy* are actions modelled directly on Hollywood movies. This is made explicit when the women first kiss in 'Seduction'; suddenly we see a dance production number straight out of the movie musical complete with a montage sequence of women (instead of the heterosexual couple) meeting – with such images as tilted neon signs and women folding laundry together at the laundromat; a chorus line; and the seductress. Film references are frequent in *Comedy*. In 'Role-Playing', the very controlled soft focus, diffuse lighting, and carefully composed close-ups suggests the 30s glamour style of photography. The under-cranked camera, quick cutting, and piano music of another section, 'Child Molester', suggests silent film comedies. Oxenberg is clearly acknowledging the power of movies to shape our attitudes and lives.

Comedy is politically important in its concern with naming and claiming lesbianism. In 'Role-Playing', Oxenberg chooses to have both women portrayed as butch not femme (femme is the much more acceptable image of lesbianism in straight society). Role playing does exist, a mimic of the oppressive heterosexist culture, and to deny its existence is to tell an inaccurate and impoverished history of lesbians. 'Child Molester' Oxenberg has the courage to confront the myth of lesbians stalking innocent children and to debunk it instead of pretending it doesn't exist. When the child molester *cum* Girl Scout leader tries to lure two little girls, they just wave at her and walk away together hugging and kissing each other. Oxenberg asks the reactionary question (don't they molest children?) and gives not the liberal answer (these things are not so) but the radical answer (girls love each other).

The film ends with the 'Stompin' Dyke' sequence. The sequence consists of the stompin' dyke, strong, powerful, and leather-jacketed, dismounting from her bike in the first shot. She walks tough down the street: a look from her and people swerve out of her way, a bicyclist stares at her and loses his balance and falls. Once again we have the image of the woman as outsider, offering a sense of both isolation and power. She walks down to the beach and disappears down an incline toward the ocean, recalling an image frequently seen in melodrama where the desolate character walks to a watery suicide (e.g., *A Star is Born, Humoresque*). But the sequence cuts to a medium shot of the dyke in front of the water; as she steps in, the waters part and she walks through unharmed. This image is crucial. It gives the last, most powerful image in the film to the most extreme lesbian stereotype, the stereotype feared by most women, that of the bull dyke. It is easy to claim the 'pretty lesbian' (see in *Playboy* layouts of beautiful women making love for the titillation of men), but to claim the most feared image is both courageous and politically important. Oxenberg gives the image of most power not to a lesbian the women's movement might accept, the chic political lesbian (e.g., Rita Mae Brown), but to the bull dyke.

The best part of Oxenberg's films is the humour that dominates them, ranging from the quiet snicker of recognition to the vulgar comedy of slapstick. Comedy is a difficult form, and Oxenberg's use of it for political ends is fairly unique in contemporary independent political films. Her films' humour is articulated in many different ways. We are shown the absurdity of stereotypes, which after all are part of our distorted history, as with the Child Molester's donning a Girl Scout uniform and trying to lure victims with cookies. We have in *Comedy* the recognition of real lesbian history, even if the actions are no longer appropriate (women do really slick back their hair, a fact no worse than permanents, yet rarely acknowledged with such sympathy). We see a joyous public articulation of lesbian culture (many lesbians' first crushes are on women culturally seen as 'mannish' – their gym teachers – for what kind of women would want to play sports anyway?). *Comedy* also has the vulgar humour of broad humour and slapstick, as in the 'Seduction' and 'Child Molester' sequences. And it provides a laugh that comes from our interpretation of the film's codes and our constant misreading of them.

Oxenberg's films, but especially *Comedy*, are made for lesbian audiences or at least those familiar with lesbian culture. And much of the humour depends on an understanding of that culture. The film plays with stereotypes; it does not make fun of lesbians. At the end of one showing to a primarily heterosexual audience, *Comedy* was attacked for being homophobic. One audience member stated, 'I like gay people – why do you make them so awful?' James Wolcott, in his *Village Voice* review of *Comedy* following its eventual showing on WNET, did not find the film funny at all, which meant he completely missed all the political points, for these are made solely through humour. He condemns the film:

> 'Child Molester' concerns a lech who dolls herself up in a Girl Scout outfit and haunts playgrounds, lusting after little girls. When she tries to entice a pair of tots with GS cookies, the girls gigglingly kiss each other and scamper off – they don't need the Scout Leader, see, because they're already budding lezzies. (With Oxenberg's sense of humor, America doesn't need the neutron bomb.)[4]

Comedy is so complex in its structure, due to its many levels of critique, analysis, and satire, that it does allow for audience's own experiences and biases. But there is a further division between viewers whose misunderstanding derives from homophobia and those whose misunderstanding arises out of their lack of knowledge and/or experience.

Oxenberg's use of humour, although it elicits a differential response from audiences, is not, I think, a limitation of her films. To make a political film for a particular primary audience is one of a number of alternative media strategies. Often, to make a film on lesbianism or homosexuality that is 'acceptable' and has a broad appeal is to whitewash or eliminate sexuality itself – which is after all the reason why homosexuality is such a taboo. Oxenberg avoids this. Equally, she avoids the opposite problem and is able to deal with the sexual/political issues involved in a non-voyeuristic way. It is difficult to depict lesbianism in film because film is a medium that historically has used women for the visual pleasure of the male audience.

There is fine line between 'naming the unnamed' and exploiting it. Oxenberg, by dealing with lesbian issues in a humorous cultural/historical way, avoids this pitfall. In her work lesbians are defined by much more than their lovemaking although she indirectly implies this critical aspect by having the characters prepare for dates, hold hands, and kiss. But lesbianism is more broadly political for her, having to do with ideological mechanisms of socialisation, male/female gender differentiation, cultural notions of romantic love, and being an outsider. Oxenberg's films deal with all these issues and in an increasingly political and sophisticated way.

This article has been cut to discuss only *Comedy*. The other film discussed was *Home Movie*.

Notes

1. The most recent case of this is WNET's controversial programming of its 1980 Independent Focus series. *Comedy* was one of the twenty-eight independently made films recommended for programming by a peer review panel. Later it was one of four films refused air time by the station. The station cited poor acting and low technical quality as its reasons. However, in the ensuing protest by the gay community, it became clear that the criterion used was the film's threatening content. Because of the pressure exerted by gay rights groups, the film was later re-programmed. The other three films have not had similar success (see *Jump Cut* no. 22).

2. For an extraordinary example of this see James Wolcott's review, 'Lesbians Are Lousy Lovers', *Village Voice*, 2 May 1980: 'I waited for the apples to come tumbling down – for Oxenberg to acknowledge that lesbians too suffer from spite, envy, jealousy. But no: She really seems to believe that her sisters leap from petal to dewy petal in a daisy chain of sapphic delight. If lesbian life is such a kissy frolic, why did all the women in *Comedy in Six Unnatural Acts* look as if they had just discovered holes in their galoshes?'

3. For wonderful reading, I suggest the letters to the editors written in response to this vicious review of *Comedy, Village Voice*, 26 May and 2 June 1980.

Reflections on Eros: 'An Epic Poem'

PAM COOK

From *Screen* vol. 23 no. 3/4, 1982, pp. 127–31.

An Epic Poem is a short, independently-made film produced with the help of Arts Association money, voluntary labour and love. It's unusual in that it manages to raise pressing questions for feminism while being witty, visually pleasurable, formally innovative and politically affirmative: qualities which our defensive politics all too often lead us to distrust. Pleasure, in all its painful contradictions, is one of the big questions feminism faces in the 80s.

The film opens with archive footage of preparations for World War I. The phallic shadow of a Zeppelin falls across the land, the male civilian population trains to take up arms, she kisses him goodbye forever and returns to work in the armaments factories. The machinery of war is set in motion. The anachronistic sound of a NASA countdown brings these images from the past chillingly close to the present, reminding us of our world shadowed by war. Feminist politics has yet to sort itself out in relation to war, or rather the many different kinds of war we are faced with today. How does feminism relate, for instance, to militarism, to women's careers in the army, to nationalist wars of liberation, to pacifism and the Peace Movement? These are urgent questions in the context of Ireland, the nationalistic war-cries thrown up by the South Atlantic crisis, and the imminent presence of Cruise missile bases, but they also have a more long-term relevance to issues of feminism and violence. Traditionally, male society has placed the ideal of femininity outside war, in the realm of love, the peaceful hearth and home which finally justifies all the political atrocities carried out in the name of war. The warlike, Amazonian woman has a function in this scenario: she represents a threat to male control, and in overcoming her, man is all the more manly, hence the erotic charge of the image; Penthesilea and her Amazons forcibly subdued by the virile Theseus, power returned to its rightful place. But not forever, as myth and history demonstrate . . .

An Epic Poem approaches the traditional division between war and love, masculine and feminine by way of myth: the story of the adulterous affair between Ares and Aphrodite in Homer's *Odyssey*.

The mythological past is set against feminist history: the struggles of the militant suffragettes, and present-day campaigns by the Women's Movement for contraception and abortion, in order to raise questions about the relationship between myth, its unconscious processes, and the real social and political gains made by organised feminist politics. The film looks back, not in order to find a lost women's history truer than prevailing male versions, but to provoke contradictions which allow us to question the past and its inevitability. It finds the past again in the present, in a new set of problems and contradictions.

The 'machinery of war' montage includes stills showing women's work in the armaments factories. A neutral voice proclaims: 'The war has left Europe with at least ten million women to live without men.' The frantic activity comes suddenly to a halt as an explosion drives the workers from the factory, and our heroine, a suffragette working to prepare bombs, stops to think. In a radical shift of point of view which shows us her feet running from her eye-view, the neutrality of the documentary sequence is shattered, and the feminist viewpoint takes over the film. The modern woman, typing the script, sees herself in the suffragette heroine of her film, and in the myth of Ares and Aphrodite which it appropriates.

In the *Odyssey* Homer tells us how Aphrodite, goddess of love, has been married off by her father Zeus to the crippled king Hephaestus in exchange for a large dowry. She is seduced by expensive gifts into an affair with Ares, the god of War, which is revealed to Hephaestus by Helios, the sun, who spies on the lovers. Hephaestus takes revenge by imprisoning Ares and Aphrodite in a web of chains, demanding that Zeus repay the entire dowry. He is finally persuaded to release Ares into the guardianship of Poseidon, so that Aphrodite is released also, and returns to her all-female sanctuary, Paphos, and her Three Graces.

A striking metaphor indeed for patriarchal power relations. Aphrodite is created in the image of man's desire for himself. Her beauty, her narcissistic sexuality, arouse all men, making them weak when they should be strong. She is the reason for, the fault of, man's forbidden desires, causing him to transgress his own social codes, here defined in terms of heterosexual monogamy. Heterosexuality is rooted in a basic contradiction: the suppression of male homosexual desire and displacement of anxiety onto the woman's body. Since the guilt is hers, man can be redeemed. Ares, of course, is also beautiful: he has his passive, feminine side, brought out by his fascination with Aphrodite. He is weakened, feminised by their affair, distracted from his duties: a victim of the love he initiated. For all the power wielded by men in the story (their control of kinship relations, of wealth, of machinery, of 'the look') it is the feminine, constantly threatening to slip out of control, that challenges the male order at its very roots. The fusion/confusion of love and war, femininity and masculinity, is the problem that the myth tries to resolve, finally returning Ares to his rightful place with the male gods, and Aphrodite to her all-female sanctuary.

What, then, is the relationship of the myth to history, and to social reality? Feminist films about women's history – *Babies and Banners* or *Rosie the Riveter*, for instance – concentrate on uncovering a past excluded from conventional histories. These films are intended to redress the balance in favour of women, and in them women are shown speaking for themselves, recounting a lost women's history which provides a truer version than the distortions of conventional accounts. More recently, feminist films have tried to present history differently, not as a lost content, or linear progression of events, but as a network of different representations, or discourses: shifting points of view which overlap with and contradict one another. *Song of the Shirt* and *Penthesilea, Queen of the Amazons* are examples of this discursive cinema, and so is *An Epic Poem*, albeit in a more amusing vein. It traces the mythological opposition between love and war through a number of historical moments, interrupting at key points to ask whether, and how, things might have happened differently. What, for example, if Aphrodite had refused to marry? Myth cannot be collapsed into history, but neither is it a false story which can be simply replaced by the 'truth'. Myth continues to circumscribe our existence because it is deeply embedded in our thought processes and in our representations – the film juxtaposes Freud, Juliet Mitchell on psychoanalysis and feminism, a pamphlet on *Women and the Census* and Homer's *Odyssey* to point up the contradictory conjunction of myth and history, which, it argues, is neither natural or inevitable. The strategy of overlapping different kinds and orders of representation produces gaps in the seamless progress of the narratives of myth and history which allow us to question their authority.

The Ares and Aphrodite myth, when brought together with the struggles of the militant suffragettes, and with the modern woman's story, whose 'sexual liberation' imprisons her in the same traps, starts to look different. The suffragettes, while campaigning around the issue of the vote, were also engaged in feminist struggles on many other levels. They fought against women's confinement within the private sphere of the Victorian patriarchal family. Although that family hardly exists any longer, the contemporary Women's Movement still finds itself campaigning around issues such as abortion law and contraception: clearly women do not yet control their bodies, or perhaps more importantly, their minds. But feminist politics takes a different route than the myth: it brings war back into the bedroom, transforming it into a battleground. Aphrodite now resists.

If history is a question of representation, it is also more often than not a process of misrecognition. Sappho's poem to Aphrodite, for instance, a passionate calling up of a warm and caring love between women, is attributed in many translations to Homer. And Velasquez' *Rokeby Venus*, which provides the central image for *An Epic Poem*, is most often described as gazing at her own reflection in a mirror, when in fact she looks out at the spectator. It's in these instances of misrecognition that the film sees the possibility of feminist intervention. Like the Homeric myth, the painting of the *Rokeby Venus* focuses on a problem of feminine sexuality, which art criticism attempts to resolve uneasily and unsuccessfully.

In *Ways of Seeing* John Berger describes the convention of the female nude in painting as one in which the woman who is the object of the painting watches herself being watched by a male spectator. Berger defines the 'male spectator' historically: in the hey-day of the female nude the function of such paintings was to confirm male ownership of trade and the arts by representing the female body as entirely available to the controlling male gaze. The female nude recognised the presence of the male spectator by looking back at him, or, in the cases where she was represented looking at herself, one or more male voyeurs would be included in the picture, to confirm the security of the male gaze. What is striking about the examples Berger chooses is the way the feminine body is constantly framed and contained, by a mirror, by a series of looks exchanged between model, artist and spectator, as though it might spill over the borders of the representation and escape. According to Berger, the female nude recognises her availability to the male spectator-owner, confirming existing male–female power relations. If the nude was painted from the back, the head often turned to look over her shoulder at the spectator. The look was both a sexual provocation, an invitation, and a recognition of male power. Berger supports his argument by suggesting a simple substitution game: if you try replacing the female nude figure with a male nude, what happens? Are the power relations reversed? As feminist art critics have also pointed out, a simple role-reversal is not enough to radically challenge the authority of the male gaze at, and control of the feminine body. However, in spite of the cogency of Berger's account, he overlooks, perhaps significantly, an instability in these masculine images of the feminine body: the body itself, for instance, so excessive that it has to be fixed in place by a complex relay of looks and system of framing devices; the look of the woman back at the spectator, an active sexual invitation which contradicts the depiction of her body as the passive object of contemplation; the function of the mirror in many of the paintings, to forestall, or delay immediate gratification of the look at the feminine body – a defence against the horror that might be revealed?

Some of these instabilities are evident in the *Rokeby Venus*, which presents the woman's nude body from the back, the front accessible only to the Cupid who holds the mirror up to it. The Venus is depicted looking into the mirror, ostensibly at her own reflection, but her gaze is deflected back to the spectator. The constant misrecognition of this fact in descriptions of the painting suggests a number of things: that the sexual provocation implicit in the representation is so threatening that it has to be displaced onto female narcissism – the look of the woman at herself allowing the spectator to contemplate her body voyeuristically, in safety; and that perhaps, since the body is presented as flawless, perfectly beautiful, this plenitude and the spectator's pleasure in it might be disturbed by the recognition that the image actively returns the spectator's look reminding him of what is at risk.

An Epic Poem takes up this instability in the *Rokeby Venus* and plays around with it. The painting is juxtaposed with the Ares and Aphrodite myth, in which Helios, the male voyeur, spies on the lovers, bringing down the retribution of male society upon Aphrodite. The myth is re-enacted in the context of the First World War. As Helios looks in on the lovers, they act out the scene of the painting, playing with the mirror to alter what it reflects. The game of substitution and role-reversal with the Venus occurs again in the film, when it is specifically linked with the sexual ambiguity that the myth tries to resolve. Aphrodite is a militant suffragette, Ares a beautiful, effeminate young man who can take the place of Cupid on one hand, or Venus herself on the other. The pleasure and eroticism of the game is underlined when Aphrodite/Venus takes the place of Cupid, holds the mirror up to Ares/Venus, and turns to look directly into camera, explicitly breaking the conventions of cinema (Don't look at the Camera!), exploiting the instabilities of its system of looking. Her glance at the spectator is intercepted by the next shot, in which the modern woman leaves her typewriter to look into camera, meeting the Venus's look, and apparently exchanging glances directly with her and the spectator, until the camera moves back to reveal a mirror-shot: the modern woman, regarding herself, smiles and returns to her typewriter. The intimacy between Venus and spectator is broken. The woman's look at herself re-appropriates her image, questioning the spectator's ownership of it, and revealing the precariousness of the spectator's control.

In recent years, feminist theory has made it increasingly difficult to think how the female body might be represented, since all representation seems to recuperate femininity back into the prevailing system of masculine domination. As a way out of the impasse, feminist cinema has, on the one hand, represented the female body as essentially feminine (vaginal, clitoral) or, on the other hand, refused to represent it at all. Rather than essentialism, or a puritanical refusal of the pleasures of looking, *An Epic Poem* prefers to exploit the contradictions and instabilities of the cinema's system of representation. In the process, the woman's body is transformed from an object of contemplation into a site of play and struggle, although there is still, always the risk of recuperation. The film is not afraid to take the risk.

The *Rokeby Venus* has a particular place in feminist history. The militant suffragette Mary Richardson, outraged by the treatment of Mrs Pankhurst in prison, decided to destroy the painting as a protest against a society which put a high price on images of woman's physical beauty, but subjected their bodies to imprisonment and force-feeding. The iconoclasm of her act brought love and war together again, challenging power relations in society. The militant suffragettes directed their violence against specific targets: the property of the male ruling class. Mary Richardson slashed the body of the Venus with an axe, attacking an image of love held dear by men for centuries, turning violence back against society in the name of a new ideal of femininity, which she defined in humanitarian terms: Justice, she claimed, was a more proper ideal for humankind than the mythological Venus.

Nonetheless, it's difficult to escape the thought that her rhetoric is belied by the sadistic desire motivating her attack. In one of the most disturbing images of the film, our suffragette heroine's face appears reflected in the Venus's mirror for a few seconds before she smashes the protective glass, smashing her own reflection. The sado-masochistic impulse behind the suffragettes' militancy is striking: as though their desire to destroy male society hinged on their own destruction. Mary Richardson's act was directed against male myths of femininity, but also at the state and legal system that supported those myths, reinforcing male control. Her transgression was punished with imprisonment, and since the suffragettes conducted hunger-strikes to acquire the status of political prisoners, with the bodily abuse of force-feeding. The sadism of the Cat and Mouse Act, which allowed those hunger strikers who became ill a temporary respite at home, before calling them back to prison for more torture, vividly exemplifies the punishment visited by society on women who actively challenge its terms in order to change it, returning them constantly to the position of victim rather than aggressor. The film uses detailed testimony from Sylvia Pankhurst's diary to describe the intensely painful experience of a hunger strike. These passages contrast sharply with the perfect beauty of the body of Venus. It's as if the woman's body can't escape its fate, the mutilation and abuse which is the other side of man's idealisation of femininity.

The suffragettes' imprisonment ended when militancy was suspended during the First World War, which brought some changes in attitudes to women's place in society, in marriage and the family. Women made a few gains in the workplace, though working conditions were still dire; at the same time, the need for a new labour force encouraged the beginnings of a welfare system for mothers, and state intervention in the family, trapping women again in the old myths. Since then, feminist and gay politics have contributed to changing traditional sexual roles, divorcing sexuality from reproduction, changing child-care patterns, giving women more control over their bodies and their lives. The contemporary Women's Movement, like the suffragette movement, organises itself around love and solidarity between women, resisting male control in the very sphere it has always most forcibly, and most precariously held sway: the female body. The feminist body is very different from the ideal figure of Venus, property and object of the male gaze. It is active, questioning, exploratory, refusing fixed sexual divisions.

Perhaps, as the film suggests, it is the fear of his own extinction that causes man to constantly try to regain his control of the female body through violence. Or the fear of incest, the forbidden desire which causes him to construct woman as 'good' and 'bad' in the image of the two sides of the coin of masculine desire: the ideal woman, to be worshipped, and the base women, to be punished. Man has created love in his image, which feminists must now confront in order to understand their own desires. *An Epic Poem* sees feminist resistance to man's concept of love in an attack on the dualism which underpins it: the feminine as the voice of heterogeneity and polymorphous desire. Our suffragette heroine rejects the fate of Aphrodite, inescapably the victim of man's love. In front of the *Rokeby Venus* in the National Gallery, she leaves Cupid holding the baby and takes action, marching out with her Three Graces to find her own, revolutionary concept of love.

Thanks to Lezli-An Barrett for her help.

'Burning An Illusion'

SALLY SAYER AND LALEEN JAYAMANNE

From *Film News* (Australia) vol. 13 no. 1/2, January/February 1983.

THE WRITING of this review was difficult for us because of the dilemma raised by the fact that it is the first black British feature film about issues of political significance to black struggles against a racist state and situation in Britain. While supporting these struggles and the making of a film about them we (one of us black, the other white) found the film didn't completely succeed for us, both politically and aesthetically.

We found ourselves in a similar position to that which we remember in relation to early feminist films; that is, supporting the effort, the commitment to acquiring the skills, the gaining of access to finance to make films about political concerns, etc., but feeling critical of the form and content of these films. In those days one was usually supportive because of the newness of the undertaking and the desire that it should develop and prosper.

Similarly, we support the fact that the British Film Institute has funded the making of this film, that it is an all black effort and that it raises some of the issues facing British blacks. But we feel that not to be as critical as we feel about the articulation of the political issues in the film as well as of the style and form of the film would be to adopt a patronising stance in relation to it.

Hence we feel bound to say that the film left us disappointed.

Burning An Illusion is the story of a young black woman's transformation from a state of 'ignorance' to one of 'knowledge'. Set in London in the 80s, the film explores issues related to gender, race and generational struggles. Pat, a young office worker, lives on her own in a council flat, reads Barbara Cartland, dresses up and dreams of meeting somebody to 'settle down' with. She meets Del, a young toolmaker who cherishes his street identity and drinking/music/gambling companionship with other black men. When Del loses his job, the conflict in their desires becomes acute. As he loafs around with his friends, gambling and messing up the living room, Pat loses patience, and Del's masculine arrogance comes to the fore. Thus the lines of gender conflict are drawn.

It is this gender question which precipitates the film into the area of race politics. A fight over a woman leads to scuffles with the police,

Del is victimised and ends up getting four years for assaulting a policeman.

The imprisonment leads to the politicisation of both Del and Pat. It is the film's articulation of this process of politicisation that we felt most dissatisfied with. The sudden transformation of Pat from a fashionable young office worker to Afro-identified militant fails to convey the complexity and contradictions involved in the development of political awareness. The film's reliance on superficial signs of militancy (dress, hairstyle, etc.) to convey serious political and personal changes leaves many questions unasked.

This superficial account of complex questions is embodied in the film's narrative structure and use of genre. Pat's conversion rests on two key turning points in the story: Del's imprisonment and her own experience of being attacked by white racists.

While already persuaded audiences will be aware that the prison experience can be a politicising one, we are not let into the process of how and why this takes place for Del – just that he sends out reading lists including books by Malcolm X. Similarly for Pat in the incident in which she is shot at. While there is no doubt at all that there is gratuitous violence and murder of black people in Britain, the use of this incident lacks credibility in terms of the narrative structure of the

Burning an Illusion

film. To make this the clinching point of Pat's enlightenment actually makes it seem less likely, less 'true'.

The rather heavy-handed way in which we are over-prepared for the incident by her friend's caution and warnings, means that the incident is even more melodramatic by being so over-determined. Ironically, the audience could feel cheated of the dramatic expectations so insistently promised by the narrative suspense, if it did not take place. So we have the politically absurd situation in which the audience may be actually desiring that an incident such as this should take place.

The point here is that when using generic conventions for political purposes it seems necessary to be aware of how they traditionally work. Otherwise, instead of using genre for one's own purposes, it will determine what one has to say, which may work against the explicit political intentions of the film.

We do not mean to say that melodrama is inimical to effective political film-making, but that the film's use of it simplifies complex processes by reducing them to a series of climaxes. The court room scene is another example of the use of melodrama which may be seen to unwittingly work against the political intentions of the film. The climactic moment when Pat verbally challenges the verdict, and the subsequent low-angle shot of Del looking grimly angry, seems to us a weak representation of the racist workings of law and black responses to it. The quality of performing in the film, which we generally found pleasing and credible, failed in this scene because the performers alone had to carry the burden of representing racial injustice in the legal system through shifting the acting mode from naturalism to histrionics.

Another question raised by the film's aesthetics is that of film technique itself being instrumental in conveying political meaning. We found the film visually bland in the way it uses the most taken-for-granted ways of looking, characteristic of the dominant visual culture (TV). We are, in this context, neither for nor against modes of representation dominant in TV but what we do find disappointing in a black political film is its apparent lack of desire to look differently. A film which is 'about' racial and cultural difference, we hoped, would at least have made a tentative gesture in this direction. We are not talking about a 'black exotic' effect, nor about a 'new language', as if the latter could happen overnight. We are registering our disappointment at the taken-for-granted use of white film language,

Given that Menelik Shabazz in interview has emphasised the importance of music in his films, saying that it is 'the bass line' which 'keeps the emotional thing going', we found the soundtrack disappointing. It seems to lack any of the vitality and sense of resistance characteristic of some black British music.

The film is principally in the didactic mode and in the early parts

88

Burning an Illusion

where it deals mostly with questions of gender relations the didacticism is entertainingly presented. However, as the film proceeds into the area of racial issues, it becomes a victim of its own limited didacticism and quest for a happy ending. By the need to get to the happy ending (all militants together in a bus, singing, with clenched fists, a sugary last frame) the film robs itself of both dramatic credibility and the possibility of exploration of the questions raised by the film itself. The last frame is the final easy way out, in a film which holds 'knowledge' to be so simply acquired and so simplistically applied. Of course solidarity and cultural and political assertiveness are hoped-for results of political knowledge, but the film's representation of it is clichéd and lacks energy and force.

The strength of the film for us lies in the part which deals with the gender relationship. This is not because we find gender relations more engrossing than race relations, but because the former is explored in less schematic filmic terms than the latter.

We also found the exploration of black sexism a very significant aspect of the film, precisely because in various class, national and racial politics the question of gender is often bracketed off as a distraction from the primary struggle. This film's refusal to do so is therefore important. Though the conflicts of race and gender undoubtedly intersect in the film, it is only to provide a catalyst for the progress of the narrative. They are left as fairly discrete areas with the gender question more or less disappearing once it catalyses the race issue in the club. There would have been more interest and credibility if these intersecting tensions had not been so separated in the film's structure.

The film has provided a window-on-the-world view for Australians interested in black British political struggles and many people have enjoyed it in this way. Our criticisms may have a utopian ring to them. However, the film itself does have some utopian aspirations and we feel it is not too harsh to address it in its own terms.

'Maeve'

CLAIRE JOHNSTON

From *Screen* vol. 22 no. 4, 1981, pp. 54–63.

THERE IS no autonomous women's movement in the North of Ireland at the present time: the dichotomy between immediate needs and long-term objectives within the context of 'the troubles' and the deepening crisis of the Northern Irish state has so far paralysed attempts to build such a movement. The general consensus within the republican movement is that specifically feminist issues should be postponed until more favourable conditions emerge. Recently such assumptions have been challenged by women's groups and the frequently uncritical support which English feminists have given the republican movement:

> The uncritical support given by some English feminists to the nationalist struggle being waged here in Northern Ireland is of little help to us, or indeed, to the women in the whole of Ireland. Not only does it serve to divide women along the traditional 'Orange and Green', it also results in a lack of attention to the feminist issues. The ability of English feminists to concentrate on the national liberation struggle is a luxury we can't afford.[1]

Similarly, writing about their work in Belfast over the past few years, the Belfast Women's Collective describe their isolation from the mainstream of republicanism:

> The problem was this – all the women within the group were agreed on their opposition to British imperialism, but we made cogent criticisms of the Republican movement, particularly of its position on women. We showed how women had been used and forgotten in previous struggles in Ireland, to demonstrate the dangers of history repeating itself. We acknowledged the importance of the national question (the campaign for a united Ireland) but stressed that it should not and could not be put before other questions – there could be no liberation without women's liberation – and unless struggle was carried out on all fronts then the 'revolution' was likely to bring little real change to women's lives.[2]

Maeve is a film which both reflects these debates within feminism and makes its own unique contribution to them. The narrative tells the story of a young woman, Maeve, who has been living in London and returns to her home in a Catholic ghetto of Belfast on a visit. The fundamental motor for the unfolding of the narrative, as it is for a significant aspect of feminist art practice and for Pat Murphy's previous film *Rituals of Memory* (1979), is the exploration of personal memory. The film juxtaposes the present of her visit to her family and friends with the past of the subjective memories of her childhood and adolescence in Belfast, of her trips with her father out into the countryside, of the move from a Protestant housing estate to a Catholic ghetto as 'the troubles' escalate, and of her relationship with Liam, a young republican and their final estrangement.

In recent years feminist film theory and practice have pointed to the need to re-assess the role of a prescriptive 'anti-realism' which ignores the central question for a politics of cinema – that of the audience defined in social and historical terms. Such a re-assessment must necessarily involve a move away from the notion of 'text' and 'spectator' conceptualised in abstract and a-historical terms and towards a more interventionist conception of textual practice seen within specific historical conjunctures, where formalist criteria for assessing whether a film is 'progressive' or 'reactionary' are secondarised. It is in this context that *Maeve* should be assessed.

Like much feminist film-making of the last decade, *Maeve* has an experimental narrative structure which works within and against the operations of the classic narrative *vis-à-vis* the spectator. The difference and the originality of the film is the way in which these narrative strategies structure the terms of the political debate the film sets up between feminism and republicanism. The film poses its critique of republicanism in the figure of Maeve, who enters the narrative from the outside as an exile. Maeve describes men's relationship to women within nationalist culture as 'like England's relationship to Ireland. You're in possession of us. You occupy us like an army'. She rejects the role women have traditionally been allowed within the nationalist struggle: 'When you're denied power, or when it's continually co-opted, the only form of protest is through your body. Our struggle is for autonomy'. Maeve represents women's negative relationship to language and the symbolic order of patriarchal nationalist culture – the outside of republican discourse. This negative positionality is embedded in the process of the film itself, and in the interaction of the narrative discourses of past and present which the film sets up. The film rejects the notion of a 'positive heroine', but at the same time attempts to create the possibility of positive images *for* women, an imaginary *for* women, which would enable them to enter history on their own terms, through the mobilisation rather than the undercutting of identification processes.

The dominant discourse of the film is the story in the present which, in its sense of documentary immediacy and realism, sets up the possibility of providing the 'reality' of the experience of the nationalist community. Within this narrative discourse, Maeve remains an outsider, a witness to the stories her family relate to her, the subject of incomprehension. The immediacy of the political situation renders her discourse meaningless and identification with her position difficult. At the same time, the film stresses the fictionalisation of these experiences, both through the process of storytelling through the way in which TV is seen to mediate that reality within the family and encapsulated in the Orange March on 12 July, which the family watch on TV as it passes their window in the street outside. If the working through of the dominant narrative discourse serves to re-produce Maeve as exile, the narrative discourse of her subjective memory told in flashback from her point of view produces the opposite effect and operates to provide an understanding of that isolation and sense of exclusion. Unlike her father's memory which serves to hold him to a past and prevent him from acting in the present, Maeve's reactivation of the past traces her political development as a feminist and provides an understanding of the present and her position within it, and through its articulation as subjective point of view, demanding the spectator's identification with it. If the dominant discourse works to naturalise nationalist ideologies and culture, the feminine discourse works to de-naturalise it, producing a space which must be filled, a problem of identity and position in the text.

Maeve's father, Martin Sweeney, is positioned in the narrative to inhabit this space. The opening scene sets him up to function as the *seannochoi,* the traditional Irish storyteller, whose position of knowledge within the narrative traditionally functions as the collective memory of the community, as he sits down at the table in the middle of a bomb scare and writes a letter to his daughter. But Martin's stories mirror his dislocation from society and remain locked in a heroic myth of the past. Through his stories he seeks to both control and distance himself from the realities of the world in which he lives. At key points in the narrative he addresses the audience directly, initially by interrupting Eileen, Maeve's mother, and taking the story she is about to tell Maeve away from her and asserting a privileged relationship to the camera by addressing the camera directly. Martin asserts his patriarchal discourse as universal, but as the film progresses it increasingly serves the function of a monologue and the position of knowledge which it seeks to hold within the narrative is undermined as Maeve retreats from his sphere of influence. The final shot of the film is of him talking to himself and looking out of frame, the privileged relationship of his discourse with the audience having been finally undermined. The storyteller finally loses control of the story: he can no longer hold together the problem of identity and of position within the film.

93

Maeve

The film is not only interpolated by Martin Sweeney's stories but by a series of dialogues between Maeve and Liam where the realist conception of character within the narrative is abandoned and they come to represent elements within an intellectual argument between feminism and republicanism. These dialogues function as a counterpoint to Martin Sweeney's stories and concretise the contradictions set up between the narratives of past and present as overtly political discourses in struggle. Liam rejects the republican tradition of his father's generation and is searching for a more progressive form of politics which can break with the myths of the past and act upon the present. At the same time he can see no place for feminism as an autonomous force within the nationalist struggle and sees Maeve's ideas as simply the products of a self-imposed exile and fundamentally depoliticising. The relationship of sound to image traces a progression from Maeve as voice-off on Cave Hill towards a greater centralising for her position in the sequence in Clifton Graveyard, but they remain at an impasse, as discourses in struggle filmed in long-shot.

An important aspect of the film is the way in which it depicts the construction of 'femininity' within nationalist culture, encapsulated in the memory sequence in the convent schoolroom where the girls are forced to recite by rote Patrick's Pearce's famous poem 'The Mother', written just before his execution after the Easter Rising in 1916, in which he associates the mother of an Irish nationalist with the mother of Jesus at the foot of the cross. Pearce's poem has become one of the cornerstones of the nationalist imaginary of women, invoking the necessity for blood sacrifice and martyrdom for a mythological notion of Ireland as the maternal, addressing her children in the name of God and dead generations to sacrifice themselves for her nationhood and for the mythical re-birth of the lost Spirit of Eire, the eternal 'nation'. In contrast to Maeve, Eileen and Roisin represent two generations of women caught in these representations of women, at the same time offering their own particular stoical and circumscribed resistances to them. They operate within a realist conception of character within the narrative to assert a marginalised and specifically female experience of the political situation (e.g. sexual harassment by the security forces, etc.) which, through reminiscence and anecdote, serves to undercut the heroics of the father's discourse. While Maeve's feminism remains irrelevant to their immediate experience, the film nevertheless, at the level of the image, through composition within the frame, conveys an intimate bond between the women which transcends the differences of generation and experience.

Maeve works towards a displacement of this nationalist imaginary of women and the construction of another imaginary – an imaginary *for* women which could, at the level of phantasy, produce a centrality for Maeve's discourse which the structure of the narrative disallows. To produce this the film invokes the landscape, which throughout the film has functioned either as a male domain (e.g. in Maeve's memories of her trips into the countryside with her father and in Liam's relationship to landscape and frame – the land as the central metaphor for generations of republican men) or as the repository of a 'Celtic' truth which lies beyond history and politics (e.g. epitomised in the Seeker of Lost Knowledge). The resolution and closure of the narrative on the Giant's Causeway depicts Maeve, Roisin and Eileen united together for the first time in the film within the image. The scene assumes the level of subversive phantasy as the demonic Causeway Man rants his mad cultural pastiche of Irish patriarchal discourse. While the women shelter under the rocks and take a swig from a bottle of whiskey, his voice-off continues to drone its empty rhetoric of blood sacrifice, 'freedom' and 'manhood'. Their final images offer a resolution and closure in terms of a displacement of the nationalist patriarchal mythology of the land and assert the need for women to reappropriate that mythology for history. If the film depicts the discourses of feminism and republicanism at an impasse, as discourses in struggle, through the dialogues of Maeve and Liam, the final images suggest a struggle within nationalist mythologies of the land on which those discourses rest, and a militant reactivation of Eire as the 'feminine', such a representation displacing the dominant nationalist ideologies which place that 'feminine' exclusively within the confines of the 'maternal' and outside history. It is a concept of the 'feminine' which draws upon Celtic mythology but is also worked through in the process of the film itself and in the representations of Eileen, Roisin and Maeve. The immense emotive power of these final images foreground the fundamental problem of cinema and images of women – the problem of how to move against the language of the cinema and the imaginary of women which underlies it to produce new meanings – another imaginary – while running the risk of identifying women with what is archaic, pre-historic – the radical 'outside' of language. It could be argued that *Maeve*, in its invocation of Celtic myth, risks precisely this essentialism, undercutting its project of placing feminism as a central issue for history: the film moves towards an essentialism both of 'woman' and of 'nation'. However, what cannot be ignored is that such an essentialism possesses a mobilising power which is crucial for the feminist politics for which the film is calling.

The intervention *Maeve* is making is bound to be problematic in the present political conjuncture.[3] Clearly, in terms of the left and the Women's Movement in England in the context of the policy of the British state to isolate nationalism, destroy it as a movement and treat it as a simple problem of crime control, the film raises questions concerning the uncritical support given by feminists and the left to the republican struggle and the implications this has for women from within that struggle. At the same time, in the context of Ireland, certain problems emerge. The intervention *Maeve* is making has to be seen within the dominant culture of the island of Ireland as defined by nationalism and Catholicism, the dominant culture hegemonised within the Southern State and the minority, subordinate culture in the North – a culture which has become almost totally synonymous with the term 'Irish Culture'. In the context of the North, in terms of the minority population, the intervention it is making reflects the debates which feminists have begun to initiate. However, within the bourgeois success story that is the Southern State where class contradictions are becoming more dominant, other problems present themselves, and are reflected in the move away from the concept of nation to that of class by such organisations as *Sinn Fein* – The Workers Party. The situation is further complicated by the fact that the critique of nationalism and the role of the Church has been mounted as much by the right as by the left, which has, in its turn, affected the politics of the Women's Movement. For instance, the internalisation of European politics within the Southern State raises the question as to how relevant republican ideologies remain for women. Eire's membership of the EEC is increasingly seen to be important for feminists and gay groups in that it opens up the possibility of challenging the State's internalisation of specifically Catholic ideologies of the family and sexuality within the Constitution of 1937. *Maeve* argues for a reworking of the republican tradition, but it is unclear to what extent Liam's discourse engages with the question of class, or simply reflects the dominant republican tradition founded on a producers' 'socialism' on the lines of Arab and African 'socialism'. There is, of course, the 'other scene' of 'Irish culture', a subordinate culture within the context of the island of Ireland, a culture which has developed historically as a profoundly stunted and defensive tradition, hegemonised within the colonial framework of the Northern Irish State, usually identified as Protestant/Unionist. It would be, perhaps, pure fantasy to envisage the film making an intervention within such a context in the present crisis, and yet it has precisely been feminists in Ireland who have done most to identify religious ideologies as a major locus of patriarchal power (e.g. in abortion and contraception campaigns, etc.). *Maeve*'s only reference to Protestant women occurs in the memory sequence at the hospital where an old woman comforts Maeve by singing 'Abide With Me', her 'otherness' underlined through Maeve's point-of-view. But the film's use of place as a signifier of memory and history points to the possibility of a republicanism which is non-sectarian, a return to the tradition of Wolf Tone[4] – the scene of the first political dialogue between Liam and Maeve takes place on Cave Hill, the scene of the famous oath taken by Tone and others in 1795 to rid Ireland of the English. In this sense the film raises the question as to the role of feminism in undermining religious ideologies and opening up the possibility of alliances between women along non-sectarian lines as a way forward.

Finally, it should be emphasised the extent to which in both its textual strategies and in its interrogation of the ways in which patriarchal ideologies lie deeply embedded in the very conceptions of national culture, *Maeve* constitutes an important contribution to the development of that emerging and problematic entity 'Irish Film Culture'. One major problem which has been identified for film theory and practice[5] in Ireland has been the weakness of visual[6] as opposed to literary culture and the way in which modernism has had very little impact on the culture itself, despite the legacy of Joyce. Strategies for ideological struggle within the context of Ireland can neither simply consist of an application of the British model nor from formalist prescriptions of the 'modernist text' outside any analysis of the cultural formation and the analysis of the counter-hegemonic and radical potential within it. A central feature of Irish national culture is precisely its populist basis which distinguishes it sharply from its British counterpart, where ideologies of 'high' and 'popular' culture are more entrenched. Similarly, the idea of the 'literary' functions vary differently within the Irish cultural formation, possessing far more radical elements. *Maeve*'s emphasis on language reflects this concern, and with it the possibility of developing the 'popular' as a radical concept along Brechtian lines. In recent years there has been a 'new wave' of Irish film-making[7] which has begun to question the construction of 'masculinity' and 'femininity' within the national culture, with films like Tom McArdle's *The Kinkisha* (1978) and Kieran Hickey's *Exposure* (1977) and *Criminal Conversation* (1980). *Exposure* in particular parallels many of the concerns of *Maeve* in its exploration of the exclusivity of the all-male group and the threat which a woman represents who enters the narrative from the outside. At the same time, textual practices have begun to develop which mark a move away from the dominant classic realist aesthetic: *The Lament of Art O'Leary* (Bob Quinn, 1974) with its exploration of a narrative structure based on the *oaoinead* or lament and *On a Paving Stone Mounted* (Thaddeus O'Sullivan, 1979) with its reworking of the documentary genre within a fragmented narrative structure. *Maeve*, however, is the first feminist intervention within this 'new wave' of Irish film-making, and in a wider cultural context in which women have largely remained invisible.

Notes

1. Statement by Derry Women's Aid, in *Spare Rib* no. 99, November 1980.
2. Statement by the Belfast Women's Collective, *Spare Rib* no. 99, November 1980.
3. For further reading, see Austen Morgan and Bob Purdie, eds., *Ireland, Divided Nation, Divided Class* (London: Ink Links, 1980).
4. Wolfe Tone was founder of the Society of United Irishmen in 1791 which aimed at establishing Ireland as a Republic along the lines of the French model. He was a protestant and a democrat and worked closely with catholic organisations.
5. See Kevin Rockett, 'Film Culture in Ireland', *Screen Education* no. 27, Summer 1978.
6. Very little work has been undertaken in this area as yet, but it is interesting to note that within the visual arts, it was largely women artists who were influenced by the impact of cubism.
7. See Kevin Rockett, 'Irish Cinema: Notes on some Nationalist Fictions', *Screen* vol. 20 nos. 3/4, 1979/80.

'A Question of Silence'

JEANETTE MURPHY

IN THIS piece I want to explore the extent to which *A Question of Silence* as a feminist text succeeds in presenting a coherent and integrated challenge to a certain set of patriarchal assumptions and taken-for-granted notions of how the world operates and has to be – namely notions and assumptions relating to heterosexuality, power relations between men and women, women's visibility and status, violence, and that curious entity, (male) 'logic'. However, while the film expresses and examines these conflicts and women's position within patriarchy, *A Question of Silence* articulates these around women's violence, anger and silence. An examination of the negotiation of these issues within the particular, woman-oriented perspective constructed by the film and the feminist politic which motivates it must necessarily expose some of the dilemmas and contradictions inherent in feminism itself. *A Question of Silence*, I would argue, presents separatism as feminism taken to its logical and inevitable conclusion.[1] It reveals women's anger as a problematic, the negotiation of which profoundly affects all women's lives, and which feminism itself has failed to resolve.

A Challenge to Patriarchal Presumption

An outstanding aspect of *A Question of Silence* is its creation and assertion, its apparent naturalisation, of a woman-oriented and identified perspective – a woman's logic and world view. This is established through a combination of the different ways in which women and men respond to the events and characters within the film. The women protagonists' responses are represented as reasonable and rational; they make sense in terms of the filmic events themselves, they are represented sympathetically, space is allowed for our identification – but not an identification associated with most mainstream (classical narrative, realist) films where the camera, camera movement, editing, lighting, etc. serve to absorb us willy-nilly into the film and its characters and plot. While *A Question of Silence* uses a realist *mise-en-scène* and story-line and a more or less conventional way of filming, it also sparingly uses and refers to modernist and avant-garde filming techniques. There are few close-ups. The camera is almost always at a distance from the characters and events and it is often still. Tracking shots – used to follow Christine to the boutique and in the boutique itself – are kept some distance from the characters themselves. The camera is often placed at a lower or higher level to the person(s) it films. The only point-of-view shots in the film (and I could find only two) are those bearing the look of a woman – that of the therapist. The difficulty in identifying point-of-view shots, and their rarity – even were I to have missed a few – is significant. Although we identify through the therapist, this identification is mainly established through her central role in and her progressive enlightenment within the course of the narrative. Thus throughout the film we are consistently kept at a distance – allowing the viewer to think and assess the meaning of events and characters' responses and make a more active and thoughtful, a more 'intelligent' identification. Inevitably, in terms of the politics underpinning the film, this identification is woman-oriented.

In contrast, the men's responses in the film are shown to be irrational, complacent and overbearing – only explicable within a structure where men thoughtlessly oppress women. In the film's narrative men are the butt of jokes – those of the film and of the women in the film. Andrea, the secretary, allows a 'respectable' man to mistake and hire her as a prostitute. An, in response to a grossly sexist statement by one of the café clientèle, tells him to throw his hat in the canal and crawl under it. Christine's husband reveals to the therapist his lack of insight or concern when he speaks of his wife's silence and withdrawal as being symptomatic only of a particular kind of woman (the 'quiet type'), denying her role in providing his home comforts and child-care (glaringly lacking now) by saying: 'I work hard . . . she didn't have anything to do all day.' All these jokes demonstrate to the viewer the nature of male presumption and power, but the film conveys this in a way which dismisses this patriarchal way-of-being as inconsequential and inappropriate. In this way constructed as 'other', lacking in authenticity, men arrogantly assume a knowledge and understanding of matters which as the film convincingly demonstrates they have no right or reason to do. The therapist's husband ignores her specialist knowledge in psychology and confidently asserts the three women's madness . . . because within *his* framework of knowledge their action makes no possible sense. This attitude is echoed by all the relevant male characters in the film. In perhaps the most painful and resonant (flashback) scene, the secretary's capabilities, competence and knowledge is – in one male sleight of hand – simultaneously dismissed and denied *and* appropriated by her 'boss' in the board meeting.

Crucially, men are shown to have no insight into their structural power, or their use and abuse of it, and since the project of the film is the therapist's (and our, the viewers') realisation of this, men – already constructed as 'other' (those with power-over and alien perception) – are structured out of the rationale of the film. Thus, patriarchal discourse, the (male) language of dominance, is disrupted on the level of representation (because films are not normally like this) and on the level of ideology (because our preconceptions about a male perspective being the 'truth' are challenged).

The therapist's central role in the film functions through our identification to lead the (women in the) audience towards a realisation of the nature of women's oppression – on a social, sexual and public/professional level; and towards a possible form of resistance – separatism. We witness her pride in her professional competence being undermined by her husband, the prosecutor, the judge. We witness her insight into the uninformed and presumptuous paternalism of the secretary's boss and Christine's husband whom she interviews after their detention. During a conversation about her three clients with her husband (who is adamant that they were 'completely deranged'), she walks the length of their spacious lounge and, attentively followed by the camera, crouches at the music centre, turns away from her husband, and directly addresses the camera (and us), saying: 'I don't think those women are insane.' At the request of her husband she rises and turns back to repeat this statement, but the scene ends and the camera/film does not wait for his response. It is our reaction – that of a woman-identified audience – which is sought and affirmed by this scene.

Thus, the film simultaneously depicts a society where women are silenced, their experience and particular insights undermined and dismissed, *and* depicts convincingly the legitimacy and coherence of women's position and experience. In this process men are portrayed as the perpetrators of women's oppression. An ever-present danger in conveying this state of affairs is that women could be constructed as victims. *A Question of Silence* avoids this pitfall – partly because it is the murder of a *man* which is central to the establishment of the enigmas and their resolution within the film, but also because it is women who are seen to initiate and take action . . . or who choose to remain silent.

A Question of Silence could equally have been called *A Question of Violence*. Many critical responses have been outraged at the murder and the way in which it is formulated and dealt with in the film.[2] Reactions from feminists have been confused, ambivalent and evasive.

It is not possible here to engage in a detailed description and analysis of the three scenes which lead to and include the murder of the boutique manager and which are presented in the form of flashbacks. My own impression was that the first three-quarters of the film was pervaded by scenes of violence; it was only on a second viewing that I realised that the murder itself took place in just one of the three scenes.

The filming of these scenes conveys great instability – mainly through the use of tracking shots, camera angles and positioning, and discordant, emphatically chorded music. The last two scenes begin with a repetition of the final moments of the previous scene, which may contribute to the impression of repetitive violence. At a crucial point in the film (which I will discuss later), still images of the three women standing over their victim's body, accompanied by crashing chords of music, are repeatedly intercut with the traumatic sex scene between the therapist and her husband. These fixed images add further to the viewers' impression of repetitive violence.

The issue of murder is constructed in the film not as one of guilt/innocence but as one of insanity/sanity. In a strange way this is an inversion of the 'expert' (and popularised) formulation of the Ripper phenomenon.[3] In the case of the Ripper, insanity somehow established innocence – or blamelessness (for male sexuality in general); in the case of *A Question of Silence* it is a sanity which establishes innocence – or blamelessness (in affirming the reality of a society which oppresses and exploits women to a degree where there is sufficient reason for them to be angry enough to kill, arbitrarily, an unknown man). In this sense it is important that the murder is not rational in male terms. Were the murder to make sense within patriarchal conventions (of justice, logic, common-sense), the most disputed and hidden features of women's oppression would be lost.

I discussed earlier the implications of certain modernist filming devices in terms of the distancing of the viewer and the effects on the process of identification. This analysis applies equally to the scenes building up to and including the murder, where – because we are distanced – we watch, are conscious of watching, and are conscious of ourselves as watchers. As with the process of identification, this facilitates our actively colluding in the murder. Distanced, we have the space to protest. Significantly, we don't protest . . . and later in the courtroom scene, when we join the women's laughter at the male prosecutor's notion that it would be the same for three men to murder one woman as it is for three women to murder a man, we cement this collusion.

It is a feminist common-sense that for women to transgress against men is to break a most rigid cultural taboo. For three women to murder, arbitrarily and with no good reason, an unknown, un-threatening and ineffectual man is unthinkable. Our knowledge of the inequity of this taboo (known not to operate in terms of men's aggression against women) does not protect us from our distaste of violence, grounded in both patriarchal society's sanctions on women's behaviour and in a feminist political stance towards violence. The film's celebration of the authenticity of women's experience and point of view combines with the complicated repercussions of the techniques of distancing to create for women a most peculiar and difficult relationship to this manifestation of women's violence. But whatever

A Question of Silence

the unease women may feel about their involvement in and relation to the film's violence, there is no doubt that the film's assertion that the three women's murder of a man could in any way be explicable and reasonable, that women viewers could in any way identify with the act of murder, that men can in no way be qualified to understand or pass judgement on any of this, is powerfully threatening to patriarchal ideology.

Another profound threat to patriarchy is the film's implicit critique of heterosexuality. *A Question of Silence* contains three scenes of heterosexual sex: the opening scene of the film and the after-dinner sex scene – both involving the therapist and her husband – and the scene where the secretary allows herself to be picked up as a prostitute.

The scenes between the therapist and her husband illustrate the way in which the viability of heterosexual sex is predicated on the man's desire for and co-operation in sexual pleasure – and his assumption that to take that pleasure is his unquestionable right. In the opening scene the therapist attempts to seduce her husband, who remains mildly irritated and uninterested until she leans over him and in play pretends to slit him open with his pen (interestingly, prefiguring the murder), whereupon he rolls her off him and leans over her himself; things get serious and the picture fades . . .

The after-dinner scene is far more sinister in its implications for heterosexuality. We can understand the opening scene as heterosexual sex requiring the activity and participation of the man. In the later scene it becomes clear that the woman does not need to be active or a participant – despite saying 'don't', despite consistently and clearly signalling her unwillingness, the husband has his way and rapes his wife. His insistent overtures and her persistent refusal of them are intercut with crashing chords and surrealist, still images of the three women standing over the body of the murdered man. The last image is followed by a disturbing dream, the motif of which is the repeated 'turning away' – of the secretary from the therapist, and of the therapist from the three women.

These images of the three women standing in varying fixed poses over the man's body are the final representations of the murder scene in the film. It is significant that they are surrealist in lighting and composition, flashing onto the screen for such brief (almost subliminal) moments. It is at this point that the murder becomes symbolic, becomes linked to our anger at men's abuse of women and takes on a political meaning which, while its feminist logic is impeccable, is possibly as uncomfortable for women as it is for men.

Shortly after this after-dinner marital rape scene is the flashback of the sex scene involving the secretary and the man who mistakes her for a prostitute. In this scene Andrea retains complete control. She is the one who moves, sitting astride the man and, in contrast to him, is fully clothed, wearing her coat and minus only her underpants and boots; she rejects any intimacy or touching, clearly feels no overwhelming pleasure and terminates the experience when she chooses to. After the murder, all three women do something which breaks the pattern of their lives. Christine, mother and housewife, takes her child for a ride on the big wheel at a funfair instead of going back to the claustrophobia and isolation of her home. An, the café worker, prepares and eats an elaborate and elegant meal. Andrea, the secretary, has sex with a man on her terms and to his disadvantage. However one might assess the meaning and morality of the murder, it seems undeniable that it was a manifestation of women taking some kind of power and control for themselves. This process is carried over by the three women into other aspects of their lives – not in achieving an ideal state of things, but in taking control of, and making the best of, things within the limitations of their experience and situation as women in society. Within this analysis *A Question of Silence* presents a gloomy prognosis for heterosexual sex.

By contrast, the silent and highly charged encounter between the therapist and the secretary presents erotic and emotional possibilities which challenge the entire fabric of heterosexuality. The secretary and therapist do not touch, the encounter has no closure (it is interrupted by a man), and as the secretary outlines the therapist with hands inches away from her body and rises to face her, so the film outlines the potential of lesbianism in the face of an oppressive and unrewarding (for women) heterosexuality.

Potentials and Disturbances within Feminism

I have already discussed the nature of the audience's collusion with the murder in *A Question of Silence*. Through various distancing devices, the film solicits from the viewer a conscious and active complicity in watching and continuing to watch the scenes of violence. Because the film's narrative places the murder in a feminist-political context, the nature of identification and collusion is likely to be different for the men and women watching the film. Most of the press reviews written by men were hostile to the film, attempting to denigrate it and render it worthless . . . in the process contradicting each other (for example, some saying it lacked humour but was technically excellent and others vice versa). A few were more open to the film and attempted to address its implications for men.[4]

In my own initial response to the film, and in discussions with friends, it has become clear that feminists have experienced some discomfort in accounting for the film's preoccupation with women's violence and in reconciling this with the very enjoyable experience of viewing a feminist film. This dilemma appears to have inspired an almost uniform account of the murder. The murder is a metaphor. It is a symbol. Therefore it has no relation to reality or to the reality of women's response to their oppression. It has no relation to feminism. It is simply a device.

The more I think about it, the more I'm sure the murder cannot be discussed as metaphoric, or symbolic, or as a device (as I was initially tempted to do, as the director did in the press conference after its first screening, and as various feminist reviewers have done subsequently).[5] It seems no coincidence that the murder of a man was chosen as the central factor motivating the narrative, and that to a large extent this act was inexplicable and 'unreasoned'. How else to expose the insidious and deeply hidden forces of male dominance? How else to express the depth and degree of women's anger?

Nevertheless, I'm equally sure that the murder and repetitive violence is not pleasurable for the audience. Not in a cinematic-voyeuristic sense where the protagonists of the murder show no pleasure and where the use of camera and editing does not encourage the viewer's pleasure; nor in a sadistic female-revenge-type pleasure. Sadistic pleasure is predicated on dominance (power over) which is not only a material situation, but crucially informed by ideology, culture, etc. – by what is in our heads. Ideology does not support women in a sadistic relation to men.

The film, in using three women's murder of a man to motivate the narrative, has been able to explore some of the more concealed aspects of sexism. It has also raised certain questions and exposed fundamental contradictions within the feminist politics which inform the film. Feminism has allowed women to identify and articulate their

A Question of Silence

experience of oppression, and legitimated their anger. What then do we do with this anger? Where do we direct it? Do we express it as wasteful, destructive energy against or in relation to men – the extreme expression of which is murder? Or do we express it, transform it, as creative, positive energy to share with women – the extreme expression of which is separatism? The film tells of both possibilities.

Lesbian experience is denied by almost all films – whether 'mainstream', avant-garde or 'art' films; whether lesbians are present in or absent from the text. The absence of lesbians and the issue of lesbianism from films is consistent with the absence of lesbianism from all other forms of representation,[6] and echoes society's systematic repression of ideologies and subcultures which oppose, challenge or undermine the hegemony of racist, sexist and capitalist patriarchy. Where lesbianism is represented cinematically it bears little relation to the complete, integrated experience of being a lesbian – the project of the particular film being either to present a perversion-from-the-norm (the perversion producing a good story or sub-plot, the telling of which inevitably recuperates and applauds the 'norm' which is broken) or to present a relatively sympathetic, and often didactic, account of those who are different-from-the-norm (often producing not-so-good stories, and never allowing the difference to be desirable, either in its own right or in relation to the 'norm'). There are films, like Chantal Akerman's *Je Tu Il Elle*, which attempt to transcend these limitations, mainly through avoiding the representation of lesbianism as having any relation to a 'norm'. It just is.

When it comes to representing sex between two women, these differing modes of dealing with lesbianism in film share the same problematic. Whether presented as perverted or different or 'naturalised', to be abhorred or tolerated or taken for granted, the representation of lesbian sex has a complex significance within the tradition of film-making. The construction of 'the look' as male, the representation of women as object and spectacle, and the use of lesbianism in pornography, are some of the factors which present themselves as built-in connotations which are carried into any scene conveying sexual passion between women.

A Question of Silence is, as Sheila Johnston points out in *Monthly Film Bulletin*,[7] dialectic – not didactic. Lesbianism is presented as part of the rationale of women's autonomy, loyalty and mutual commitment, as well as a positive alternative to draining, unrewarding and positively negative relations with men. The scene between the secretary and the therapist avoids the problem usually posed in representations of sexual exchange between women through the studied absence of point-of-view shots, the lack of edited fragmentation of bodies, the absence of harsh breathing, the absence of nudity, the respectful distance of the camera (the viewers) from the women, the distance of the secretary's hands from the therapist's body. All this establishes space for the audience to make imaginative leaps. The space between the women refers to the taboo, the impossibility, of women touching. At the same time it refers to the separateness and difference of each woman. It also refers to the possibilities of women touching.

It is notable that neither the press reviews nor critical assessments by feminists that I have read have mentioned this feature (or scene) of the film. Ti Grace Atkinson once said, 'Feminism is the theory, lesbianism is the practice.' A polemic which heterosexual feminists both dispute and are vulnerable to, and which radical feminists both agree with and would qualify. A debate which has created profound tensions within feminism. In my limited analysis of the film, it appears that Atkinson's dictum is one of the messages of the film – *not* presented as a dictate, but as a possibility. The final scene outside the courtroom, where the therapist turns from her husband across the road and lifts her head to join the silent witnesses to the murder, suggests that accompanying the message of the possibility of lesbianism is the message of the possibility of separatism – the disinvestment of women's energy from men, the commitment of women's energy to women.

Conversations with Charlotte Brunsdon, Chris Doherty and Tessa Perkins have helped me immeasurably in thinking about and writing this piece, which was commissioned and completed in 1984.

Notes

1. Arguments for and against separatism are dispersed over time and through various publications. For an accessible account of the debate, see *Love your enemy? The debate between heterosexual feminism and political lesbianism* (London: Onlywomen Press, 1981). See also Lucia Valeska, 'The Future of Female Separatism', and Charlotte Bunch, 'Not for Lesbians Only', in *Building Feminist Theory: Essays from Quest* (New York: Longman, 1981).

2. Particularly vehement examples of these are reviews by Michael Wigan, *Scotsman*, 21 August 1982, p. 6; Nigel Andrews, *Financial Times*, 18 February 1983, p. 17; Philip French, *Observer*, 20 February 1983, p. 30; Janet Maslin, *New York Times*, 18 March 1983.

3. For a critique of the construction and interpretation of the Sutcliffe trial by the media, legal profession, etc., especially in relation to the mad or bad dichotomy, see Wendy Hollway, ' "I just wanted to kill a women." Why? The Ripper and Male Sexuality', *Feminist Review* no. 9, Autumn 1981.

4. Patrick Gibbs' review in the *Daily Telegraph*, 18 February 1983, p. 13, is the most positive example of this, with Derek Malcolm, *Guardian*, 5 August 1982, p. 11, and Ian Bell, *Scotsman*, 21 May 1983, p. 4, trying hard. The following are reviews which demonstrate contradictory, but mainly negative, responses to the film: Richard Cook, *New Musical Express*, 4 December 1982, p. 26; David Hughes, *Sunday Times*, 20 February 1983, p. 43; Tim Pulleine, *Guardian*, 17 February 1983, p. 13; Geoff Brown, *The Times*, 18 February 1983, p. 11. Women reviewers fit into this category, but are even more contradictory: Jackie Skarvellis, *Morning Star*, 18 February 1983, p. 2; Lindsay Mackie, *Glasgow Herald*, 4 September 1982, p. 8, and 26 May 1983, p. 4.

5. See Sheila Johnston's review in *Monthly Film Bulletin* no. 589, February 1983, p. 48. See comments from the director, Marleen Gorris, in *City Limits* no. 72, 18 – 24 February 1983, pp. 13–14.

6. For an account of the absence and presence of lesbians in film, see Caroline Sheldon, 'Lesbians and Film: some thoughts', Richard Dyer, ed., *Gays and Film* (London: British Film Institute, 1977). For a general account of the invisibility of lesbians within society, see Adrienne Rich, *Compulsory Heterosexuality and Lesbian Existence* (London: Onlywomen Press, 1981).

7. No. 589, February 1983.

The Political is Personal: Margarethe von Trotta's 'Marianne and Juliane'

ELLEN SEITER

From *Journal of Film and Video* vol. XXXVII no. 2, Spring 1985.

> . . . if *Die bleierne Zeit* were really what it claims to be it would not
> have gotten any support, distribution or exhibition.
>
> Charlotte Delorme[1]

MARGARETHE VON TROTTA'S 1981 film, *Marianne and Juliane* (*Die bleierne Zeit*, released in the UK as *The German Sisters*) raises critical questions about feminist film-making, political narrative film, and the interpretation of German films in the United States. The director has achieved considerable critical acclaim and commercial success making films with exclusively female, and often feminist, protagonists: *The Lost Honour of Katharina Blum* (*Die verlorene Ehre der Katharina Blum*, co-directed with Volker Schlöndorff, 1975), *The Second Awakening of Christa Klages* (*Das zweite Erwachen der Christa Klages*, 1977), *Sisters or the Balance of Happiness* (*Schwestern oder die Balance des Glücks*, 1979), and most recently, *Friends and Husbands* (*Heller Wahn*, 1982). Particularly noted has been von Trotta's attention to intimate relationships between women and the psychological dimension of these relationships. *Marianne and Juliane* stands as an especially problematic work in this regard because it is based in part on the life of Gudrun Ensslin, member of the Baader Meinhof group (Rote Armee Fraktion), and explores her personal history from the point of view of Ensslin's sister, Christiane. Set during the 1970s with flashbacks to the sisters' childhoods in the post-war period, the film is bound in German history so inextricably that it exemplifies the problems of interpreting the New German Cinema outside the context of German history and culture.

Margarethe von Trotta is one of a handful of women directors making narrative feature films to gain an international reputation on the art film circuit; she is also the women director most often identified in the United States with the New German Cinema.[2] While there are many women directors working in Germany whose films are more strongly feminist than von Trotta's, they have failed (with the possible exceptions of Danièle Huillet, Helke Sander, and Helma Sanders-Brahms) to receive the same recognition in the US.[3] This may be attributed in part to von Trotta's collaboration with Volker Schlöndorff, her association as an actor with the New German Cinema, the production of her films by Schlöndorff's company, Bioskop-Film. To some extent, von Trotta's protagonists can be seen as the female counterparts to Wim Wenders' alienated heroes of the postwar generation; her films, like Schlöndorff's, resemble a genre familiar to American distributors, the thriller – as Thomas Elsaesser has argued.[4] Von Trotta's films can also be compared to the work of other women directors who have had some success on the American art film circuit, and whose films are distributed there in 16mm. Many of these films have focused, like von Trotta's last three films, on a relationship between two women, such as Vera Chytilova's *Daisies*, Diane Kurys' *Peppermint Soda*, Marta Meszaros' *Women* and Agnès Varda's *One Sings the Other Doesn't*. What distinguishes von Trotta's films from these is the absence of comic relief, nostalgia, heterosexual romance or careerism. Von Trotta is unremittingly serious about relationships between women in her films, and the relationships she portrays tend to be rather tortured.

In *Sisters* . . . and in *Marianne and Juliane*, von Trotta examines the relationship between women in the context of the nuclear family – the characters are sisters – and aspects of personal life which have been studied by feminists: feminine identity, identification, ego formation, competition and jealousy among women. In the first film the older sister, Maria, and the younger sister, Anna, are characterised as disparate in personality, world view, relationship to others and to their work, yet their relationship is one of intense and destructive interdependence. Flashbacks and dream sequences convey the psychological relationship between the sisters. Anna remembers her sister reading a fairy tale to her about children lost in the forest, and a scene standing with her sister before a mirror, putting on make-up and fascinated by their multiple, doubled reflection. After Anna's suicide, Maria obsessively tries to establish a similar relationship with another woman. In her dreams she looks into the mirror and sees, not her own reflection, but her sister's. At the conclusion of the film, Maria gains a painful understanding of their relationship and resolves to integrate Anna's attributes into her own personality.

In *Marianne and Juliane* the relationship between sisters is more solidly grounded in the nuclear family and social institutions, while von Trotta retains a strong emphasis on its psychological dimension. The story is told from the point of view of Juliane (Christiane Ensslin) and concerns her attempts to resolve her troubled relationship to her

Marianne and Juliane

sister Marianne (Gudrun Ensslin), to understand her sister's commitment to violent political action, and to come to terms with her death (Gudrun Ensslin was widely believed to have been murdered in prison). As in *Sisters*, the differences between the women are emphasised. At the beginning of the film Juliane is involved in a stable, childless relationship with a man and is deeply committed to working for women's rights through journalism and legal reform. The film's first dialogue scene consists of a conversation between Juliane and Marianne's husband, Werner, in which it is revealed that Marianne is involved in terrorism, has deserted her husband and her son, Jan, and that Juliane perceives her as selfish, spiteful and irresponsible. Marianne's first scenes in the film, meeting her sister clandestinely and storming into her apartment in the middle of the night demanding coffee and clothing, tend to reinforce this view. Juliane (played by Jutta Lampe, who appeared as Maria in *Sisters*) is responsible, dedicated, sensitive; Marianne is hard, cynical, contemptuous of others. In the scenes between the sisters at the prison after Marianne's arrest, they confront one another and their personal and political differences in exchanges which are alternately tender and violent. When Marianne dies in prison, Juliane engages in a desperate search for evidence to prove that her sister's death was a murder, not a suicide, and sacrifices her work and her personal relationship to do so. Her actions prove to have no public usefulness, however, and, rebuked after one attempt to make the information public, she accepts the role of guardian to the now physically and emotionally traumatised Jan.

Marianne and Juliane resembles *Sisters* in its emphasis on psychology, its sustained emotional intensity, and its confinement, in a majority of scenes, to domestic space. Stylistically, the films are realist: eye-level camera, moderately long takes, naturalistic lighting, location shooting. Von Trotta's sisters are usually suffering, and we are invited, in several lingering facial close-ups, to scrutinise them. All these characteristics would suggest that the films belong to the domain of the domestic melodrama. The characters are angry and alienated, however, ill-suited to the kind of sentimental treatment which melodrama demands. The families are the site of strained and constraining relationships and a desperate struggle for identity. Von Trotta subjects the family itself to scrutiny, as well as the individuals within it. It is this investigation of the past and of the relationships which, among other things, gives the films the emotional tenor of the psychological thriller rather than the melodrama. In *Marianne and Juliane*, the investigation takes the form of flashback sequences which occur seven times in the film and cover, with one exception, the childhood period from 1945–55. These flashbacks situate the relationship between the sisters in history as well as in the family. The film's original title, 'The Leaden Times', refers to Germany during the 'unemotional, dreary 1950s', according to von Trotta, from a line of the Romantic poet Friedrich Hölderlin.[5] This emphasis on historical period is lost in the retitling of the film for American distribution, with its emphasis instead on the female characters.

All of the flashback sequences in *Marianne and Juliane* derive from Juliane's point of view, as E. Ann Kaplan has demonstrated.[6] The first meeting of the sisters is followed by a flashback to them as small children, watching the skin form on their cocoa while their stern-looking father recites his morning prayer. When Juliane attempts to visit Marianne in prison for the first time, there is a flashback to the sisters playing in the yard together, racing each other home. Other flashbacks present the emotional impact of German history on the sisters: at four and five years old, woken in the night and taken by their mother to air raid shelters, as teenagers watching scenes of the concentration camps in a film projected by their father. The longest flashback sequences are set in 1955. Juliane has a rebellious spirit while Marianne is submissive and well-behaved. Juliane breaks the dress code, challenges her father and her teacher, smokes in the hallway at school, and, on a dare from her sister, gets up to dance alone at a staid social occasion. Marianne, on the other hand, appears to be father's and teacher's pet, practises the cello, and dreams of joining a missionary group. The flashbacks do not appear in chronological order, and only one flashback is set in the time period after 1955: the sisters as adults are watching a film about Vietnam, and Marianne leans over and whispers, 'I'll never accept that nothing can be done about that.'[7]

Conventionally, flashbacks create the expectation of an explanation, a filling-in of the information necessary to solve the narrative enigma. *Marianne and Juliane* is structured in such a way that the flashbacks address the narrative question posed by the film's present: how did the sisters turn out so differently? The film can be read, then, as an effective dramatisation of the feminist slogan, 'the personal is political', locating as it does the characters in their experience in the nuclear family within a specific historical, national and cultural instance, as E. Ann Kaplan has demonstrated in her psychoanalytic interpretation of the film.[8] A very different interpretation of the flashback sequences is offered by Charlotte Delorme in her review in *Frauen und Film*. Delorme suggests that von Trotta offers the same psychological motivations for terrorist activity that were popularised by the German tabloids (*Bildzeitungen*) in the 1970s, that the political is entirely personal. Delorme summarises the explanation: '(a) unresolved (*unbewältigen*) conflicts with authority in childhood lead directly to terrorism and (b) right equals left.'[9] Radical politics are reduced to rebellion against the authoritarian father, and all such actions are equated, regardless of political position. In this interpretation, Juliane serves as a model of responsible, social democratic oppositional politics, while Marianne epitomises irresponsible, pathological opposition.

The flashbacks reinforce this polarisation of the two sisters, for in childhood as well as in adult life they are unalterably opposed, and in the intervening years (1955–75), when Marianne made the transition from daddy's girl to terrorist, we have no information about the characters. The contrast between the sisters, and the flashbacks' explanation of the adult characters, resembles the conventional melodramatic treatment of women as opposite figures: the vamp versus the straight girl, the good mother versus the bad one. In domestic melodrama, the genre which has offered the most narrative concentration on women, this has usually meant that the positive characterisation of a female character was achieved through comparison to another female character who was morally condemned, thus emphasising normative definitions of women's roles and a narrative interest in the punishment of women who did not comply with them.

Von Trotta's concentration on pairs of sisters with disparate attributes is similar to this conventional narrative polarisation of women characters. The question becomes, then, whether the films withhold moral judgment of the characters and concentrate instead on the conflicting demands on women in patriarchal society. Two widely divergent interpretations have been given by feminist critics. E. Ann Kaplan describes von Trotta's characters, '. . . as actively engaged in a struggle to define their lives, their identities, and their feminist politics in a situation where the dominant discourse constantly undermines their efforts, or forces them into destructive positions through controlling what choices are available.'[10] Charlotte Delorme interprets the film as a reactionary and anti-feminist diatribe against Gudrun Ensslin, in which she is constantly compared to her sister, Christiane (to whom the film is dedicated), and thereby condemned. The vehemence of Delorme's attack must be seen from the perspective of someone reading the film in terms of German politics and history, as well as the representation of women. In von Trotta's depiction of Marianne, Delorme sees the image of Gudrun Ensslin offered by the government, and the way that image was used to justify wide-spread political repression. E. Ann Kaplan's analysis of the film is theoretically grounded in semiotic and psychoanalytic interpretations of film from a feminist perspective and is restricted to the text of the film;[11] Charlotte Delorme's review is sociological and historical in focus, and very influenced by the kind of press the film received in Germany, as well as by von Trotta's and Christiane Ensslin's comments about the film. The difference between these perspectives is also characteristic of differences in German and American film criticism, and the problems of interpretation of New German Cinema in the US, typified by Rick Rentschler as '. . . a concentration on the formal attributes of the film without taking into account the socio-historical setting they reflect or issue from: the primacy of text over context.'[12]

If *Marianne and Juliane* is read as an historical film about Gudrun Ensslin, a number of questions can be asked. Why does the film concentrate on the psychological ordeal of the character based on Christiane Ensslin? How deterministic is the film in its representation of childhood experience? To what extent is the narrative discourse that of melodrama? If the film is read historically, what is missing from the film becomes important: the broad impact of the terrorists' actions on German society and the way that the RAF was used as a rationale for the repeal of civil liberties. The narrative structure conspicuously excludes information such as Ensslin's involvement in the student movement in Berlin in the 1960s, the reaction to media coverage of the Vietnam war, the terrorists' isolation from the political left in Germany. Von Trotta's avoidance of these aspects of Ensslin's history relates, as well, to questions about the funding system for German films and the self-censorship of film-makers on such politically charged subjects as terrorism.[13]

These omissions can be seen as detracting from *Marianne and Juliane*'s feminist potential. Gudrun Ensslin and Ulrike Meinhof were tragically misguided, but their treatment by the German government and the way that their media images were constructed are feminist issues. For it was precisely because they were women engaging in violence, and because they had rejected the roles of wife and mother, that they were subject to the greatest moral outrage. Gudrun Ensslin and Ulrike Meinhof are hardly figures for a 'positive image' type of cinematic treatment, but they are crucial figures to understand, especially since their history has been so obfuscated. In *Marianne and Juliane*, we see the consequences of the terrorist actions of Marianne portrayed as personal tragedy – her husband's suicide, her suffering and death in prison, the attack on her son – but we never understand the decisions which led to those actions. There is a resemblance to the melodramatic mode in the narrative emphasis on victimisation and the emotional rendering of events. Juliane comes to an understanding of her sister by the end of the film, but she seems to have done so primarily by inflicting on herself some of the physical suffering endured by Marianne in prison. In the film's final scene, Juliane tells Marianne's son: 'Your mother was an extraordinary (*aussergewöhnliche*) woman.' But her change of heart appears to derive primarily from her understanding of Marianne's act of self-sacrifice and her victimisation, and Juliane has made a parallel sacrifice by finally assuming responsibility for Marianne's son.

The introduction to the paperback edition of the script of *Marianne and Juliane* reads: 'This is not a film about terrorism, nor about the motivations to join a political underground. Neither is it a documentation of the fate of the sisters Gudrun and Christiane Ensslin.'[14] That statement is perhaps more easily accepted in the United States than in West Germany. What von Trotta's films do offer is an exploration of primary relationships between women, where the tension reflects the difficulties for women in securing an identity in a culture where they are devalued. It is typical of the New German Cinema that a film so fraught with political contradictions is, at the same time, a quite important women's film in the United States.

Notes

1. Charlotte Delorme, 'Zum Film, *Die bleierne Zeit* von Margarethe von Trotta', *Frauen und Film* no. 31, 1982, p. 55.
2. See Eric Rentschler, 'American Friends and New German Cinema: Patterns of Reception', *New German Critique* no. 24–5, Fall–Winter 1981–2, p. 33.
3. Other German women film-makers are discussed in Renate Mohrmann, *Die Frau mit der Kamera* (Munich: Carl Hanser Verlag, 1980), and Marc Silberman, 'Cine-Feminists in West Berlin', *Quarterly Review of Film Studies* no. 5, Spring 1980, pp. 217–32.
4. Thomas Elsaesser, 'New German Cinema: How German is it?', paper

given at Oregon State University, Corvallis, Oregon, 24 October 1983.

5. Raimund Hoghe, 'Balanceversuch einer Rebellin', in *Die bleierne Zeit*, ed. Hans Jürgen Weber and Ingeborg Weber (Frankfurt am Main: Fischer Taschenbuch Verlag, 1981), p. 79.

6. E. Ann Kaplan, 'Discourses of Terrorism, Feminism and the Family in von Trotta's *Marianne and Juliane*', in *Persistence of Vision* vol. 1 no. 2, Spring 1985, p. 61–8.

7. '*Ich werde mich nie damit abfinden, dass man nichts dagegen tut*'.

8. E. Ann Kaplan, 'Female politics in the symbolic realm: von Trotta's *Marianne and Juliane*', in *Women and Film: Both Sides of the Camera* (New York and London: Methuen, 1983), pp. 104–12.

9. Charlotte Delorme, *Frauen und Film* no. 31, 1982, p. 52.

10. E. Ann Kaplan, *Women and Film: Both Sides of the Camera*, pp. 104–5.

11. Kaplan also analyses the image of the terrorist in her article 'Discourses of Terrorism, Feminism and the Family' referred to in note 6 above.

12. Eric Rentschler, p. 24.

13. See Jan Dawson, 'The Sacred Terror: Shadows of Terrorism in the New German Cinema', *Sight & Sound*, Autumn 1979, pp. 242–5.

14. *Die bleierne Zeit*, inside cover.

PART THREE

Hollywood

Introduction

IN 1971, *Klute* and *McCabe and Mrs Miller* initiated a cycle of films made in the 70s which bear the traces of feminist struggles elsewhere, even if it is only in the attempt to capitalise on a discernible new audience: the modern women.[1] These films include: *Three Women* (1977), *Alice Doesn't Live Here Any More* (1974), *A Woman Under the Influence* (1974), *Julia* (1977), *The Romantic Englishwoman* (1975), *The Turning Point* (1977), *Looking for Mr Goodbar* (1977), *Girlfriends* (1978), *Coma* (1977), *An Unmarried Woman* (1977), *Norma Rae* (1979), *Gloria* (1980), *Nine to Five* (1980) and, fairly recently, *Personal Best* and *Lianna* (both 1982).

These are all pictures which – to some extent – are 'about' women, whether through the device of a central female protagonist, a concentration on relations between women, or narratives that concentrate on the personal and familial – the classically feminine sphere. There has, however, been considerable disagreement among feminists about both the political significance of the films, and also about the methodologies it is appropriate to use in assessing this significance. While some women have given a cautious welcome to these films, arguing that they do indicate shifts in definitions and representations of femininity, others have been particularly angered, feeling that political ideals have been exploited to provide fashionable – and profitable – entertainment. The main criticisms of the films have been that the heroines are not sufficiently representative or ordinary, and that the dilemmas and problems are made personal rather than the result of the subordination of women as a group. It is the way in which the films really do seem to engage with some of the dilemmas of contemporary femininity which has been seen as most politically dangerous.[2]

The cycle of 70s Hollywood women's films raises a range of important critical questions about how we read films and how we understand the political significance of representations that are offered to us in movies. Two ideas have been particularly significant in these debates: firstly, the idea of 'recuperation', and secondly, the notion of a 'progressive' (or 'reactionary') text.

'Recuperation' involves conceptualising continual and flexible cultural processes whereby radical and oppositional ideas, images and movements are taken on, or sucked in by dominant culture(s), to become part of the culture of domination. Not only do the oppositional ideas and practices lose their bite, but they can function to make it appear as if change has been effected. The relevance of this notion to the analysis of a rash of 70s Hollywood films dealing with 'new women' is obvious, and Elizabeth Cowie discusses the concept critically using the example of Virginia Slims cigarette advertisements. Another example would be the Lovable advertisement which appeared in women's magazines after the feminist campaign against the film *Dressed to Kill*. It is the memory of that feminist opposition to the perceived misogyny of the film which is being mobilised in the advertisement, but now it is looks (the look of the underwear) that kill. And, of course, it is men who will fall victim. The moment of recuperation is the harnessing of feminist opposition to give the promise (threat) of power to a very stereotypically fetishistic feminine image.[3]

Dressed to kill.

Creations of purrfection by Lovable
Chic. The Co-ordinated Collection For The Young At Heart.

In some ways, the sense of ceaseless cultural movement which is present in the idea of recuperation is very illuminating. That a look which was unacceptable and oppositional in 1977 – punk – is now a must for tourist postcards of London, and could be used to sell electricity in cinema commercials in 1983, must make us wary of ascribing immutable political values to particular cultural practices. Watney's Red Revolution does, precisely, sell us beer – not politics. But the outraged cry with which these instances are met frequently implies a static opposite – a purity of opposition – which often means merely that oppositional ideas can't be allowed out, in case they get dirty.

So although the idea of recuperation does perhaps explain one movement in cultural practice, its implicit opposite – that oppositional practices should retain a kind of radical copyright – makes it very difficult to imagine any kind of social change. While it is true that the connotations of the term 'liberated women' resonate more with 6os ideas of sexual liberation – she'd do it anywhere – than with anything the Women's Movement has ever meant by 'liberation', it is also the case that ideas of appropriate feminine behaviour have changed radically since the late 6os, and that this is partly because of the way feminist ideas have been 'taken on'.

Similarly, the idea of a 'progressive' text can be rather unsatisfactory, the first problem being that it often implies that a film has got one, fixed meaning. Thus it has been argued that *Alice Doesn't Live Here Anymore* isn't 'progressive' because in the end she finds happiness by settling down with the Kris Kristofferson character. This uncontradictory reading privileges the ending of the narrative over the rest of the film, ignoring the strength of the depiction of female friendships and the possibility that the film sets in play more elements than can be resolved by the narrative closure. Another problem with the idea of a 'progressive' text, or textual device, is the idea that particular films or strategies are progressive (or reactionary) for all time, for all audiences, in all contexts. In a way, this is the same problem, because it assumes what the 'meaning' of a film is in the sense that it has behind it an idea of meaning as something that is always already there and complete in the film, so that, for example, there wouldn't be any difference between watching *Julia* when it first came out – when it felt very 'new' to be watching a contemporary commercial film about women's friendships – and watching it now, maybe as part of a course about the representation of women.

If the criterion of 'progressiveness' is going to be used, it seems important that films are recognised as complex objects which can offer more than one meaning, and can achieve varying and contradictory scores on the progressiveness ratings. *Kramer vs. Kramer*, for example, which has been read as a very direct response to, and attack on, the concerns of the Women's Movement, must also be recognised as providing a rare filmic representation of a nurturing father. The use of this directly political criterion – progressive in whose terms? – frequently involves a somewhat naive understanding of the relationship between text and audience, implicitly assuming a rather knee-jerk model of audiences as if you get 'progressive' ideas as a reflex reaction to watching 'progressive' films.

It is not possible to separate ideas of the political significance of a film text from critical questions of how we 'read' a film, and how we understand the relation between a film and the social context in which it was made and is shown. If these critical ideas are not made explicit, it is often because the methods that are being used are assumed to be obvious. Radical critics looking at commercial cinema sometimes just compare the films with Life, and criticise the films for not being sufficiently 'realistic'. Life, of course, can mean rather different things, but, in this context, it could mean: life doesn't have happy endings (*Alice, An Unmarried Woman*); not all women look like film stars (all the films except *Girlfriends*); life isn't just white/middle-class/heterosexual/able-bodied/youngish people (all the films at one point or another). Alternatively, critics may concentrate on what happens in the narrative, at the expense of any attention to how these events are constructed for us as a narrative.

Underlying all these strategies is a range of essentially realist positions. The function of the artwork (film) is being assumed to be to offer a representation of contemporary everyday life. This representation, it is argued, should be socially extensive rather than concentrate on privileged groups – such as white middle-class women – and should not, through fictional devices such as legacies, obscure the problems that most people face.

These are historically honourable and politically necessary arguments, and have, for obvious reasons, been associated with and developed by socialists and the range of disenfranchised social groups. However, they are not the only demands that can or should be made of an artwork. We stand in danger of impoverishing both our own traditions, and our future, if we persist in treating films as if they were political, historical or sociological texts *manqués*, and do not allow for the non-discursive aspects of art.[4] The deep ideological complicity of traditional aesthetic criteria such as 'the good' and 'the beautiful' and, indeed, the historical role of aesthetic judgment in the maintenance of social power, should not lead us to abandon the terrain of critical judgment to the Right. The shortcomings of 'ideological assessment' as sole critical method are particularly obvious in relation to the cinema, which is, after all, regarded by most preople as a form of entertainment. The argument that entertainment is never politically or ideologically neutral – which is a crucial argument to win – should not allow us to ignore the fact that it is also, at the same time, by the same textual strategies, entertaining.

All the writings in this section attempt to give some account of the types of pleasure provided by these Hollywood films for women, as well as trying to think through the politics of this type of film production. Several of the essays point to the way in which the strategies of many of these films include appeals to different, and even incompatible, audiences. Thus Richard Dyer traces the way in which *Mahogany* attempts to hold on to both black and white audiences, and Linda Williams shows how *Personal Best* both is and isn't about a lesbian relationship. Both Elizabeth Cowie and Christine Geraghty point to the way in which *Coma* attempts to provide traditional thriller/suspense elements as well as a female protagonist. This multiple appeal, the extreme ambiguity of the politics and address of many of these films, is noted by Annette Kuhn to be one of the defining characteristics of this cycle of movies as part of an attempt both to cater for newly defined audiences and maximise box office appeal.[5] The final essay in this section, Mandy Merck's analysis of *Lianna*, could easily have been included in the second part of the book. I have placed it here because, although its production circumstances do differ from the other 'Hollywood' films discussed, it seemed very useful to be reminded of the generic characteristics of Art cinema in the context of discussion of 'New Hollywood'.

Notes

1. Christine Gledhill, 'Klute 1: a contemporary film noir and feminist criticism', E. Ann Kaplan, ed., *Women in Film Noir* (London: British Film Institute, 1978), pp. 6–21; Judith Gustafson, 'The whore with the heart of gold: a second look at *Klute* and *McCabe and Mrs Miller*', *Cinéaste* vol. 11 no. 2, 1981, pp. 14–17, 49.

2. See Julia Lesage, 'The hegemonic female fantasy in *An Unmarried Woman* and *Craig's Wife*', in *Film Reader* 5, pp. 83–94, and Charlotte Brunsdon, 'A Subject for the Seventies', *Screen* vol. 23 no. 3–4, 1982, pp. 20–29, for two differing accounts. Susan Clayton, 'Cherchez la Femme', in D. Morley and S. Blanchard, eds., *What's this Channel Four?* (London: Comedia, 1983) provides a clear overview.

3. For a comment on an earlier Lovable advertisement, see Rosalind Coward, 'Underneath We're Angry', *Time Out* no. 567, 27 February – 5 March 1981, pp. 5–7.

4. For discussion of some of these issues, see: Terry Lovell, *Pictures of Reality* (London: British Film Institute, 1981); Janet Wolff, *Aesthetics and the Sociology of Art* (London: George Allen and Unwin, 1983), and Michèle Barrett, 'Feminism and the Definition of Cultural Politics', in Rosalind Brunt and Caroline Rowan, eds., *Feminism, Culture and Politics* (London: Lawrence and Wishart, 1982).

5. Robin Wood, 'The Incoherent Text: Narrative in the 1970s', *Movie* 27/28, Winter 1980/Spring 1981, pp. 24–42, provides more general arguments about the incoherence of 1970s Hollywood films. See also Peter Biskind and Barbara Ehrenreich, 'Machismo and Hollywood's Working Class', *Socialist Review* no. 50/51, 1980, pp. 109–30.

Hollywood and
New Women's Cinema

ANNETTE KUHN

Extract from *Women's Pictures, Feminism and Cinema* (London: Routledge and Kegan Paul, 1982), pp. 135–40.

SINCE the years of ascendancy of the Hollywood studio system, the industry has undergone many institutional changes which have had a number of implications regarding the textual organisation of Hollywood films. Molly Haskell and Marjorie Rosen have charted shifts in representations of women in Hollywood films which have accompanied these institutional changes (Haskell, 1975; Rosen, 1973) and both writers conclude that during the 1960s Hollywood films became increasingly violent, that women characters were increasingly represented as victims, and that the days of the powerful female star and the 'independent woman' as a character were gone. Haskell offers a sociological explanation for this finding, arguing that: 'The closer women come to claiming their rights and achieving independence in real life, the more loudly and stridently films tell us it's a man's world' (Haskell, 1975, p. 363). The rise of the second wave of feminism, according to this explanation, brought about a backlash effect: the threat posed by the liberated women was actually contained in films, often by a literal containment, at the level of story, of female protagonists. This might range from confinement within home and family, or in mental institutions, through to containment by various forms of physical violence up to and including murder.

At the same time, however, since the middle 1970s – after Haskell's and Rosen's books were first published – a number of Hollywood films have been made which may be read as indicating an opposite trend. In these films, the central characters are women, and often women who are not attractive or glamorous in the conventional sense. Narratives, moreover, are frequently organised around the process of a woman's self-discovery and growing independence: instances of this genre include *Alice Doesn't Live Here Anymore* (Scorsese, Warner Brothers, 1975), *Starting Over* (Pakula, Paramount, 1979), and *An Unmarried Woman* (Mazursky, Fox, 1977). The existence of this 'new women's cinema' might be explained in terms of direct determination: that it simply reflects the growth and influence of the women's movement.

On its own, however, such an explanation is perhaps rather one-dimensional, in that it cannot take into account the simultaneous existence of, say, films portraying violence towards women. By what process, in any case, are 'social climates' translated into cinematic signifieds? Given the complexity of the institutional structures of the film industry, not to mention the coded operations of film texts, the relationship between social climates and the content of films is obviously not a simple one. Explaining the co-existence of dissimilar types of Hollywood films calls for an examination of a variety of structures in their historical specificity. For example, if the cinema audience is composed of segmented 'sub-audiences' with different interests, films will address themselves to these various audiences. Thus the 'new women's film' addresses itself in particular to women, even to women with some degree of feminist consciousness, while other film genres will be directed at quite different social audiences.

In what ways do new women's films embody realism, and what is their relevance for feminism? As dominant cinema, their realism rests on the credibility of texts which construct identifications for the spectator on the levels of character and narrative, within a fictional world constituted as coherent and internally consistent. The spectator may, in other words, be drawn fairly readily into the identifications offered by the films. The pleasure for the female spectator of films of this kind lies in several possible identifications: with a central character who is not only also a woman, but who may be similar in some respects to the spectator herself; or with a narrative voice enunciated by a woman character; or with fictional events which evoke a degree of recognition; or with a resolution that constitutes a 'victory' for the central character. The address of the new women's film may thus position the spectator not only as herself a potential 'winner', but also as a winner whose gender is instrumental in the victory: it may consequently offer the female spectator a degree of affirmation. Two questions may be posed at this point, however. First, how do these various identifications operate in relation to one another in the address of film texts? And second, what are the implications for feminism of a classic realist cinema which is 'affirmative' of women?

These questions are best dealt with by reference to specific films. I shall look at Claudia Weill's *Girlfriends* (1977) and Fred Zinnemann's *Julia* (1977), both of which take up a genre popular in the 1960s and the 1970s, the male 'buddy movie'. *Girlfriends* and *Julia* become women's films by virtue of the simple fact that the buddies in these cases are female. A primary requirement of the new women's film is thus immediately met – the central characters are female, and they are sympathetically portrayed. *Girlfriends* goes a step further than this by presenting its main characters as not at all glamorous. The heroines of *Julia* conform much more to the Hollywood 'star' model, however:

Lillian Hellman (Jane Fonda) is a famous writer and Julia (Vanessa Redgrave) an obscure but highly courageous revolutionary. The star system is obviously at work here: while the central characters in *Girlfriends* are played by little-known actresses, who play 'ordinary' women, the casting of two world-famous figures – both of them also highly visible as political activists – as the stars of *Julia* has important consequences for the meanings generated by the film. Neither Julia nor Lillian as 'fictional' characters can be regarded as ordinary, and the casting underlines this: the point of identification for female spectators lies not so much with the characters as with the relationship between them.

Both *Julia* and *Girlfriends* may be seen as departing somewhat from the classic realist model in their narrative resolutions. In each film the questions set up by the narrative are not fully resolved by the closure. In *Girlfriends*, in fact, full closure is perhaps impossible, given the nature of the structuring enigmas of the narrative. The story begins with one of the women friends moving out of their shared apartment in order to get married. Anne's departure seems to motivate a series of events in Susan's life, all somewhat unconnected by anything other than the fact of her friend's absence. In the classic narrative model, resolution of this absence would be brought about by the restoration of an equilibrium. Within the trajectory of lack to liquidation of lack (see Chapter 2 of *Women's Pictures, Feminism and Cinema*) which marks variants of this model, resolution in *Girlfriends* might be brought about by the establishment of love relationships for Anne and Susan: either with each other, or with new partners. Although the first option would fit in well with the structural demands of classic narrative, as well as with the powerful Hollywood 'romance' model, its content is excluded by rules, conscious and unconscious, currently governing representations of homosexuality in dominant cinema. But at the same time the second option – re-establishment of equilibrium through the setting up of new relationships – is also ruled out, in this case by the demands on the narrative set up through the characterisations of the two women: it would simply not be plausible. However, although there is a constant movement towards the latter resolution – in Susan's relationship with a rabbi, for instance, and even in Anne's with her husband – it is never quite brought off, partly perhaps because it would undermine the 'buddy' structure that governs the organisation of the narrative. And so, caught in its own contradictions, the narrative cannot be resolved in the classic manner. We are left instead with a relatively 'open' ending: the women's relationship continues to be problematic and contradictory, and yet important enough to be continued. It may be argued, of course, that such an open ending is in fact more 'credible' than any classic resolution which ties all the ends of the narrative together.

Julia, too, possesses a degree of openness, which in this instance operates not so much in the film's resolution as through its entire narrative. This openness is crucially related to the film's articulation of plot and story, and the fact that its discourse is pivoted on memory. The film's enunciation involves at least two layers of memory. First there is the overarching discourse of Hellman's memoir, rendered in the film as her voice-over and as the temporal 'present' of the narrative, and marked by the representation of the writer's relationship with Dashiell Hammett. Secondly, there is the memory within the memoir, constituted as the 'past' of the film and marked cinematically as subjective, as Hellman's fantasies and dreams, most of them involving Julia. The two levels are brought together only in those sequences in the film's 'present' when Lillian and Julia meet – in a Vienna hospital and in a station café in Berlin. Since the relationship between the women is largely told discursively through Hellman's narrative point of view, and exactly because of its status as memory within memoir, it is relativised. What we see is Hellman's impression of a remembered relationship, doubly marked as subjective. We can therefore read the film in several ways. The openness of *Julia* centres less on the film's closure (which is in any case not entirely inconclusive, in that the past and the present of the narrative are brought together with Julia's death and Lillian's dealing with it in her relationship with Hammett), than on the nature of the relationship between the two women. This is encapsulated in a scene – a flashback, in fact – in which Lillian slugs a drunken male friend for suggesting that 'the whole world knows about you and Julia': that, in other words, the women have a lesbian relationship. The scene may be read in at least two ways: either Hellman's reaction is to the slur on lesbianism implied in 'the whole world's' uncomprehending gossip, or the 'accusation' of lesbianism is itself a slur on the relationship (see Julia Lesage in *New German Critique* no. 13, 1978, p. 92). A reading of reviews of *Julia* certainly upholds this suggestion: while most reviewers agree that the relationship portrayed between the women is central to the film (although it might in fact be argued, to the contrary, that the way the Hellman–Hammett relationship is represented, and also its place in the film's 'present', serve actually to enclose and relativise that of the women), there are almost as many opinions as there are reviews concerning the precise nature of that relationship.

The question of openness in these two examples of new women's cinema may be considered in relation to some general formal and thematic shifts within recent Hollywood cinema. These shifts have been regarded as significant enough to constitute a 'New Hollywood Cinema'. The mobilisation in New Hollywood Cinema of certain cinematic codes – zooming, telephoto shots, slow motion and split screen – have, it has been argued, 'destroyed the dramatic and spatio-temporal unity that founded the classical *mise en scène*' (see Steve Neale in *Screen* vol. 17 no. 2, pp. 117–122). Another mark of New Hollywood Cinema is a degree of open-endedness or ambiguity at the level of narrative – a defining feature of both *Julia* and *Girlfriends*. Two points of relevance to the question of realism, feminism and the new women's film may be made here. The first is that although New Hollywood Cinema is something of a departure for narrative cinema, it reworks rather than destroys the textual operations of dominant cinema: 'Ambiguity and open-endedness are sustained and articulated *within* the limits of the dominant discourse, within the text. They are not of the kind likely to fracture the unity of position of the reader' (Neale, 1976, p. 121, my emphasis).

Secondly, although the openness of New Hollywood Cinema operates across a range of cinematic genres and narratives, it may be argued that, precisely because of its subject matter, the new women's cinema is particularly prone to such openness. Although feminism and new women's cinema are by no means coterminous, new women's cinema does raise, at some level at least, the question of feminism. Feminism is controversial, however, and it would be problematic for a cinematic institution whose products are directed at a politically heterogeneous audience overtly to take up positions which might alienate certain sections of that audience. Films whose address sustains a degree of polysemy – which open up rather than restrict potential readings, in other words – may appeal to a relatively broadly-based audience. Openness permits readings to be made which accord more or less with spectators' prior stances on feminist issues. *Julia* illustrates this point quite well: while lesbians may be free to read the film as an affirmation of lesbianism, such a reading – just as it is not ruled out – is by no means privileged by the text. *Girlfriends* works similarly with regard to the question of feminism. On its release, the film was widely received as charming, warm, amusing and likeable. It was not regarded as threatening largely because, despite its status as a female 'buddy' film, it does not demand a reading as a feminist film. Nevertheless, at the same time, the 'buddy' structure can equally well justify a reading of the film in terms of woman-identification.

The possibility that this kind of openness may actually be a defining characteristic of new women's cinema is pointed to by Julia Lesage, who argues that: 'The industry wants to let everybody have their ideological cake and eat it, too. In other words, you'll see deliberate ambiguities structured into almost every film to come out about strong women' (*New German Critique*, 1978, p. 91). Whether or not this process is as conscious or deliberate as Lesage suggests, one of the most significant effects of this ideologically-implicated ambiguity must be to buttress the textual and institutional operations of dominant cinema. Whatever positive identifications it offers to those who choose to make them, new women's cinema cannot in the final instance deal in any direct way with the questions which feminism poses for cinematic representation.

References

Haskell, Molly, *From Reverence to Rape: the Treatment of Women in the Movies* (London: New English Library, 1975).
Neale, Steve, ' "New Hollywood Cinema" ', *Screen* vol. 17 no. 2, 1976, pp. 117–22.
New German Critique no. 13, 1978, pp. 83–107.
Rosen, Marjorie, *Popcorn Venus: Women, Movies and the American Dream* (New York: Coward McCann & Geoghegan, 1973).

'Mahogany'

RICHARD DYER

From *Movie* no. 27/28, Winter/Spring 1980–81, pp. 91–4.

NO DOUBT some wag has already pointed out that the theme tune of *Mahogany*, 'Do You Know Where You're Going To?', is an unfortunate give-away. It is a question that applies not only to the main character in the film, but to the film itself, the career of its star, Diana Ross, and the development of blacks in mainstream film in the 'seventies.

It is hard not to feel that, in the case of *Mahogany* itself, this lack of direction springs from pure opportunism. As a vehicle for Diana Ross, it chucks in something for everyone in her audience. The white audience is given a story of 'success' and of how 'success doesn't bring happiness' that both celebrates the American way of life and keeps people (blacks) in their place; the conservative black audience is given a black star, validated by the dominant media, whose success is measured by her commanding as extravagant a vehicle as this; the radical black audience is given, in the Billy Dee Williams character, a noble black rights politician, validated partly by the feelings of guilt he inspires in the Ross character; and the gay male audience, long followers of Diana Ross, is given two gay characters, one male and one female. As happens with opportunism, most of these acknowledgments of the audience are back-handed, the more so as the given audience identified is situated outside normalcy. Thus the radical black audience is no doubt supposed to be especially gratified that 'their' character is played by a performer so near in appearance, barring skin colour, to such handsome hunkiness as Burt Reynolds's; and gays are supposed to be grateful for being recognised in the form of a neurotic and sadistic closet queen and an ineffectually predatory dyke.

Opportunism, however, is only one way of putting it and has the effect of singling out a film like *Mahogany* from other Hollywood films. Another way of seeing it would be in terms of the overriding imperative for films to sell, and the concomitant need to identify audiences as potential buyers. Doing this is a project of consumer manipulation, but it actually involves recognising real cultural/ political formations in the society that film wishes to sell in. Films hope to take a lead in categorising and harnessing these formations (for economic reasons, though with political/cultural consequences) but they do not spirit them out of the air, nor are these formations so readily or inexorably bought. Appealing to more than one audience looks like box-office sense, but it also requires *Mahogany* to draw on values and sensibilities that can only tortuously be reconciled.

A black star for a racially mixed audience already has problems. How does she or he retain the specificity of her or his race, without that specificity seeming a threat to the white audience? Traditionally, it was done either through cultivating a 'white' image (e.g. Sidney Poitier) or through occupying the safe space of entertainer, set apart from daily life and therefore not constituting a role model (e.g. almost all other pre-seventies black film stars). Post Black Power and post Tamla and disco, however, these are not such ready options – in particular, it is less certain that they will carry the black audience or even the radical white audience with them. Ross sidestepped this with her other two films – *Lady Sings the Blues* celebrates someone who has attained the status of Great Artist (hence above social divisions) and can construe racism as individual bigotry in the past, while *The Wiz*, an all-black musical based on a children's story, occupies the space of entertainment with no white in sight. *Mahogany* – precisely *because* it wants to pack everyone in – does take on the problem. Indeed, the problem is the plot – is Tracy (Ross) going to choose white success (the fashion business) or black struggle (local politics)? Well, both, so as to please everyone: but how is this to be effected?

The key lies in the treatment of the world of fashion. The world of politics, embodied in Brian (Billy Dee Williams), is only minimally represented. Insofar as it is, it is not a Black Power insurrectionary or separatist form of politics, but rather the long march of transformation through the existing institutions. The film thus translates the problem into an opposition that is really the acceptable balance in bourgeois society between political reformism and individual endeavour. Set against respectable political activism, Tracy Ross's initial commitment to the world of fashion has to be *both* vindicated as an area of activity for a black person *and* shown to be inadequate.

The first job, vindication, is done in two, contradictory, ways – first by introducing black culture into the white fashion world, and then by avoiding this race question altogether. The film tries to establish that the entry of blacks to the world of fashion signifies enrichment for both parties. The very title of the film suggests how black models can lend to fashion the luxuriance of something highly valued by the white, high aesthetic sensibility. Sean (Anthony Perkins) gives Tracy the name Mahogany: his previous, very blonde white model he had called Crystal. More tellingly, a shot early on in the film, as Tracy is returning from design school on the subway, her sketch pad on her knee, shows her deliberately colouring her designs by analogy with

Mahogany

some bright graffiti she has just watched some black kids spray on the wall. She is, as it were, incorporating the colours of black street culture into her designs, and her tendency to do this is suggested by her teacher's admonition to her not to design bright and gaudy clothes. She ignores this, and her subsequent success vindicates her.

In a wider sense, Diana Ross herself embodies the reconciliation of black and white modes. In the film, her/Tracy's ability to handle dazzling street argot to ward off a pestering male and later to 'improvise' gospel-style on the words of a slogan to promote Brian illustrate – even assert – that she's still got soul, even if her name, normal speech and singing style are mainstream American (i.e. white). Even her appearance reconciles black and white and, in the film, most strikingly so in the first shot of her. Her face is hidden behind a mask; she lowers it and throws her head back, in a gesture reminiscent of the first shot of Rita Hayworth in *Gilda*. Her hair is straight: she could be a sun-tanned, black-haired Hayworth, but for her mouth, which she opens in a huge smile with dazzling white teeth, an unmistakeably black mouth. At this moment, her face does fuse black and white – that is, in case there is any misunderstanding, it fuses the socially constructed categories of 'female', 'black/white' 'beauty'.

Tracy's – partly because it is so insistently also Ross's – progress up the world of fashion draws black and white together. Yet, since the film is also about the opposition of black and white and since the fashion world is also shown to be racist (see below), it cannot do this too much, and Tracy's final moment of triumph, her own fashion show, sidesteps it altogether by the simple expedient of making all the clothes (Western-style) Japanese, thus neither black nor white. The film has already recognised the shock of a real incursion of black aesthetics into the tasteful fashion world when Tracy wears her own designed, shiny orange dress, instead of a simple white one, at a charity fashion show, to be humiliated first by audience derision and then by the dress being bought by Christian obviously because of his interest in the wearer (though Tracy is not shown to be fully conscious of this). The film could not then go on to a whole-hearted, black-inspired fashion show, and so goes East and away from the problem altogether, for what is Tracy's greatest moment of affirmation in the film.

But also her greatest moment of doubt: the film is actually structured around a freeze frame (leading to flashback), immediately after the show, where Tracy's triumphant cries of 'success!' are counterposed by an expression of fear or doubt on her face. In order to get in politics and Brian as well, the film has also to reveal the inadequacy of the world of fashion. (Because of the flashback structure, this vindication and undermining of fashion occur simultaneously – or muddledly – in the film as it actually proceeds.)

Here we might distinguish three moves. First, the fashion world is shown to be racist, not only in its implicitly white canons of taste (anti-'black' gaudiness), but also in some of its exploitative structures. Sean cannot use Tracy as a model in America because, as the fashion house owner puts it, it is a 'conservative' market. White female models are posed, in a very sixties Vogue style, in a black slum, while local blacks are patronisingly (and, the film hints, very cheaply) placed around for local colour.

Second, there is an attempt to suggest an equivalence between the two worlds of fashion and politics, and the experience of Tracy and Brian within them. Neither option is unproblematic, which makes the choice of fashion understandable while preparing us for its inadequacies. Both characters are seen to be splendidly ambitious – there are intimations of self-seeking, but they remain well within the ethos of classic American individualism. Both characters also have rough rides, and in a central sequence these are directly paralleled in a series of cross cuts. Brian has things thrown at him and is beaten up at an outdoor political meeting; Tracy is forced into bed with Sean who is then unable to have sex with her. The cross cutting and emotional tone tell us that these are meant to be equivalent, but it is of course supremely significant that Tracy/Ross's humiliation is sexual.

It is, third, by a displacement on to sexuality that the fashion business is finally downgraded. As the film progresses, the world of fashion is gradually revealed as sexually degenerate. Tracy gets to be a model courtesy of Gavina's lesbian interest in her and Sean's thoroughly sexually screwed-up promotion of her. (Sean's characterisation draws on Perkins's twitchy, nervous performance style to indicate a photographer-voyeur, a man who can't make it with women and resorts, in a scene that remains impenetrable on repeated viewings, to almost sexually teasing a man (Brian) by pretending that he's going to shoot him . . .) She gets to be a top designer courtesy of Christian, an ageing aristocrat who promotes her but wants her to pay by sleeping with him.

All of this sexual ambiguity and degeneracy is in direct contrast to the representation of black sexual relations. Billy Dee William and Diana Ross could hardly be bettered for impeccable embodiments of standard masculinity and femininity respectively, and Brian/ Williams's decidedly straight masculinity is further heightened by his visit to Rome, his embarrassment at going to fancy menswear shops there with Tracy and the sheer visual contrast of his still macho with the writhing androgyny around him at the party. When, at the end of the film, Tracy runs back to him (having not slept with Christian), they are re-united through a gag used earlier. He is addressing queues in a welfare office; she, a voice from the rear, pretends to be 'a widow from the south side with six kids'. He proposes welfare but she says she wants 'my old man back'. Through a series of questions lifted more or

Mahogany

less directly from the marriage ceremony, Brian says she can have her old man back. (Welfare is no substitute for female dependence on men.) Tracy's return to Brian can appear to be a return to politics, but it is also, because race is dropped as an issue and sexual decadence replaces it, a return to heterosexual normalcy.

It may be apparent that in many ways *Mahogany* is very nearly incoherent. Nor have I mentioned, for instance, the 'women's lib' lines that Ross is given to say, nor the forceful bitterness of Christian's response to her when she refuses to sleep with him after her great success that he has made possible. The film barely holds together, because the discourses it seeks to reconcile are not in fact reconcilable. If it does hold together at all, it is partly because star charisma is often about the magical resolution of the irresolvable, and partly by the importance of certain sequences in the film that operate on a predominantly experiential level. In a way, it is rather like a musical – the problems of the narrative are solved by the irresistible appeal of the numbers, except that the numbers here are montage sequences. These include the opening 'Japanese' show, the arrival in Rome, Tracy being photographed in Rome by Sean. The use of the song over the credits, over the Rome arrival and at the end, each time with a more spectacular use of camerawork and/or editing, also reinforces this effect. The experience aimed at is similar to that of those sensuous, materialistic ads for Martini and other life-style products. Most of the images connote expense, jet-setting, the beautiful people and so on, but whipped up into a dreamy delirium of zooms and dissolves that almost overrides any direct social signification. The power of these sequences, as embodiments of a sensuousness that wants to know nothing of social issues and ideas, is seductive, and partly because straight-laced Brian does not appear in any of them. However admirable the Brian world, the film also knows it is dreary, not only in the problems with which it has to deal but in its approach to them. Tracy/Ross even points out that a little fashion/show-biz bezazz would not do politics any harm. It is a thought that *Mahogany* clearly hopes will cement the film together, since it is itself a fusion of razzle-dazzle and 'issues'.

How far it gets away with it, for all or any of the time, depends a lot on how much you go for Diana Ross and sensuous montage. For me, there is only one moment in the film that really works and that is that first appearance already described. Head thrown back and lips parted, Ross suddenly, momentarily shudders, then widens the smile again; her fragile cheek-bones are bared to the terrifying storm of applause and success. In that moment she condenses all the contradictions of the film and her image (and, though I haven't argued it through, blacks in films in the seventies) into herself and embodies the lived experience of them. If she could only tap that vein of expression, she might yet make a film that really uses the charisma so brilliantly present in her records.

Three Women's Films

CHRISTINE GERAGHTY

From *Movie* no. 27/28, Winter/Spring, 1980–81, pp. 85–90.

THE LAST few years have seen the rise not only of the spectacular film aimed with massive publicity at a wide audience but, running parallel with this, films made with less money and aiming at a more specific audience. Ironically, one of the most prevalent of these minority films appears to be a revival of the 'woman's film', suitably revised for the seventies. Some of these films have been made by women, some by men but apparently with women as the audience consciously in mind. This article attempts to look at three of these films which, sometimes surprisingly, have been commercially successful; it tries to analyse the effect of the shift of a woman to the centre of the narrative and to indicate the strategies used to engage the audience. The three films use different styles at the formal level, and I have tried to show how this formal difference affects the way they approach their subject. *Girlfriends* is a text leaning towards naturalism, *An Unmarried Woman* a realist/narrative film, and *Coma* a fantasy/narrative film, which is aimed at a more traditionally commercial market than the other two.

Girlfriends is a naturalist work in the sense that it relies for much of its effect on the accumulation of surface detail. The camerawork almost draws attention to itself in its simplicity. Characteristically, the camera remains still while the characters, in particular Susan, move across, towards or away from it. Whereas in *An Unmarried Woman* the camera follows the woman around her flat, in *Girlfriends* the camera is often positioned in one room of Susan's flat, looking down the corridor into the other room. Positioned like this, the camera offers us the details of the flat, the changes in its colours, furniture and decorations as evidence of Susan; the point at which she puts up her own photographs on the wall is not emphasised but is there if we want it. Susan is seen in her environment and the creation of that environment ('We'll paint the walls red,' she says to Anne. 'Trust me.') is an indication of her struggles elsewhere.

Similarly, in the presentation of Susan as a character, there is an emphasis (made much of by reviewers) on Melanie Myron's physical differences from a usual film actress like Geneviève Bujold (Susan in *Coma*). When Susan goes to the hairdresser, he dismisses her picture of the style she'd like as not being possible for her. Wandering around the flat in shorts and socks she seems to be having a rest from trying to be attractive and looks (in conventional terms) large and ungainly. There is considerable play within the film between women's bodies as art (the statues in Eric's flat, the pictures in Eric's bathroom and Mr Carpel's office) and their reality; the images are fixed and static while the reality, as presented to us, is variable and shifting.

It seems that this emphasis on Susan's physical appearance operates two strategies to involve women in the audience with the film. The first is that of reassurance, for if Susan is not physical perfection, she is still witty, ironic and attractive. It is after all, as we were always told, not looks that count. The possibility of identifying with someone who looks like us, rather than a film star, is held out, and we are potentially confirmed in our identification with her via the second strategy, that of recognition. This seems to be a very common device in these 'women's films', and it is significant that in *Girlfriends* naturalistic details are used: her resigned acceptance at the hairdressers when her own ideas of how she wants to look are ignored, the surreptitious way she removes her spectacles before the lunch date with the Rabbi, the rush to the mirror when Eric arrives unexpectedly, her rage when the electricity suddenly goes off – everyday happenings which we recognise and which seem to offer hooks for identification.

With this emphasis on detail, the film offers not so much a straightforward narrative but a series of episodes which show different aspects of Susan's character and struggle. We see her alone, with her various girlfriends, with the older, married Rabbi, and with the younger Eric. None of the relationships is presented unambiguously and the conversations are not rounded off or summed up. 'How can you be so sure,' she asks Anne when she announces her engagement, 'when you're so unsure?' and this uncertainty, the lack of an answer, is a powerful motif in the film. 'I don't know what's best for you,' Susan tells Anne and the film emphasises her difficulty in recognising what she herself wants. She likes living alone but also finds it difficult and depressing; she loves Eric but also wants her 'own place' and that dilemma is not resolved; she loves Anne but can't always talk to her. Discussions of these issues are not reflective (as they are, as we shall see, in *An Unmarried Woman*) but always take place under pressure, as if to get over the experience, the feeling of these confused emotions. Perhaps the key scene here is the confrontation with Anne when they argue about their different positions:

Anne: I'm still the same person.
Susan: No, you're not. You're married . . . I felt betrayed.
Anne: You're so selfish.

Within the film, both the betrayal and the selfishness are held as possibilities. The final scene between Susan and Anne resolves nothing intellectually but re-establishes the friendship which contains these difficulties. The film has emphasised Susan's individuality, her quirkiness, her unconventionality, in order to make us feel that she is more 'real' than the heroines we are normally given. In a sense, Susan (unlike Erica in *An Unmarried Woman*) is not presented as progressing very much in her relationships; she simply exists and lives them. The film closes on a close-up of Susan's face, at rest but still troubled; it is the person who is seen to hold these ambiguities together.

Working within a similar field, *An Unmarried Woman* concentrates on the situation rather than the individual, with Erica (Jill Clayburgh) as a representative rather than unique. The credits of *Girlfriends* feature crude (and therefore more conventionally real) booth photographs of Susan and Anne making faces; during the credits of *An Unmarried Woman*, the camera sweeps the New York skyline and through the streets before homing in on Erica. I have categorised this film as realist/narrative – realist in the sense of contrasting with naturalist and fantasy narratives because of its emphasis on a story which in some way reveals the meaning of the film. The story is presented as that of a woman who does learn, who does make progress. The situation (Erica's marriage) is established in the first scenes of the film; it is disrupted by the revelation of her husband's love for someone else and the rest of the film shows how, in various ways, she re-establishes herself. Dramatic devices are used to pull the audience along with this story. Thus, while the music in *Girlfriends* is in the background, it is used in *An Unmarried Woman* to give dramatic force to particular episodes. When Erica walks away after her husband Martin's revelation, the theme music wells up, reaching the loudest point when she is sick in the street. Similarly, music is used to emphasise certain points within a scene (a kiss, for example) or to tie into the film less narratively dramatic moments such as the skating scene. When Erica goes to visit Martin at his office, the sequence starts with her coming out of the subway and walking to the office – events of no intrinsic importance – during which the theme music is emphatic in order to retain our interest. Music is absent when she first talks to Martin but at the end of the conversation it is used to emphasise the drama and importance of the final lines when he tells her that he does still love her and she retorts, 'I was your hooker.' While *Girlfriends* uses rather cool, classical music, that of *An Unmarried Women* is emotional and dramatic, developing and returning to a recognisable theme.

In a similarly dramatic way, the camerawork, rather than appearing to reveal reality, actively explores it. First, the camera concentrates on Erica, in particular her face, and follows her in the flat, on the street, at the skating-rink. The camerawork is particularly important in what it indicates to us about her male relationships. In the scenes with Martin and Charlie, Erica, although obviously with them, is seen often

Girlfriends

isolated in close-up; in her conversations with Martin, the editing gives us their faces separately. When she is with Saul, however, even when they are not embracing but are talking at the party or sitting on a street bench, we are given both their faces in close-up in the same frame, and the idea of the strength of their relationship is conveyed in such framing as much as in words.

The other function of camerawork and editing is to maintain our interest in the narrative. Characteristically, scenes open by posing an enigma which the camera explains, beginning with a close-up of a face or an object which is only explained or placed when the camera pulls back. Many scenes begin with a close-up of Erica, so it is a moment before we know where she is. The first meeting with Saul begins with a close-up of a part of his painting, then a cut to the whole painting and then to Saul, supervising the hanging of the picture. A later scene, in Saul's flat, starts with two close-ups, one of paint sloshing over canvas, the second of raw eggs slithering into a bowl; Saul is then revealed painting and we learn that Erica is making an omelette. Put like this the techniques sound obvious, as indeed does the film's use of music, but the devices do serve relatively unobtrusively to engage audience attention.

These devices are much less in evidence in the central scenes with the psychiatrist. If *Girlfriends* tries to work on the level of communicating the experience of emotions, the scenes with the psychiatrist in *An Unmarried Woman* seem to emphasise, in contrast, a reflection on such experience, so that being a woman, in the film's terms, becomes not a matter of living it out (as it is in *Girlfriends*) but is raised to the status of a problem. Erica is *told* of the importance of feeling; her sense of confusion and lack of control is explained and placed as being understandable and normal. Her friendships with the women in the 'club' are commented on as being valuable. The possibility of relationships with other men is put to her by the psychiatrist and, indeed, the lunch date and the picking up of Charlie are experiments in following this advice. In the presentation of Erica there is much more of a sense of control and thought-out action than there is in Susan, where the emphasis is on her impulsiveness. Similarly, Erica's conversations with her girlfriends are reflective about life, men, relationships and self-esteem. Although they do disagree, there is no equivalent to Susan and Anne's struggle to understand each other's situation and by the end even Elaine's sharpness and cynicism have mellowed.

I have argued that the shifts and ambiguities in *Girlfriends* are held together in its heroine. *An Unmarried Woman* operates similarly, but with important differences. Erica, like Susan, is presented as struggling, uncertain, sometimes lonely, sometimes afraid, but in the end she is finally identified and placed by Saul. At the end of the film, when she tells him that she is not going to Vermont with him, he sums her up. 'Am I only a sexual object to you?' she jokes. The music emphasises his words and the close-up on his face gives them force as he defines what she is – 'a bright, wilful, curious woman who is also a sexual object . . . an independent, vicious, honest woman who is driving me mad.' While Saul does not escape criticism in the film, at this point music and editing give weight to his words so that they seem to sum up not only Erica but also women in general. It is at this point that the narrative, the story of this woman, and the emphasis on reflection are joined in this reflection on what it is to be a woman. In a sense it does not matter whether Erica lives with Saul or not. The answer to the central question of the narrative – what is it like to be a woman today? – has been answered, and the words are given to a man.

Coma operates within an awareness of the 'women's issues' raised in the other films, but does so from a rather different perspective. In describing the film as fantasy/narrative, I should stress that the term fantasy is not meant to describe the film *per se* but to differentiate it from the other two. In other words, while the film is perfectly plausible in its own terms and operates from the realistic base of the hospital scenes, it offers, as an agent of the plot, a person of intelligence, resource and courage who acts not as we believe we behave but as we would like to behave. The notion of identification is a difficult one, but it seems crucial to these films and it is this notion (rather than, for example, the issue of medical ethics) which I wish to examine in *Coma*.

As in the other two films, the opening credits are interesting, placing the heroine, Susan (Geneviève Bujold), firmly in relation to her work: we see her drive up to the hospital and then at various points during the day – describing a case (in highly technical terms) to colleagues and students, scrubbing up, performing an operation, etc. Thus, when the credits end, we have had economically established the fact of Susan's work and an indication of her professionalism and confidence. This is important because it puts into context Mark's demand to shower first and his off-hand request to 'grab me a beer', and it allows the quarrel to be seen not as a silly tiff but as a battle Susan has to wage to get him to respect her work. Having established this, the film also quickly establishes the importance to Susan of friendship with other women: Susan insists on going to the dance class despite Mark's incomprehension. The grace, rhythm and laughter of the dancing class establishes a different area to that of the hospital with its uniformed order, and the conversation between Susan and Nancy in the changing room confirms its importance. With these two issues of respect for work and for friendship made clear, the narrative tightens as the operation on Nancy sets into motion the rest of the plot.

The issues that have been raised here are familiar to us from *Girlfriends* and *An Unmarried Woman*, and perhaps the audience is beginning to feel that the film will explore these problems in Susan's relationships. But if *Girlfriends* emphasises feeling and *An Unmarried Woman* reflection, *Coma* suddenly shifts genres and goes for action. It is not entirely unusual for women to initiate action in films. They do it normally, as in *films noirs* or some melodramas, through the manipulation of sexual power and of feelings. What is interesting about *Coma* is that the action which Susan takes is based on her professional abilities, which have already been established. She notices that Nancy had been given a tissue test for a routine operation; she is able to spot the suspicious cases on the long printout of coma discharges; she is able to walk into labs and morgues without blinking a squeamish eye and she can carry out intelligent conversations with the pathologists and technicians. But, most interestingly, she is able to defeat the man who is trying to kill her in the central chase sequence by drawing him into her professional area. He is distinctly unnerved, as is the audience, by the mortuary, nervously shooting at an already dead body, and it is this which enables Susan to take him by surprise, push the bodies on top of him and run.

An examination of the narrative shows up another quite sharp contrast with the other films, to do with attitudes to feeling and emotion. Emotion, in our society and in film, is often cast as a peculiarly female concern, and *Girlfriends* and *An Unmarried Woman* both take the realm of feeling as their area of concern (though not perhaps in the conventional way). In *Coma*, on the other hand, giving in to emotion spells danger and it almost acts as bait for the men to trap her. Susan is continually criticised by the men in the film for not showing her feelings. One male doctor, attending Nancy Greenly, comments on Susan's reactions, 'If it had been a friend of mine, I doubt if I'd have been that cool.' While she studies Nancy's notes, Mark insists that she is upset and should go home. The psychiatrist wants to know how she *feels* about Nancy's death, not what she is doing about it. Most sinister of all, it is Dr Harris (Richard Widmark) who urges her to explore and express her feelings, telling her that, 'Our emotions are what make us human.'

But it is when she does express feelings of grief or fear that Susan comes closest to giving up or being stopped in her pursuit of truth. In her second interview with Dr Harris, he asks her how she feels and she weeps for Nancy – 'she was my best friend, she understood me.' As she leaves the room, she appears to have given up until the stranger follows her and alerts her suspicions again. Similarly, after the chases in the hospital, she goes to Mark, crying with terror. He soothes her and she grows more relaxed – 'you're so great, Mark' – and while she is feeling relaxed and comforted, Mark telephones the hospital. It is difficult to talk definitely about audience reaction. It is however likely that, whereas normally we gain enjoyment from women in films feeling emotions of love, anger or grief, in *Coma* at these points the audience is actually concerned that Susan should not give in to these feelings.

This kind of play on the normal role of women in films can also be seen in the ending, though this does depend on how the audience chooses to read it. Certainly it is possible to believe that the ending shows that it finally requires a male to sort the business out, to save Susan from death at the hands of Dr Harris. But it seems to me that what the audience *feels* is rather different. In traditional thrillers, if women have a part to play, we are used to feeling rather worried and anxious when a woman is required to take responsibility for part of the action (as, for instance, in *The Getaway*). In *Coma*, it seems at least possible that when action is put into the hands of the male, Mark, the audience experiences exactly that feeling of anxiety about whether he is capable of pulling it off. Our faith is in Susan who has proved her competence; our doubts centre on Mark, who has blundered and betrayed her. The fact that he does succeed, in the interests of a happy ending, does not negate or make less important the audience's initial feelings.

It may be possible to see a new set of conventions emerging for mainstream 'women's films' and in particular the establishment of the main areas of concern. All three films accept as an initial premise that these concerns should be the problem of relationships with men, the importance of friendships between women and, though this comes a poor third, the difficulties of combining these things with holding down a job. Although they are very different in their dramatic strategies, *Girlfriends* and *An Unmarried Woman* both seem to end with a notion of women being different from the norm, as an enigma or problem. Their point of reference is society outside the film; they ask women to recognise the problems from their own experience and to identify with their heroines. *Coma*, on the other hand, because of its shift to the thriller mode and its placing of the woman in the traditionally male role, calls into question the form of the film and the traditional role of the heroine, at the level not only of content but also of feeling, of experiencing the tensions of a thriller. It is interesting both in its use of a different genre and its manipulation of the audience.

I am grateful to Jim Cook for helpful discussions about *Coma* on which much of this section is based.

'Personal Best': Women in Love

LINDA WILLIAMS

From *Jump Cut* no. 27, October 1982, pp. 1, 11–12.

ROBERT TOWNE'S *Personal Best* is a film about two women pentathletes who meet at the 1976 Olympic trials, become friends and lovers, then separate and meet again at the 1980 Olympic trials as competitors. Basically a sports movie, it differs from the genre's male pattern of individualist competition in its representation of female athletes who not only perform their 'personal best' but also support one another in doing so.

The film has been much praised for its realistic representation of athletic female bodies at the moment of concentrated performance, for picturing the 'wild beauty of young women with the mystic gusto usually reserved for young men' (Michael Sragow, *Rolling Stone*), for 'presenting fresh images of women on screen . . . a special treat' (Gene Siskell, *Chicago Tribune*), and for daring 'with great delicacy and insight, to show a loving sexual relationship between two young women, not as a statement about homosexuality, but as a paradigm of authentic human intimacy' (Jack Kroll, *Newsweek*).[1]

Just about everyone found *something* to like in the film. Straight women like the 'positive' portrayal of (literally) strong female protagonists committed to excellence in their field. Men like the sports subject and the fact that it provides the occasion for the relatively unclothed spectacle of female bodies in competitive contexts that excuse the usual voyeuristic pleasure of the way men look at them. Many (though certainly not all) lesbians like the guilt-free portrayal of a lesbian relationship. Runners of both sexes like the celebration of running itself.

Like most Hollywood films, *Personal Best* broadly appeals to a wide variety of contemporary social attitudes and tastes. Although the film presents itself as 'daring' in its depiction of a sexual relationship between two women, it is not daring enough to delve very far into the emotional details of that relationship or to suggest that such a relationship could endure. As a result there are many lacunae and motivational puzzlements in the basic narrative. Not the least of these occurs at a point two-thirds of the way through the film when a line of dialogue indicates, much to the audience's surprise, that what has seemed to be a relatively short-term affair has been going on for three years. What may at first appear to be the ineptness of a first-time director is in fact a confusion arising from the strain of juggling so many diverging social attitudes into a package that would titillate, but not offend, most viewers. In what follows I would like to examine the qualities for which the film has been most praised – its iconography of physically active, powerful women and its lesbian love theme – in order to discover the ways in which they are contradicted or undercut by predominantly patriarchal attitudes and points of view.

Female Iconography
Many of the discussions of *Personal Best* have centred on the photography of the track and field sequences. What is somewhat surprising in this discussion is that very often, among the film's relatively few negative reviews, male critics have attacked what they consider to be a voyeuristic presentation of female bodies. Female critics, however, have tended to defend the film against these very charges. Robert Hatch, for example, writes in *The Nation*:

> During track and field events, the cameras focus obsessively on the women's crotches – most outrageously during a slow-motion passage when six or eight of them practice the high jump by turning back-somersaults over the bar. This is cheesecake; it demeans women, and the lubricious chuckles in the audience suggest that it does so successfully.[3]

Veronika Geng, however, writing for the *New York Review of Books*, defends these very same shots:

> The idea that cinematographer, Michael Chapman, and Towne are using the camera voyeuristically, and that women must be protected from them by several manly, heroic film critics, is preposterous. Visually, *Personal Best* is designed around the autonomous movements of the women. When they are still, the camera never prowls their bodies. When they move, they make their own trajectories through the frame. If the camera moves with them, it goes from the general to the specific – from the sources of athletic power, the legs and pelvis, to a particular face. (Pornography looks at a specific woman and then debases her into generalised body parts; with Towne, looking at the body parts makes him fall in love with the whole woman.) In the high jump, the hinge of the movement is the crotch (and too bad if you can't stand seeing it), but each character pushes her entire body into the frame, and the payoff is the unique reaction on her face. Every photographic choice – the distance of the camera, a change from slow-motion to normal speed – is attuned to the women's feelings and picks out the individuality in physical movement.[4]

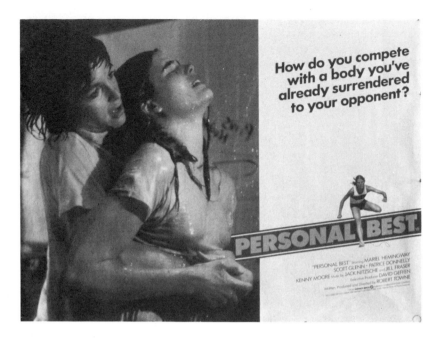

What Hatch sees as the cheesecake of the unindividuated and fragmented body, Geng sees as the autonomous expression of individuality through movement. Who is right? Or do men and women simply respond differently to the same images?

This issue is a complicated one and I do not pretend to have all the answers. It would be tempting to reply that where men see cheesecake women see autonomous beings. We could thus relegate the entire issue to the 'eye of the beholder' who sees what he/she is sexually programmed to see. But if we look closely at Geng's defence of Towne, we will see that she is not at all describing what *her* eye beholds but creating a rather elaborate defence of the male director's point of view – as both creator and consumer of these images. The defence is telling. For I strongly suspect that such images invite women to consume them from a temporarily assumed male point of view. If women could not learn to at least partially assume the male viewpoint in consuming such images, they would experience constant visual displeasure in the bombardment of female body parts provided by the media. Geng reveals the extent to which women have become complicit in the objectification of female bodies.

The assertion that the various fragments of the female body add up to a whole that is attuned to the subjective expression of the woman's feelings might be possible in an innocent world that had not already appropriated female bodies to the measure of male desire. But in the context of our already fallen, patriarchal world, Eve's body is no longer innocent, no longer her own.

Nor can activity alone constitute the autonomy of the female image. Even the briefest glance at television ads and magazine covers – from *Runner's World* to the *Playboy* issue that features *Personal Best* star Mariel Hemingway on the cover and interviews Towne within – reveals the sleek active bodies of an increasingly androgynous feminine ideal displaying the 'new cleavage' of ass to leg. From the breast fetishes of the fifties we move to the ass, crotch and muscle fetishes of the eighties. At this point in time, when commercials have already fetishised the fragmented female body to sell the most mundane commodities, analytic slow motion montages of athletic bodies in motion merely confirm the current style of fashionably fetishised female bodies constructed to the measure of male desire. Where that desire once consigned women to a passive voluptuousness, it now represents them as so many trained seals flexing their muscles to male awe and approval. Thus even Jane Fonda finds herself, in *On Golden Pond*, obliged to perform a muscle-flexing back-flip to resolve the father-daughter differences of that film, thereby proving to her father Henry – in one of the least satisfying plot resolutions ever concocted – that she is really just as good as the son he always wanted her to be.

The point, however, is not to berate Geng for an 'unliberated' enjoyment of female bodies. Women viewers, traditionally deprived of active women characters with whom they can identify, are naturally inclined to celebrate *any* female images that break out – however slightly – of the traditional molds of passive and decorous objects. (I recently found myself applauding Lauren Bacall's graceful ability to catch the match box Humphrey Bogart tosses her in *To Have and Have Not*, even though the vast majority of her movements are self-consciously and narcissistically calculated to please both Bogart and the male viewer.)

The question then arises: what would a non-patriarchal representation of the athletic female body be? There is no answer that works for all time. In 1982 a slow-motion analysis of female athletes will be read in the context of the patriarchy's commercial and sexual appropriation of those very same images. It could very well be that what we need at this point in time is to restore the integrity of the whole body in real time and space.[5] Even the *Wide World of Sports* allows all athletes this much integrity before launching into the slow-motion replay.

Women in Love
Personal Best's other claim to originality is the lesbian relationship between its two female characters. Here the film makes more explicit a female love relationship that was hinted at in *Julia*, the last decade's enormously popular epic of female friendship and love. In *Personal*

Best the track and field sports context of the narrative permits an emphasis on the physical and sensual that renders the women's erotic relationship a 'natural' by-product of their highly physical existence. This, I think, is the source of the almost overwhelming acceptance of the film's treatment of the normally taboo subject of homosexual love.

In box office terms, the combination of sports and sex was a stroke of genius. Those who would normally be shocked or at least irritated by a lesbian relationship in any other context find it quite 'natural' among female athletes who, it is presumed, are simply more physical than other people. The film thus capitalises on public awareness of, and curiosity about, lesbian athletes like Billy Jean King while evading any real presentation of lesbian identity. Thus Kroll, in the statement quoted above, can take Chris and Tory's relationship not as a 'statement about homosexuality but as a paradigm of authentic human intimacy'. Authenticity for Kroll seems to consist of avoiding the very issues of sexual identity that the lesbian relationship raises. My own criticism of *Personal Best* is not that it should have made a 'statement about homosexuality,' but that in studiously avoiding even mentioning the *word* lesbian – let alone the word love – the film's notion of 'authentic human intimacy' tends to reduce this relationship to a kind of pre-verbal and pre-oedipal regression to narcissism.

The first lovemaking scene between the two athletes, Chris and Tory (Mariel Hemingway and Patrice Donnelly), occurs early in the film. It is presented as the outgrowth of a prolonged and herculean arm-wrestling contest whose ups and downs prefigure the various ups and downs of the two women's competitive careers. Only the physicality of the arm-wrestling and the proximity of the two remarkably fit and beautiful bodies prepares us for their sudden passion. In the very next scene they celebrate their love in an ecstatic work-out along the beach. A three-year love affair follows.

What we see of this affair is somewhat confusing. At times it is presented as an idyll of sensuality; at other times it seems tense and troubled. The two women both live and train together. Under Tory's guidance Chris at first gains confidence and skill. But as Chris improves, Tory begins to decline. A key moment in their relationship occurs at the Pan Am Games in Colombia. When Chris becomes ill with stomach cramps, Tory spends the night nursing her, cradling her in her arms on the floor of a dressing room shower in a pose that recalls that of a madonna and child. The next day Chris is well and performs magnificently while Tory is tired and does poorly. Although Chris clings desperately to the maternal care and support that Tory gives her, it becomes increasingly obvious that she performs best under adverse conditions and needs not to depend on Tory. As Chris's skills improve, she reluctantly begins to challenge Tory in the pentathlon. Tory seems able to accept this challenge and still love Chris, but her concern for Chris's well-being tends to hurt her own performance.

The real problem, however, is not that they must compete with one another but that they must do so within the context of a personal relationship of unequals. For Tory's relationship to Chris, as the madonna and child scene in the shower clearly suggests, is that of a mother. This mothering is the real impediment to the growth and endurance of their relationship. Yet this mothering also renders the relationship safe in the eyes of the film's ultimately patriarchal system of values. The film can afford to celebrate nostalgically the sensual lost eden of a female-to-female bond precisely because it chooses to depict this bond as the non-viable pre-oedipal dependence and narcissistic identification of mother and daughter.

Chris and Tory's love affair is doomed not because they are lesbians, the film seems to say, but because of the regressive nature of their narcissistic relation. The failure to define the lesbian nature of their relationship as anything other than a regression to mother–daughter narcissism is one of the major disappointments of the film. The remarkable fact that the film goes to great lengths to avoid giving a name to the lesbian nature of Chris and Tory's relationship indicates the extent of the evasion.

The closest the film comes to defining their relationship is Tory's statement: 'We may be friends but every once in a while we fuck each other.' This definition of a three-year love affair as friendship plus occasional sex seems hopelessly inadequate. The very language of the formulation 'fuck each other' assumes an oppressively phallic model for its sexual content. If ever two people had a chance *not* to 'fuck each other' (with all the manipulation and abuse the term implies), it would be these two women.

In other words, we find in *Personal Best* what we have so often found in the action films of male bonding: a gratuitous and decorative love interest with no organic relation to the real concerns of the film. Chris and Tory's love remains an emotional and sexual interlude in a larger configuration that cannot deal with its implications. Thus, having put the two women together, the film must then find a way to drive them apart.

If Chris and Tory were driven apart by the pressures of competing in a patriarchal system of ruthless competition, then we could clearly blame this system and celebrate the women's triumph over it in the end. But what actually drives them apart is a blatantly contrived scene in which Tory accidentally moves a marker that causes Chris an injury. Because neither of the women can account for the accident, the coach can drive a wedge of suspicion between them. Although we deplore the evil suspicions of the macho coach, the melodramatic contrivance of the unlikely accident actually effects the separation. The coach is ultimately proven wrong in his suspicions and in his ruthless handling of the two women, but nothing in the film proves wrong their contrived separation. Quite the contrary. From this point on the film shifts focus (from Chris and Tory to Chris alone) and tone (from serious melodrama to comic relief) as it recounts Chris's initiation into the joys of adult heterosexuality.

Another evasion of the lesbian theme occurs in the contradictory presentation of Tory, played by the novice actress and former hurdler Patrice Donnelly. Although Tory looks and acts a good ten years older than Chris, she appears in a role that would make her roughly Chris's contemporary. Similarly, although provided with an ex-boyfriend (mentioned briefly) and no previous experience with other women, she is visually coded – short hair, square features, tailored jackets – to look the part of the 'dyke' in opposition to Mariel Hemingway's more feminine long hair, unassertive presence, and general girlishness. Tory takes the initiative in their first sexual encounter, appears jealous of Chris when she is in the company of men, and, after they separate, seems to lurk in the background of Chris's life, a frustrated lesbian.

The film thus delivers a double message: on the one hand it presents two heterosexual women who 'simply' fall into an affair without examining the meaning of their relationship; on the other hand, it indirectly implies that one of them is older, more experienced and a 'real' lesbian. The fact that Tory is almost completely dropped as a character after she and Chris separate suggests that Hollywood has not entirely given up the old policy of punishing the homosexuals in its stories. Instead of death or suicide, the punishment has simply been reduced to narrative banishment.

The repression of the lesbian woman-identified content of Chris and Tory's relationship is all the more remarkable given the film's ostensible moral: that women athletes can be both tough and compassionate, that the 'killer instinct' that motivates male competition, and which is advocated by their coach, can be tempered with a female ethic of support and cooperation that is not only good for the soul but can also win in the end. In other words, the film asserts on the level of its sports theme what it is afraid to assert on the level of its sexual theme.

By the end of the film Chris, who began as a whiny little girl in terror first of her father then of her male coach, finds the strength to oppose her coach's order not to associate with Tory. At the climactic meet she helps Tory win a crucial event by taking out the competition too fast. The plan works, cooperation in competition prevails, and both women qualify for the Olympic team, which never went to Moscow, with the satisfaction that they have performed their 'personal best'. But the personal best of competitive sports has here clearly supplanted the personal best of relationships. Again, what the film offers on the level of its sports theme – that women can be competitors with a positive difference – it takes away on the level of its sexual theme – that they can also be lovers with a positive difference.

The shift in tone is quite remarkable. Chris achieves her rite of passage under the tutelage of Denny, an ex-swimmer whose ingratiating buffoonery comes as a literal relief to the emotional intensity of the Chris/Tory relationship. Denny functions as a modified and reasonable substitute for the excessive and unreasonable patriarchal authority of Chris's father and coach. It is Denny who delivers the final moral of the film's title, 'The only ass you need to whip is your own.' And it is Denny whose (full frontal but briefly spied) penis becomes the final symbol of Chris's delighted reconciliation with patriarchy: a comic scene in which Denny goes to the toilet accompanied by a curious and enthusiastic Chris who stands behind him to 'hold it'.

In this scene, what appears on the surface to be a clever role-reversal – woman objectifying and fetishising a male body part – is really a not-very-subtle comic expression of Chris's embrace of a newly-found adult heterosexuality. Chris's maturity is then proven in the very next scene when she defies her coach to befriend the now weakened and child-like Tory. Although Chris's support of Tory prepares the 'happy end' of both women's mutual triumph in the final meet, the moral is clear: Chris's strength and maturity derive not from Tory, who mothered her, but from Denny whose laid-back fathering has finally made her a woman.

And so, what began as a promising depiction of women in love and competition becomes a series of dirty phallic jokes whose function is to dispel the seriousness and tension of the original woman-to-woman relation: 'What's gotten into you?' says one of Chris's friends, and Chris, in dreamy reply, simply looks at Denny.

If the phallus has become a running joke throughout the film, first for its absence and then later (with a vengeance) for its presence, it never really becomes the butt of the joke; everything is ultimately envisioned from its point of view. Denny's function in the film makes this painfully clear. If we have had any early doubts about the voyeuristic presentation of women's bodies in the first half of the film, Denny's bug-eyed appreciation of Chris's body must dispel them. His comic, knee-jerk reactions to Chris's athletic beauty stand for the pleasures of the male viewer who is 'wowed' by the power and beauty of the newly streamlined feminine ideal. Scenes in which he bumps his head on the side of a pool as punishment for too much underwater looking, or does bench presses while blowing air up Chris's crotch are pure burlesque, and like all burlesque render the involuntary male sexual response comically forgivable.

The women in *Personal Best* do not define for themselves the challenge their relationship poses to patriarchy. This allows the film to recuperate their (unnamed) sensual pleasure into its own regime of voyeurism. Ultimately, the many nude scenes and crotch-shots can be enjoyed much the way the lesbian turn-ons of traditional heterosexual pornography are enjoyed – as so much titillation before the penis makes its grand entrance. For all its lyrically natural and guiltless sensuality, for all its celebration of women athletes as possessed of both excellence and integrity, *Personal Best* fails to provide a genuinely feminist depiction of women in love or competition.

I would like to thank Judy Gardiner, Richard Gardiner, Meg Halsey, Kathy Minogue, Michelle Citron, Julia Lesage and Chuck Kleinhans for either contributing their own valuable ideas on this film or for helping me to clarify my own ideas.

Notes

1. These statements are gleaned from the current newspaper ad. for the film.
2. Male critics who deplore the film's voyeurism include: Vincent Canby in the *New York Times*, Carlos Clarens in *The Soho News*, Robert Hatch in *The Nation*, and Dave Kerr in *The Chicago Reader*. Female critics who defend the film's presentation of the female body include: Barbara Presley Nobel in *In These Times*, Pauline Kael in *The New Yorker*, and Veronika Geng in *The New York Review of Books*. Of course, many male critics have also praised the film extravagantly, as demonstrated by the excerpts quoted above. But it does seem significant that, among the male critics who dislike the film, so many of them isolate the issue of voyeurism as an important element of their criticism and that, similarly, female critics feel obliged to defend the film on this very issue. I have not conducted a survey of the gay and lesbian and feminist press; opinion on the film appears to be somewhat divided in it.
3. *The Nation*, 27 February 1982, pp. 251–2.
4. 18 March 1982, p. 45.
5. This is, in fact, what a great many current feminist film-makers have chosen to do. See, for example, the films of Chantal Akerman, Marguerite Duras, Yvonne Rainer, Michelle Citron, Helke Sander and Ulrike Ottinger.

A Discussion of 'Coma'

ELIZABETH COWIE

Extract from 'The Popular Film as a Progressive Text – a discussion of *Coma*', in *m/f* no. 3, 1979, pp. 59–81.

The Detective

MARJORIE BILBOW in her review of *Coma* says: 'It is not the who and the why that makes the story an entertaining mixture of suspense and black humour but the macabre how of Susan's investigations.' *Coma* is thus not exactly a classic detective story or 'whodunnit', which has been loosely defined as 'works which may or may not include a classical detective, but whose narrative is organised around the movement towards a final revelation which rationally attributes criminal culpability to at least one among a group of more or less equally treated characters.' The detective narrative must play fair with its readers, or audience, and allow them to make a calculated guess as to the solution. Introducing the murderer on the last page is not 'fair', so the 'clues' must be present but disguised in a number of ways. While *Coma* has a detective – Dr Susan Wheeler – it does not have a series of suspects; or rather, Susan suspects a number of characters as *all* involved in a conspiracy, and they act suspiciously in relation to her investigation (Dr George, the Chief of Anaesthesia, in particular, is picked out by the camera a number of times, staring 'suspiciously' at Susan). However no clue is offered beyond the hostility and lack of help from certain characters, until the 'revelation' at the Jefferson Institute of 'George' as the head of the conspiracy. But it is in fact only another clue – George refers not to the Chief of Anaesthesia but to the first name of Dr Harris. Harris however has been unsuspected within the film, and by Susan, though possibly not by the audience.

In any case the film does not start with a criminal act; the enigma is not one of murder initially and hence of who did it, but the problem of how normal, healthy patients undergoing minor surgery are becoming comatose following the operation. It is initially, therefore, a problem of medical knowledge and part of the project of the investigation will be the reconstitution of the problem as a criminal act, of the comas as unlawful deaths; the film however, despite the abundance of corpses, cadavers and moribund bodies, lacks evidence in terms of a body defined as murder victim. Of course the audience will presume that murder and sinister intent have been involved all along, reinforced by prior publicity of the film in terms of 'someone is getting away with murder', but the initial detection within the film is the *establishment* of this possibility.

It would be quite typical, too, within a detective film for the protagonist to suspect sinister underpinnings, where other characters deny it (the suicide or accident which is really murder) though usually they are fortunate enough to have a body. However in *Coma* this is not quite the case either, since Susan commences her role as detective not in order to reveal, to prove, but to understand *how*. 'I just want to understand' she says, which narratively is given as her response to grief over the condition of her best friend Nancy. As a result this places Susan in a position where she, as it were, doesn't know what she is doing – the knowledge she seeks is not the one she can or will obtain. She is given a pre-eminently masculine trait, the desire for knowledge, but she is seeking a medical knowledge to understand a criminal act and hence is doubly ignorant of what she seeks to understand though her attempt to discover the truth of the first will bring about the exposure of the second. Since she effectively reveals the crime through her attempts to solve a 'medical' mystery, her investigation is therefore literally a spectacle,[2] and her position as detective/protagonist in possession of knowledge clearly qualified.

A similar process can be seen in Hitchcock's *North by Northwest* where the hero Thornhill (Gary Grant) is forced to find a man called Kaplan who in fact does not exist but is a cover for a female agent. He too, like Susan, has the wrong question, or quest, but in this film the 'blindness' of Thornhill is presented as comic, which is narratively extended in the character of Thornhill through his relationship with his mother. In *North by Northwest* Thornhill is forced to take on the role of detective, seeking knowledge, but is never in the position of detective, is never knowledgeable, or rather never has true knowledge in the film until the end.[3]

Coma uses this same narrative device but covertly. Susan appears to be a place of knowledge, agent of the discovery of knowledge, but she is consistently displaced from this position, this time not by comedy but by a denial and dismissal of the knowledge she asserts and seeks, i.e. that the coma cases are suspicious at all. The ending where she does not perform the final decisive act, is thus simply a culmination of this displacement rather than a contradiction of her role as protagonist; it is not a cop-out but the logical conclusion. The moment Susan has 'true' knowledge, that Dr George Harris is the villain, she is 'returned' to the role of woman as victim, literally prostrate on the operating table (see also here the still of her being undressed by nurses, and its uncanny similarity to the pose in the earlier shot with Mark, the later image appearing as an 'echo' of the earlier one, as part of the same order of being held in place).

Coma

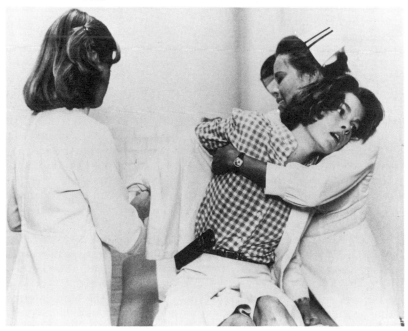

Coma

For the detective story, however, the position of the detective as knowledgeable is crucial. The detective will always know more than any other character, and also more than the audience or reader, though he will not know the whole truth of the enigma or else the film or novel, as a process of 'unravelling' the truth, would be manifestly a fabrication (in *The Big Sleep*, for example, this can be seen in the way that Humphrey Bogart, as Marlowe, always seems to know already what has happened or is going to happen). This problem of the detective knowing, or at least knowing more, is extremely difficult for narration, leading to devices like the figure of Dr Watson in the *Sherlock Holmes* stories, who relates the narrative of detection and therefore speaks from a position of ignorance ostensibly equivalent to that of the reader, while being able to point to and reveal the knowledge of Holmes.

In addition the detective story needs to relate the tale of the detection in a way which will hold the interest of the reader or audience in 'how' rather than simply 'who' (the how of detection rather than the crime), since otherwise the reader will simply go to the end of the book to learn the answer, or the film will be made pointless if the audience has already 'found out' the answer. While the narrative is predicated on a question and its answer, its existence lies in the telling of the tale – but a telling which must be effaced since the telling is always a *delay*, a rhetorical device which if 'seen' will expose the contrivance and hence disrupt that 'suspension of disbelief in favour of knowing' which is central to narrative. The problem arises most severely for the detective narrative because it is formed on such a simple enigma, of who perpetrated the criminal act.

To return to *Coma*: Susan is clearly never in command of more knowledge than the viewer. On the contrary, the viewer at times has knowledge unknown to her; the conversation between Harris and the psychiatrist is an important example. Nor can she be said to have greater knowledge of the enigma than the other characters, since they don't even recognise one; and certain characters withhold knowledge – the charts of patients, etc. Finally, she gives away knowledge to other characters in the course of the film – to Mark and to Dr Harris. This is important since the role of detective as possessor of superior knowledge is central to the detective format.

I have been concerned to look at *Coma* as a detective narrative because it is within that genre that Susan Wheeler can have the role of protagonist[4] as dominant initiator and principal agent of the action and hence narrative in the film – an important point for feminist interest in the film. Susan *appears* to have that role inasmuch as she sets in motion a train of events as a result of her investigations – though the links are not immediately clear – and she actively pursues her investigation, which involves strenuous physical effort and danger, a would-be assassin (male) whom she effectively disposes of beneath a pile of frozen cadavers. Yet, like Thornhill in *North by Northwest*, she does so *blindly*, and she is denied the definitive action, the capture of the villain (which is achieved by Mark but shown by the arrival of policemen at the operating theatre). She doesn't really know, but nevertheless acts; the Jefferson Institute seems important in her investigation, for example, as simply a link between coma cases rather than as part of any general hypothesis she is formulating. And despite the clue we already have, that another link between the cases is that all of them have been tissue-typed, Susan doesn't seem to be anticipating what she will find at the Institute.

The Conspiracy of 'Coma'

If Susan is not a true detective in *Coma*, then what is the status of her investigation, and of her as investigator? It is not a question of discovering the 'real' detective within the film, but of recognising the absence of such an agent. Yet a mystery is posed, and solved, within *Coma*, and the problem is how this comes about. In fact there is a shift from mystery to suspense; that is, the issue of knowledge in the film moves from one of 'answer' to one of 'what will happen'. The interest is now no longer in detection and solution, but in how the characters will act, and hence in *re*solution. Suspense here is thus the 'waiting to know'.

This shift is not, however, simply fortuitous – that there just isn't a detective – since in *Coma* Susan is clearly offered as one; thus *Coma* seeks to operate through the conventions of both the detective and the suspense genre, the shift between them being effected through the narrative's construction of an enigma of both a mystery and a *threat*.[5] This is not simply to refer to the danger inherent in tackling the mystery but to suggest that the protagonist within suspense never narratively has the 'upper hand', but is always a potential victim to the mystery under investigation. This I will argue later is integral to suspense in a number of ways, but first I want to consider the shift in *Coma* from a detective story to a suspense thriller and how this is brought about in the narrative.

As noted already, one of the problems within the film is that while the investigation is central, its object has to be asserted and then justified in the process of the investigation. Susan's response to her best friend's coma following a straightforward operation is to try to understand why it happened. She establishes the issue of coma for herself and then asserts it as a general problem, since she cannot understand Nancy's condition from within the (medical) knowledge she has. Checking all the cases of unexplained coma at the hospital over the past year, she discovers that the rate for these cases is far higher than could be statistically expected. The basis on which she is trying to make sense of Nancy's condition thus shifts from the purely individual to one of the enigma of unexplained coma cases in general. However her investigation is never recognised within the film, in the sense of being either authorised or reasonable. The hospital authorities reject the need for her investigation – all aspects of the coma cases have already been covered and therefore by continuing it she is implying negligence on the part of the hospital and staff. Hence it is also viewed with hostility and there is an active attempt to stop her – the reprimands from Dr Harris, the argument with Dr George, the enforced visit to the psychiatrist.

Such an 'opposition of disbelief' is seen in many films, where the hero must do battle against a bureaucracy as well as with the 'real' villain, but these difficulties or 'trials' put before the protagonist operate as simple forms of delay in the narrative. This is not quite the case in *Coma*. First of all Susan's investigation is not directed towards a suspected third party, but at the hospital itself; since she doesn't initially recognise the criminal nature of the cause behind the coma cases, hospital malpractice and cover-up must be assumed to be involved (though the film never reveals Susan's suppositions on this); therefore the hospital management's response is logical and expected, in fact quite 'reasonable'. Secondly, not only her investigation but Susan herself is set up by the hospital as unreasonable – the opposition to her investigation becoming an opposition to her. The status of the investigation, therefore, while central is also highly problematic. The film at this point could simply be a psychological drama about the 'problems' of Susan Wheeler, the personal difficulties of a woman doctor in an all-male world.

This means that the status of Susan as protagonist is crucial, for both she and the investigation must seem plausible, her suspicions well-founded and reasonable, and the investigation therefore necessary and justified. Two factors inter-relate in confirming Susan's credibility as protagonist: first of all there is audience expectation, created through cinema advertising, prior publicity and reviews, that *Coma* is not a psychological drama, and that a conspiracy will soon be made apparent. The problem of the coma cases immediately fits as the 'sinister mystery', so that the audience will accept all along that the investigation is justified, and see its questioning in the film as a narrative twist. Secondly, this expectation will confirm Susan Wheeler as the investigator inasmuch as she has already been offered within the film for identification as the protagonist. This can be seen in the film in a number of ways: the film opens on Susan driving to the hospital – her place of work, which is a conventional way of introducing the chief character. The following scenes at the hospital, of Susan taking a conference on a patient, in the operating theatre, etc., present her as a doctor, in charge, authoritative, in possession of knowledge. After the row with Mark, we see Susan in her flat, the narrative thus following Susan rather than Mark, confirming the bias of the opening shots. In addition Susan is presented as having a number of positive traits which encourage identification with her as protagonist: she holds a position of moral rectitude in her rejection of the hospital politics and careerism expressed by Mark, or the political wheeling and dealing of Dr Harris. Her care and concern for patients is contrasted to the general theme in the film of the typical de-personalised care given in hospitals, of doctors' insensitivity – while the surgeon operating on Nancy Greenly says, 'I just want to get this mother off the table.' Susan is later shown giving lollipops to a small boy patient (he in fact needs a kidney transplant, a typical example of the narrative over determination in *Coma*).

What then of the narrative twist, of the 'opposition of disbelief' to her investigation within the hospital? I want to argue that this is more than just a narrative twist, that it is a crucial narrative strategy which in effect sets up a kind of second, 'false' conspiracy within *Coma* on to which the real conspiracy and threat are displaced for much of the film. What makes this second conspiracy possible are the very features which provided the basis for a feminist reading of the film, that is, the construction of Susan as a *strong independent woman* prepared to think and act on her own. As such she is shown as continually 'difficult' in the film in relation to other characters. This is set up in the row with Mark at the beginning of the film which both establishes Susan's strength and independence, securing the credibility of her investigation and of subsequent 'heroic' scenes, *and* sets her up as a difficult woman, a problem as a woman. As she walks out of his flat she says, 'I just want some respect', but Mark replies, 'You don't want a relationship, you run away from it. You don't want a lover, you want a Goddam wife'. Against the reasonableness of her demands for Mark to 'help out' is set his accusation that she can't handle her femininity, can't cope with a relationship. Her independence is identified with 'her problem' in their relationship and thus also portrayed as a weakness – she is also vulnerable – and this theme is continued in the next scene where she arrives at her own flat (strikingly tidy and peaceful in comparison with Mark's) as the phone is ringing, which she finally answers, too late – the caller has hung up. Poignant, the 'too late' evoking a sense of loss, we assume the call was from Mark. Suggesting that, yes, she does want him really. Expelling an image of Susan as totally domineering, it also reinforces the theme of her vulnerability. This theme recurs subsequently, always related to her position as a woman: for instance she herself repeats Mark's accusation to the psychiatrist; and earlier, in insisting on pursuing the investigation, she says to Mark, 'You think that just because I'm a woman I'm going to be upset. I just want to understand. I wish you'd stop treating me as if there was something wrong with me'. Dr Harris, too, says, 'I can protect you cos you're good. And a woman'; and Susan says again to him that people seem to think there's something wrong with her, and not that the problem is the cases of coma.

Susan is quite right. Her independence, as it is constructed in the film, is played on within it in commonsense sexist terms: if she is so independent then there must be something wrong with her. Which is also a way in which her investigation is denied in the film by the other characters. This takes the form of a kind of male conspiracy, of a collective male prejudice against the idea that a woman could be right – that if a woman is saying something disagreeable she must be neurotic. The 'opposition of disbelief' sets her up as overwrought and upset at her best friend's condition, as unreasonable and paranoid – 'shown' by the way she does not react as a woman should, but yet *over*-reacting, as a woman would. Harris comments after their second interview 'Women. Christ', and the psychiatrist's report is that she's 'rather paranoid and upset'. This locks into the exploitation of the connotations of the independent women, the idea that she's a problem to those around her, i.e. to men. A sense of conspiracy builds up and is developed, for example, in the scene where Mark is exhorted by the Chief Resident (whose job he hopes, and is encouraged to believe, he will get) to 'Do something about her', though Mark can only repeat that 'she likes to do things her own way'. Importantly, these scenes are unknown to Susan; the audience has a privileged position of knowledge: of an apparent conspiracy to control her, to stop her investigation, on the basis that she is really simply paranoid.

The scene in which Susan is apparently followed by a suspicious-looking man (who later proves to be the hired killer) culminates this narrative strategy. Following the frustrations of that day, she leaves to go home and finds that her car won't start. It's too much and she collapses in rage and frustration, uselessly beating the roof of the car with her fists, her aggression ineffectual and defeatist, the position of victim. The violence emphasising her lack of control, her 'feminine' position. The scene is shot to encourage our cinematic identification with her position, alternating close and medium-long shots of Susan, from a position to the side of her, with only a few reverse shots close-up from the other side of the car. We see her turn around and notice something, and only then are we given a full reverse shot which reveals a man standing in shadows opposite her. Susan hurries to the subway and as the train pulls away we turn with her to see the face of the same man, left standing on the platform. The scene suggests that Susan suspects this man tampered with her car, is following her; we are led to identify with her projection of threat from this man although such a reading is not yet narratively supported but could simply be further evidence of Susan's paranoid and hence unfounded fears. Thus the scene both introduces the first mark of the 'true' conspiracy and completes the construction of Susan as paranoid: she goes to see Mark who reassures her that her car is always breaking down, and then 'proves' the absurdity of her theories of carbon monoxide poisoning as the cause of the coma cases when they go and check the operating room's equipment.

They then go away for the weekend (as Dr Harris suggested), for Susan to 'recover'; where the narrative requires it Susan is weak and 'feminine', against character. The idyllic weekend extends this, with images of the classic romantic couple and the portrayal of love and tenderness within conventional male/active, female/passive roles. Susan has been put back, in place. This sequence is, though, a false resolution, a hiatus, which seems narratively unnecessary (and unfortunate in terms of a progressive reading of the film). But it does serve to complete the 'male conspiracy', and to hold a tension about whether it really is 'all over'. An opposition is set up between the safety of this sequence where Susan is 'normal' and the scenes where she is actively pursuing her investigation – the end of the film repeating this structure with Susan's rescue by Mark, the last shots showing her prostrate on the stretcher, her hand held by Mark, ceasing to be 'independent' once the narrative ends.

The weekend has one important function in advancing the investigation: passing the Jefferson Institute, Susan makes Mark stop the car and she goes in to have a look, the camera revealing very well the ominous architecture of the building. She is met by a woman who informs her that 'there is no staff' and that 'I am in charge', telling Susan that she must visit during official times. Here, where Susan will find the real conspiracy (it is a long-term care hospital for brain-damaged patients to which all the coma cases have been transferred, and is the locale for the auction of 'spare parts') she finds another woman; this balances her as protagonist, setting the two up as adversaries. But even more it avoids rupturing the 'male conspiracy' by not presenting at this point a man as bearer of the real conspiracy, but a woman instead. (Susan's assailant cannot stand for the conspiracy itself, since he is simply an agent rather than a locus for the conspiracy. Her ability to deal with him, but not with the true locus, Harris, is important.)

My argument has been, therefore, that suspense is created within the film around a second, 'false' conspiracy, while the true one is elsewhere; it is not in fact Dr George, despite the clues foisted on us when the camera picks him out, staring at Susan in the coffee-room, or in the lift before her final meeting with Harris; nor is it Mark, whose suspicious phone-call when she arrives at his flat after discovering the gas line and disposing of the assassin, was actually to her mother. There is excitement around Susan's successful engagements with the 'enemy' but anxiety that she has not dealt with the main enemy. This has a number of consequences. It produces a certain confusion in the ending since the 'false' conspiracy is not resolved, but disappears with the emergence and resolution of the 'real' conspiracy, located in the figure of Dr Harris who can now become the sole bearer of the 'false' conspiracy as well. In addition, the basis for a feminist appropriation of Susan Wheeler's role as a strong woman is radically changed since to extrapolate just this element from the narrative now becomes a wilful denial of the film's work. It is not a question of recuperation, however, since it is impossible to make any such separation of a progressive content from the narrative strategy as a whole; not only is it not a story 'about' an independent woman, but that independence itself is the mode of constructing her as victim. What is interesting in *Coma* is not any element of progressivity nor its supposed recuperation of such an element, but the way in which the 'independence' of Susan Wheeler is constructed in order to fulfil a certain narrative strategy through which a different kind of suspense and tension (the holding off of the solution through a 'false' conspiracy) can be created than with a male role – commercially a 'good gimmick' with the added bonus that it is 'socially relevant'. The political evaluation of the film must be affected by this understanding of its filmic process in terms of the production and circulation of images and meanings. Thus the problem, politically, of *Coma* is not that it recuperates its progressive meaning (or any other) but that the meaning and image produced within it can be judged inadequate and unacceptable to the feminist political project.

It has been argued that the 'false' conspiracy is only possible because the protagonist is a woman and that this strategy is crucial to the effectivity of the narrative as suspense. *Coma* can now be considered in relation to its specific production within this narrative strategy, and the consequent implications for the construction of its representation of a woman protagonist. To do this it is necessary to relate the 'false' conspiracy to the narrative production of suspense, which will require an examination of the notion of suspense itself. Part 2 ('Discussion of *Coma* part 2', *m/f* no. 4, 1980, pp. 57–69) will show that to reconsider *Coma* as a suspense thriller is to reorganise the assumptions of knowledge in the film; Susan Wheeler will then become victim to the events she seeks to engage with – the film becomes about how little she knows rather than how much. As a character she is 'strong' but as an actant within the narrative she is 'weak'. And this is a narrative strategy across the film as a whole rather than in 'moments' of suspense. Certain other questions will also be taken up: that of the relation of the spectator to the protagonist in the suspense film, of the forms of identification in play and how the *gender* of the protagonist might be implicated as a factor in the position of the spectator in relation to the film. These will be addressed in the second part of this article in the context of *Coma*'s narrative juggling of its suspense structure and its female protagonist.

Notes

1. Charles Derry, 'Towards a Categorisation of Film Narrative', in *Film Reader* no. 2, p. 111.
2. The issue of spectacle, of the look within film, will be taken up in the second part of this article in relation to the place of the spectator within the structure of suspense as paranoia. Here I am referring to the concern with *display* in the film, the display of bodies, the revelation and framing of characters through glass doors, windows, characters seemingly discovered for us by the camera as it cuts to a new shot. There is also the spectacle of the revelation of the conspiracy, we *see* Susan discover how the comas are produced in patients, we follow her through the innards of the hospital as she traces the gas line; in particular we see her discover the real nature of the Jefferson Institute as she *watches* the removal of organs from a patient *after* we, but not Susan, have seen the head nurse conduct an auction of 'spare parts'.
3. Thornhill's place as one of knowledge is explicitly undermined at the beginning of the film, to be 'refound' at the end. For a discussion of this oedipal journey, see Raymond Bellour, 'Le Blocage Symbolique', in *Communications* 23 (1975), and Kari Hanet's summary of this article, 'Bellour on *North by Northwest*', Edinburgh '76 Magazine, pp. 43–9.
4. The term 'protagonist', indicating the chief actor, character or combatant, is used here in preference to 'heroine' to describe Geneviève Bujold's role as Dr Susan Wheeler in order to emphasise the narrative function of the hero; the 'heroine' is not normally the female equivalent of 'hero'.
5. The film is full of half-completed narrative strategies – the 'horror' of the hospital setting, the autopsy and cadavers, etc., the melodrama of the two lovers, the theme of medical ethics in relation to definitions of death and 'spare-part surgery'.

'Lianna' and the Lesbians of Art Cinema

MANDY MERCK

IN 1977, Caroline Sheldon's pioneering study of 'Lesbians and Film' noted that art cinema had gone 'relatively unexplored by feminists given that feminist film culture emerged at a time when Hollywood was the cinema being assessed'.[1] Interestingly, this remains true, despite (or perhaps because of?) that cinema's increasing deployment of feminist and lesbian themes and its consumption by feminist audiences. (Contemporary examples might range across films with specifically lesbian themes or implications, like *Another Way* (1982) or *The Bostonians* (1984), to the broader considerations of female friendship in those directed by von Trotta.)

In the face of this neglect, I want to argue here that if lesbianism hadn't already existed, art cinema might have invented it. To a cinema which affects an attitude of high seriousness in matters sexual, the lesbian romance affords a double benefit. It provides a sufficient degree of difference from dominant cinematic representations of sex and sexuality to be seen as 'realistic', 'courageous', 'questioning', '(saved) from Hollywood fudging', 'true to itself' (all terms from reviews of *Lianna*). Yet it does this by offering – quite literally – more of the same (the same being that old cinema equation 'woman = sexuality'[2] which art cinema, despite its differences with Hollywood, has rarely forsaken).

Narrative cinema has traditionally looked to the figure of the woman to signify sexual pleasure, sexual problems, sexuality itself – placing her 'as erotic object for the characters within the screen story, and as erotic object for the spectator within the auditorium'.[3] And none of those differences upon which art cinema founded its fortunes (realism, cultural specificity, authorial expressivity, episodic narratives structured by symbolic congruence or psychological re-action rather than linear ones driven by a protagonist's activity) preclude the eroticisation of the female body.[4] If anything, art cinema heightens that effect. Its ancestry in movements like the French avant-garde of the 20s provided connections (notably via the interventions of Dada and the Surrealists) with the erotic conventions of fine art, including the female nude. Thus Man Ray's 1928 *Etoile de Mer*, which intercuts the

166

phallic regalia of skyscrapers, chimneys and starfish tentacles with the figure of a woman seen naked on a bed through frosted glass. (The compositions and conventions of European oil painting persist in art films as varied as Bertolucci's *1900* and Godard's *Passion*. *Coup de foudre* presents its nudity largely in terms of representation: Madeleine is an amateur artist whose studio is filled with figures of naked women. In an intriguing reversal of the film's recurring use of an onlooker in scenes of sexual intimacy, her sculptures seem to watch the characters.)

These high culture values were available for invocation in the debates which surrounded European cinema between the Wars. At a time when the Hays Code forbade representations of nudity and sexual activity in Hollywood films, the French cinema, for instance, found a defence from censorship on the grounds of the 'adult' and 'realistic' nature of art. When the resumption of international trade and the anti-trust suits of the 40s relaxed Hollywood's grip on US exhibition, European films were able to capitalise on their reputation for an aesthetically-defensible explicitness in the American market. By the mid-60s to mid-70s, much of this work – from *Last Tango in Paris* to *The Night Porter* to sundry Pasolini films – had coalesced into an explicitly erotic form: the soft-core art film.[5]

It isn't surprising, then, that art film titles (*Les Biches, Rome Open City, The Conformist, Les Stances à Sophie*) figure extensively in Caroline Sheldon's filmography. Not surprising either, given the period's interest in positive images and female authorship, are her objections to the institution for its stereotypically 'mysterious or childlike' women and 'the male-defined world' of its narratives. But where Sheldon decries this cinema in favour of women's experimental work (Oxenberg, Deren, Dulac, the scripting of *Céline and Julie Go Boating*), other lesbian critics of the late 70s sought the naturalism urged by Susan Griffin:

> This is from a film I want to see. It is a film made by a woman about two women who live together. This is a scene from their daily lives. It is a film about the small daily transformations which some women experience, allow, tend to, and which have been invisible in this male culture. In this film, two women touch. In all ways possible they show knowledge of what they have lived through and what they will yet do, and one sees in their movements how they have survived. I am certain that one day this film will exist.[6]

With its penchant for the 'real' and its low-budget bias towards small casts and intimate settings, art cinema has an awful tendency to grant such wishes – and seven years later [1984] close approximations of this description have arrived in our cinemas. *Coup de foudre/At First Sight* (France, 1983, directed by Diane Kurys) might have been

tailored to Griffin's design, while *Lianna* (US, 1982, directed by John
Sayles), though more problematic in its male writer-director, has the
advantage of an explicitly lesbian narrative. (Reviewers tend to deal
with the physical ambiguity in *Coup de foudre* by citing the director's
own statement that 'it was a little more than a friendship and a little less
than a passion between them'.[7] This extra-textual 'evidence' itself
reflects the conventions of art cinema, guaranteeing the film's realism
with the biography of the director's mother; placing it as a 'prequel' to
the also autobiographical *Diabolo Menthe* in the director's canon; and
directing us towards a 'broad' – non-lesbian – reading of the film.)

By contrast, *Lianna* – as a product not only of the United States but
of a writer-director with a considerable background in Hollywood
exploitation (*Piranha*, *Alligator*, *The Howling*) – may seem a perverse
example of a cinema which originated as an alternative to American
dominance. However, subsequent events, notably the importation of
art elements into Hollywood's New American Cinema and the
development of independent production elsewhere in the US, have
seen the rise of indigenous American art cinema(s). But even had
Lianna lacked clear national precedents, its narrative, style and
publicity strategies are markedly within the art cinema tradition.

The chief of these may be the sort of realism which tends to produce
the plaudits cited above, particularly the film's very knowing dialogue
about sex. Where *Coup de foudre*'s 'honesty' resides in its correspon-

Lianna

dence with an 'actual' unspoken desire, that of *Lianna* is emphasised by the extent to which it is voiced. From her first tentative recollections of teenage homosexual experimentation, the heroine's speaking of her desires becomes an important part of the story, with her candour positively contrasted to others' euphemisms. This has endeared *Lianna* to critics who regard *verbal* sexual explicitness as a crucial part of the practice of 'coming out'. Penny Ashbrook, for example, remarks on 'Lianna's recognising and embracing her lesbian sexuality in a process of experiment, excitement and discovery, encapsulated in the moment of comic shock when we see her announcing to the mirror, "Lianna Massey eats pussy", immediately after her night with Cindy, trying the words out and pleased by the result. It's another reminder of the physical reality of sex – none of the obscure tickling of *Personal Best* here – and an assertion of the film's recognition of the importance of naming.'[8]

The paradox that this very naming, this speaking of sex, historically made 'possible a strong advance of social controls into this area of "perversity" ', to cite Foucault,[9] remains an important problem for gay politics. My own point is merely that both this politics and art cinema are constituted within discourses which privilege the body, particularly its sexual functions, as a source of truth about social relations in general. The connection which Ashbrook suggests between these moments of 'physical reality' in *Lianna* and 'lesbian experience' *per se* participates in the art film's general impulse towards allegory – in which everything tends to mean something else.

The result is to assign that cinematic convention, the love scene, a particular symbolic function: the ability to represent 'lesbian experience'. (If this seems completely natural, consider whether cinema's heterosexual embraces function in the same way. . . .) Ironically, critics like Penny Ashbrook, and Ruby Rich before her, reject readings of lesbian scenarios which treat them as 'a metaphor, a coded text about something else, something other than what appears on screen'.[10] Yet Rich, in her assertion that *Maedchen in Uniform* 'should have been a warning to lesbians then living in Germany', and Ashbrook, when she suggests that 'a film can be about lesbianism and also throw light on universal aspects of human experience'[11], produce their own extrapolations on film texts. And how can they avoid doing so? For a film, like any other representation, is *always* a coded text about something other than what appears on screen.

Art cinema both intensifies and reveals this process, foregrounding its own encoded status. In its suppression of action in favour of visual style, in its display of authorial signatures of technique and theme, and in its deployment of enigma in everything from narrative to spatio-temporal codes to diegetic ontology (is this really happening or is she dreaming it?), this cinema positively incites allegorical readings. As we emerge from the Gate or the Plaza or the Screen, interpretation goes into overdrive (to the sound of loose ends being tied): what was the director's message? what did such-and-such symbolise? what did it all really mean? Indeed, these acts of exegesis are one of the chief pleasures art cinema offers, especially to audiences schooled in traditional literary criticism, with its own emphasis on authorial expression and textual unity – and also to the similarly trained reviewers of our newspapers and magazines.

Thus, Philip French in *The Observer* (5 February 1984):

> The film's subject is only superficially lesbianism and sexuality. It could have been a religious experience or the discovery of a new vocation that made Lianna take the vital step. What the picture is about is the sudden confrontation of a highly responsible person with the demands of self, the problem of being forced to establish an independent life after years of emotional dependency and the acceptance of our essential human loneliness.

Cynthia Rose in the *New Musical Express* (3 February 1984):

> It's not a 'gay film' or a 'feminist film' or a 'low-budget cult film'. It's just a modest and realistic portrayal of the costs which can be inherent in decision-making.

David Castell in the *Sunday Telegraph* (5 February 1984):

> The result is a delightful, gentle and quietly questioning film, more about starting over – in a new flat, a new relationship, a new sexual role – than about homosexuality *per se*.

Phillip Bergson in *What's On and Where to Go in London* (2 February 1984):

> . . . *Lianna* is a humane and courageous focus on the endless mystery of love and sex.

and Virginia Dignam in the *Morning Star* (10 February 1984):

> Ostensibly the film is about lesbianism. . . . Under the superficial story of a wife and mother of two leaving her husband to live with another woman, is a whole minefield of emotions.

The extraordinary unanimity of these responses undoubtedly owes a great deal to the reviewers' aversion to lesbianism, but it is also a product of art cinema, which characteristically solicits essential humanist readings founded on psychologistic saws and authorial (i.e. the director's) declarations of a given film's general relevance.

John Sayles is not only credited as writer/director/editor on *Lianna*; he also performed in it (in the not-really-reflexive role of a lecherous lecturer in film-making). Furthermore, Maggie Renzi, with whom he lives, functioned as co-producer and played the role of Sheila. This personal investment in the film was literalised by financial backing from both Sayles' and Renzi's mothers; but low budgets (here $340,000) are anyway understood as indicators of individual artistry in the cinema – no Hollywood assembly-line for *Lianna*. The film was presented in the press as Sayles' 'personal statement', and his own interpretative comments granted considerable weight. And as he frequently observed, 'I chose *Lianna* because people I knew, both gay and straight, have been through the same experiences.'[12]

Art cinema's emphasis on character and psychology (often manifested in narratives which deal explicitly with breakdown and therapy, such as Bergman's *Persona*) tends to focus attention on the individual protagonist rather than groups or classes. The realism of such films is measured in characterological terms – motivation, consistency, depth. Thus Penny Ashbrook praises the scene in which Lianna recalls her adolescent love for a camp counsellor as giving the character 'a personal lesbian history that is echoed later when we are told that she feels she has always felt "that way" without having realised it',[13] while *Jump Cut* reviewer, Lisa DiCaprio, criticises the film's 'one-dimensional characters lacking in emotional depth'.[14] Where reviewers fail to discover the appropriate degree of motivation for Lianna's sudden romance with Ruth, their explanations switch – in typical art cinema terms – from the individual to 'humanity': 'why Lianna loves women isn't any more explicable than why some women love men – anyone loves anyone, for that matter . . .'.[15] As David Bordwell observes, 'The art film is non-classical in that it foregrounds deviations from the classical norm – there are certain gaps and problems. But these very deviations are placed, re-situated as realism (in life things happen this way) or authorial commentary (the ambiguity is symbolic).'[16]

These readings of Lianna may also be encouraged by the film's deployment of its academic *mise en scène*. As Tom Ryall has argued, the art cinema reverses 'the subordination of formal qualities to narrative clarity which characterises the classical cinema'.[17] Here, the college setting – with its background of campus, lecture rooms, playing fields and faculty parties – is particularly emphasised. Lianna, the once and present student, leaves a male lecturer for a female one – a childless child psychologist whose subject suggests a related process of maturation on the part of her lover/pupil/would-be research assistant. Furthermore, Lianna's (homo-)sexual initiation (set off, remember, by her own recollection of adolescent experimentation) is paralleled by scenes in which her children read about sex together and by one in which her son discusses the sexual behaviour of *his* teacher. The film's linking of sexual initiation to teaching in general is underlined by Ruth's pointed parting remark to her evening class (and a reverse shot of Lianna): 'You can learn from plenty of other people'.

To present a woman's inauguration into lesbianism under the aegis of the sentimental education is to evoke the sort of 'live and learn' aphorisms cited above. Stories about the initiation of a younger lover by an elder often suggest more about the power of age and experience than that invested in gender or sexual norms. Flaubert's young lover, after all, was a heterosexual man. . . . In *Lianna*, the parallels with heterosexual romance are underscored in the intercutting of Lianna's final night with Ruth and a dance sequence in which a man and woman part.

Ironically, Lianna's story can only signify *everyone's* experience by remaining peculiarly ahistorical, unspecified, thus troubling art cinema's canons of realism. The heroine seems remarkably immature, even for a coming-of-age narrative, because, despite living the present day US, she – like the film – seems scarcely to have registered the gay or women's movements. The contending forces which would threaten the representative status of any single character have to be masked off: 'Lianna and Ruth's relation exists in a social and political vacuum.'[18]

But if Lianna really is 'about' learning, what does the heroine learn? To love women? (Ruth: 'You love women, Lianna, not just me.') That she always loved women? (Sandy: 'She said it wasn't new, that she had always felt that way.') That loving women won't save her from unhappiness? (Lianna: 'I thought, when I found somebody, every-thing would be all right.') These are the lessons recited in the dialogue, but they ignore another one: the heroine's induction into the film's own voyeurism. From her first, wide-eyed gaze at the moonlit posterior of the woman student she discovers with her husband (a sight which she later reprises to Ruth in her story about watching the camp counsellors: 'we could see his bare bottom shining white in the moonlight'), to her eager gaze at passing women the morning after her first visit to the lesbian bar, Lianna learns to look. As in *Coup de Foudre*, with its strongly-marked looks (stares, in the case of Madeleine) between the two women when they first meet after the school recital, Lianna's romance with Ruth is conducted through emphatically visual exchanges (in the classroom, in the coffee bar, after their first dinner, at the pool, in bed).

Both films match this diegetic perspective to that of the spectator in mirror scenes, in which the characters turn their backs to the camera and look with us at their own semi-clad bodies (Lianna, when considering whether to discard her bra for her first date with Ruth; Lena and Madeleine while dressing after *their* swim). Both films also write public spectacles of femininity into their narratives: Lena and Madeleine watch women model fashions in a Paris salon; Lianna watches the woman dancer as she cues the lights.

In a similar way, the sexual curiosity incited by both films is rendered innocent by their use of children as both fascinated onlookers and auditors. Lena's husband – who experiences the film's one, very displaced, primal scene when he interrupts Madeleine and her art teacher dressing after sex – may 'wonder who's kissing her now', the soldiers may spy on Lena's seduction on the train, but then so do the little girls when they watch the maid kissing her boyfriend ('Look, they're licking tongues!'). And Lianna's husband Dick only asks *his* question ('How was it? Like a drugstore paperback?') after we've seen her children consult a variety of texts on what appears to be the film's unseen revelation – oral sex: 'Lianna Massey eats pussy . . .'.

It is this legitimation of the feminine spectacle which makes lesbianism such a gift to art cinema. When Lianna complains that 'everybody's staring at us' in the My Way bar, she's right: not only because the film cuts repeatedly from her own fascinated gaze to pairs of eyes in extreme close-up, but also because *we're* staring. The scene's upbeat rock accompaniment displaces other, more diegetic sounds without adding the distraction of contradictory or particularly pre-occupying lyrics – thereby permitting us to concentrate solely on the sight of women dancing together.

This displacement of diegetic sound occurs whenever Lianna and Ruth make love. Their first sex scene runs the gamut of display techniques, and also is the most 'arty', the most redolent of certain European films: blue filter, slow motion, montage cutting, bodily fragmentation. Nor does the soundtrack disturb the spectacle (as it does, for instance, by its volume in the bed scene of Akerman's *Je, Tu, Il, Elle*). Instead, a soft murmur of dubbed endearments is voiced over (under, really) in English and French. (The unsuitability of the latter for sex in New Jersey led one reviewer to conclude that Ruth must teach, not psychology, but modern languages!) If, as Tom Ryall remarks, ' "foreignness" (is) perhaps the most generalised characteristic' of art cinema, this may explain its use here.[19] In any case, the soundtrack's low level of volume and intelligibility again enables the visual register to assume pre-eminence.

It can be argued that both the bar and bed scenes integrate the relay of looks in the first instance and the mannered style of the second into an overall theme of initiation, as experienced from the viewpoint of the central character. Thus, the first sequence of glances in the bar seems unfriendly, even menacing to the anxious initiate. But when Lianna relaxes into a swaying *pas de deux* with one of the previously staring strangers, the looks are reprised – with smiles. A similar case can be made for the stylistic devices so fulsomely employed in the first love scene. Their emphatically arty connotations may convey suggestions of an extreme, almost disorienting ecstasy, as well as a certain ritual character (slow purposeful gestures, incantation, low light).

My purpose here is not to rule out such interpretations, but to remind readers that such switches between omniscient and subjective perspectives are characteristic art cinema fare; and that arguments which fit such scenes into an overall intelligibility are simply beside the point. These devices may indeed 'make sense' within the narrative – they may have been consciously intended to do so by an 'author'. But they also renew the sense, the meaningfulness, of that venerable tradition in which the woman functions as the object of both the gaze of a film's characters and of its spectators.

What are the consequences of a cinema which frees the woman's look in order to vindicate that of the spectator? In classical Hollywood, the heroine's investigations trespass the male prerogative and are punished accordingly.[20] In art cinema, lesbianism has also been punished, often by death (*Les Biches*, *The Conformist*, *Another Way*). Although Lianna, Lena and Madeleine survive, they suffer. They suffer for their stares in a way which we spectators escape: our looks are not returned by their mirrors, our curiosity is gratified without jeopardy. Ultimately, these characters suffer as the objects of a cinema which cannot come to terms with its own pleasures. (Witness Sayles' own defiance when discussing queries at the London Film Festival over why he hadn't made the film about homosexual men. . . .[21]) Despite Dick Massey's classroom quotation of Heisenberg's Uncertainty Principle to debunk the 'purity' of documentary film, *Lianna* – like so much of art cinema – remains studiously unaware of the effects of its own observations.

(This article was commissioned and written in 1984.)

Notes

1. Caroline Sheldon, 'Lesbians and Film: Some Thoughts', in Richard Dyer, ed., *Gays and Film* (London: British Film Institute, 1980), p. 18.
2. Laura Mulvey and Colin MacCabe, 'Images of Woman, Images of Sexuality', in Colin MacCabe, ed., *Godard: Images, Sounds, Politics* (London: British Film Institute and Macmillan, 1980), p. 91.
3. Laura Mulvey, 'Visual Pleasure and Narrative Cinema', *Screen* vol. 16 no. 3, 1975, p. 11.
4. The above equation is actually deduced from the films of Godard, in Mulvey and MacCabe, op. cit.
5. See Steve Neale, 'Art Cinema as Institution', *Screen* vol. 22 no. 1, 1981, pp. 30–33.
6. Susan Griffin, 'Transformations', *Sinister Wisdom* no. 3, 1977, quoted in *Jump Cut* no. 24/25, p. 21.
7. See John Gillett, 'Coup de Foudre', *Monthly Film Bulletin* vol. 50 no. 598, November 1983, p. 301.
8. Penny Ashbrook, 'Lesbians at the Movies – Who's Watching Who' (to be included in a possibly forthcoming book entitled *Changing Gear*, to be published by Tyneside Cinema).

9. Michel Foucault, *The History of Sexuality* vol. 1 (London: Allen Lane, 1979), p. 101.

10. Ruby Rich, 'From Repressive Tolerance to Erotic Liberation: *Maedchen in Uniform*', in Mary Ann Doane, Patricia Mellencamp and Linda Williams, eds., *Re-Vision* (University Publications of America, Inc., Frederick, MD, in association with The American Film Institute, 1984), p. 100.

11. Penny Ashbrook, op. cit.

12. Quoted in James Woudhusen, 'The Un-American Movie That Shook the Box Office', *Sunday Times Magazine*, 5 February 1984, p. 57.

13. Penny Ashbrook, op. cit.

14. Lisa DiCaprio, 'Liberal Lesbianism', *Jump Cut* 29, p. 45.

15. Barbara Presley Noble, *In These Times*, 9–22 March, 1983, p. 13, cited by DiCaprio, op. cit.

16. David Bordwell, 'The Art Cinema as a Mode of Film Practice', *Film Criticism* vol. 4 no. 1, Fall 1979, pp. 56–64.

17. Tom Ryall, 'Art House, Smart House', *The Movie* no. 90, 1981, p. 8.

18. Lisa DiCaprio, op. cit., p. 46.

19. Tom Ryall, op. cit., p. 7. (The exoticisation of the lesbian is parodied in the recent horror film, *The Hunger*, when the Susan Sarandon character attempts to explain the unusual attentions of vampire Catherine Deneuve: 'She's *European*.')

20. See Mary Ann Doane, 'The "Woman's Film": Possession and Address', in Doane, Mellencamp and Williams, op. cit., p. 72.

21. See Paul Kerr, 'Web-Footed in Harlem', *Monthly Film Bulletin* vol. 51 no. 600, January 1984, p. 28, where Sayles is quoted: 'And finally, I don't give a shit. In *Secaucus Seven*, the men were naked and the women weren't, and there was a point to that.'

PART FOUR

Exhibition and Distribution

Introduction

IN AUGUST 1984 the Ritzy cinema in Brixton had a festive women-only screening of *Supergirl*, which opened with a set from the Mint Juleps, an all-women acapella group who sing mainly 60s numbers like 'Jimmy Mac'. Although *Supergirl* had moved to local cinemas all over London the previous week, the screening was packed, with women sitting in the aisles, and everyone cheering and booing at appropriate moments. The evening couldn't have happened ten years earlier – a women-only screening of a Hollywood film at which the power of the collectivity could accept, reject and transform the product which had obviously been made with half an eye on us as potential audience.

The history which made such an event possible is one of political struggle in which there has been a whole range of interventions by women *as* women in the distribution and exhibition of films. From the first festival-based events in 1972 – the Women's Event at the Edinburgh Film Festival and the New York International Women's Film Festival – through the founding of feminist film magazines (*Women and Film*, 1972, USA; *Frauen und Film*, 1974, West Germany; *Camera Obscura*, 1976, USA), and the development of feminist film criticism, we now in Britain have two feminist distributors (Cinema of Women and Circles) and many repertory cinemas operating women-only screenings. This section tries to document some of these interventions in distribution and exhibition which have taken place between, on the one hand, the general growth of feminist cultural politics and, on the other, the explosion of feminist film-making since the early 70s.

To be shown in public, a film must usually be placed with a distribution company, from whom it will be hired by theatrical (cinema) and other exhibitors. Some film groups – like Cinema Action, and film workshops – distribute their own films, but films bought by, for example, a relatively large radical distributor like The Other Cinema are likely to reach larger audiences. Usually, distributors buy the rights on a particular film, sometimes just a print. So before there is any change of seeing a film outside a film festival, a whole set of decisions have been made. It's no good trying to run a 'women's film' season if none of the films you are interested in are in distribution. Feminist intervention in both exhibition and distribution has affected not only the availability of particular films, but also the type of exhibition films receive. For example, it is now possible to see the 1931

German film, *Maedchen in Uniform*, directed by Leontine Sagan – one of the few women to direct a feature film in Weimar Germany. This film, with its reputation as a tale of lesbian love, was widely shown in women's film festivals before it acquired a British distributor (Cinema of Women).[1] Similarly, Circles have now acquired *Olivia*, directed in 1950 by Jacqueline Audry and premièred in Britain as part of the 1983 GLC 'September in the Pink' Festival.[2]

Changes in availability also mean changes in the way in which the history of cinema, and women's place in this history, are constructed.

Supergirl

At the level of representation, both *Maedchen in Uniform* and *Olivia* offer narratives concerned with passion in communities of women; both are set in boarding schools, and are exceptional for their lack of heterosexual narrative motivation. Both films are directed by women, and are now available because of feminist interest. Directors such as Wendy Toye and Dorothy Arzner have become more 'present' in film history. The mainstream television review programme, *Film 84*, used Judy/Maureen O'Hara's 'voyeurs' speech from Arzner's *Dance Girl Dance* – a part of the film highlighted by feminist criticism – as a prelude to a review of Sally Potter's *The Gold Diggers* (1983) in order to indicate that she was not the first woman director.[3]

The ways in which feminists have organised in relation to the cinema are drawn from the political practices of the Women's Liberation Movement. Women have worked – usually in small, avowedly non-hierarchical groups – to explore and promote the interests of women as a gender group. Sometimes, as the first piece in this section (the women's statement from the 1979 Arts Council *Film as Film* exhibition) indicates, this has led groups of women to refuse to participate in events in which they feel that there has not been a structural commitment to feminist principles. The political choices involved in this type of refusal are often painful, as the result can be the absence (rather than token presence) of feminist and women's work. However, many women in different circumstances have used this strategy of refusal, and it seems important to document it in a collection of this type.

Partly as a sequel to the *Film as Film* statement, I have included Arts Council programme notes by Lis Rhodes and Felicity Sparrow, both signatories of the Statement. These notes come from a 1983 booklet published by the Arts Council which packages four short films by women film-makers as a potential programme for exhibitors. Putting together several short avant-garde films in this way provides a particular context in which to view each film, and also offers an opportunity for an audience to make links between the films. It is a strategy which, in combining key historical works with more contemporary ones, attempts to find an audience for each.

Second-wave feminism has undoubtedly offered support – and audiences – to women working within the art sector of independent film, such as Joyce Wieland, Annabel Nicolson, Lis Rhodes, Margaret Tait and Marjorie Keller, but this support seems often to be premised on the extent to which the work explicitly engages with feminist or women's concerns.[4] Thus, women working in film, but outside the agit-prop or feature area, are subjected to two different forms of pressure, both of which appear to militate against abstract and art-identified film work. Firstly there is the institutional masculinity, not only of art schools and film training, but of the cultural identity of The

Artist.[5] The second pressure, which often arises from the answer or response to the first, comes out of feminism itself, where there are very strong prejudices against difficult and avant-garde work, usually on grounds of accessibility. The demand is for work that is relevant and can be related to (all) women's lives, the pressure being towards representational work. As a distributor, Circles has specialised in 'art-identified', or formally innovative, film work by women, as well as pursuing women's history as film-makers, with films like *Olivia* and *The Smiling Madame Beudet*.[6]

Cinema of Women, the distributor of *A Question of Silence*, has always been more explicitly movement-oriented, as is clear from their account in the Appendix. Both distributors have insisted always that their work be seen as complementary and both have been involved in supplying films for exhibition events like the Norwich Women's Film Weekend and groups such as the Birmingham Women and Film Consortium.[7] The account of the Norwich weekend here shows clearly the changing political climate in relation to exhibition for women. It also points to some of the issues – such as choice, availability, independent/popular, local/national – that face organisers of exhibition spaces that are congenial to women.

Frequently, 'congenial' has meant women-only. The early women-and-film events were, for many of us, the first time that we had been part of a consciously gendered audience. Certain genres of films have always been made and marketed for female audiences, and when you go to see them you watch with a mainly female audience. This is not the same experience as watching with an audience which is conscious of itself as having come together, on the basis of gender, as a new political collectivity to consider the way in which we are/were constructed and represented in the cinema. Watching films in this type of audience changes the atmosphere in which we view and can affect the way we understand and look at films. What might be a suppressed snort in another context can now be a loud laugh. Suddenly you can get an intimation of the power and pleasure boys feel as they guffaw their way through horror films. There are circumstances in which the audience can be 'stronger' than the text.

The question which underlies so much of the debate in the early part of this book, 'what does/should a feminist film look like?', becomes transformed if we pay attention to the power of the audience in this way. Many of these debates were informed by the assumption that meaning is something which is already and immutably there in a film text. Thus a particular device – for example, showing the camera, or the process of editing, to indicate that the film is constructed – has a particular political value, related to its assumed meaning. This is not to suggest that anything can mean anything, but that – particularly when it comes to what can rather crudely be called 'the politics of a representation' – significance is not fixed. The context of viewing and the constitution of the audience can work against what might seem the obvious imperatives of the text. Thus, a heterosexual pornographic text, one which is organised to achieve masculine sexual arousal, will generally have a rather different significance to feminists viewing in a women-only context. Similarly, but less frequently specified, it is a white feminist reading of a film like *Imitation of Life* which sees its central concerns as those of family melodrama, rather than the construction of racial difference.

The arguments to set up women-only viewing contexts and film distribution have been accompanied by critical attempts to theorise the place of female spectators – to gender the spectator/audience so often assumed in criticism, and to begin to understand how gender positioning may affect viewing, identification and pleasure.[8] How do women watch and enjoy films? However, this unitary 'women', although it marks a crucial political naming, is much too simple, and forgets that anyone in the gender category 'woman' is also socially constructed in other categories such as social class and ethnicity. It is important that we develop accounts of the way in which different women, and different groups of women, watch films which recognise the diversity and heterogeneity – and different determinations – of cultural experience.[9]

The 'Notes' on the Black Women and Representation Workshops held in London in 1984 document part of this process. As well as continuing the critical examination of the reductive and repetitive range of representations of black women imposed by white film-makers and industries, these workshops also aimed, through discussion and practical sessions, to work on counter strategies. Unlike all the rest of the articles in this book, parts of this dossier include an address specifically to black women. The 'difference' of this address, which has its own political urgency, also serves to remind white readers and writers like myself of our complicity in the construction of white experiences as 'experience' and black experiences as unitary and 'other', thus constituting and sustaining the 'natural' dominance of white ethnic identity. The difference of the address marks precisely the way in which white feminism's inclusive 'we' conceals its exclusions.

Historically, the cinema has always been seen as a particularly effective means of propaganda. With what accuracy it is difficult to gauge. However, for feminists – as for other social and political groups – this has raised two related issues. Firstly the question of organised intervention – through, for example, leafleting, picketing and, sometimes, the disruption of screenings – against films which are seen as particularly misogynist or offensive to women. The campaigns against *Dressed to Kill* in Britain in 1981/2 are one example of this type of activity, a mobilisation against the perceived role of a particular film in reinforcing and perpetuating dominant ideas about women.[10] Secondly, there is the question of how to use films to extend both the accessibility and influence of feminist ideas.

Sheila Whitaker discusses both these issues in her article which draws on the experience of programming one of the subsidised repertory cinemas in Britain in the wake of the *Dressed to Kill* campaign.

This section closes with Jane Root's account of the distribution of *A Question of Silence* by Cinema of Women. Most of this collection is historical, and offers documentation of the 1970s – the first decade of widespread feminist activity around film (*pace* the pioneers at the beginning of the century). Jane Root's article, in contrast, seems very 80s, revealing the contradictory intersection of the necessity for survival in Thatcher's Britain with the political ideals of 'counter-cultural' collectives. The description of the strategies used by Cinema of Women to negotiate the institutional determinants on a film's existence *for audiences* (as opposed to in the can) brings together many of the questions and terms that have been circulating in this book.

Notes

1. The role of criticism in circulating knowledge of these hidden histories is obviously important. On *Maedchen*, see Caroline Sheldon, 'Lesbians and Film: some thoughts', in Richard Dyer, ed., *Gays and Film* (London: British Film Institute, 1977), pp. 5–26; B. Ruby Rich, 'From Repressive Tolerance to Erotic Liberation', *Jump Cut* no. 24/25, March 1981, pp. 44–50, and Nancy Scholar, '*Maedchen in Uniform*', in Patricia Erens, ed., *Sexual Stratagems* (New York: Horizon, 1979), pp. 219–223.

2. 'September in the Pink' was a Lesbian and Gay Arts Festival funded by the Greater London Council in Autumn 1983.

3. Claire Johnston, ed., *The Work of Dorothy Arzner* (London: British Film Institute, 1975), and Karen Kay and Gerald Peary, 'Dorothy Arzner's *Dance, Girl, Dance*', *The Velvet Light Trap* no. 10, Fall 1973, pp. 26–31.

4. The list of film-makers given here is necessarily selective and limited by my own viewing. Arguably, Yvonne Rainer and Chantal Akerman are the most notable cases in point. For Akerman, see Part Two. For Rainer, see her own *Work 1961–73* (Halifax: Nova Scotia College of Art and Design and New York: New York University Press, 1974) and the interview in *Camera Obscura* no. 1, 1976, pp. 76–96, which exemplifies this point. See also the interview with Marjorie Keller in *Camera Obscura* no. 11, 1983, pp. 72–85, and Anne Friedberg's article on Keller, 'Misconception = the "Division of Labor" in the Childbirth Film', *Millenium Film Journal* no. 4/5, Summer/Fall 1979, pp. 64–70. On Joyce Wieland, see Pam Cook's review of *Pierre Vallières*, *Monthly Film Bulletin* vol. 50 no. 596, September 1983, pp. 256–7.

5. The masculinity of the cultural identity of The Artist is documented by Griselda Pollock and Rosziska Parker in *Old Mistresses* (London: Routledge and Kegan Paul, 1981), and from a different perspective, Frances Borzello, *The Artist's Model* (London: Junction Books, 1982).

6. The Circles catalogue, ed. Felicity Sparrow, is most informative here (see extract in Appendix), as were the programmes of women's work, 'Women Direct', selected for *The Eleventh Hour* in January 1985.

7. See Jo Imeson's interview with Felicity Sparrow (Circles) and Eileen McNulty (Cinema of Women), *Monthly Film Bulletin* vol. 49 no. 583, August 1982, p. 184. I do not wish to set up a crude 'art' versus 'movement' opposition between these two feminist distributors – a glance at both catalogues shows this to be incorrect – but some sort of differentiation along these lines does seem to be possible.

8. Much of this work is resumed in Annette Kuhn, 'Women's Genres', *Screen* vol. 25 no. 1, 1984, pp. 18–29.

9. On audiences, see Gertrud Koch, 'Why Women go to the Movies', reprinted in *Jump Cut* no. 27, 1982, pp. 51–3; Annette Kuhn, 'Dear Linda', *Feminist Review* no. 18, 1985, pp. 112–120, and David Morley, 'Interpreting Television', U203, *Popular Culture*, Block 3, Unit 12 (Milton Keynes: The Open University, 1981).

10. The major historical precedent for this type of campaign were the black campaigns against *The Birth of a Nation* in 1915, which also involved debates around the demand for censorship (Cripps, *Slow Fade to Black*, New York: Oxford University Press, 1977, pp. 41–69). More recently, gay protests at *Cruising* raised related issues (Guthmann, 'The *Cruising* Controversy', *Cineaste* vol. 10 no. 3, Summer 1980, pp. 2–8).

Women and the Formal Film

ANNABEL NICOLSON, FELICITY SPARROW, JANE CLARKE,
JEANETTE ILJON, LIS RHODES, MARY PAT LEECE, PAT MURPHY,
SUSAN STEIN

From *Film as Film*, ed. Phillip Drummond, Arts Council of Great Britain, 1979, p. 118.

As the only woman involved in planning the 'Film as Film' exhibition [in 1979] Lis Rhodes decided to concentrate on the history of women making films and invited Felicity Sparrow to join her in this research. They focused on the work of Alice Guy, Germaine Dulac and Maya Deren, making personal contact with Ester Carla de Miro in Italy, who has been researching into Germaine Dulac for several years, and Millicent Hodson, Catrina Neiman, Veve Clark and Francine Bailey in America who have been making a comprehensive study of Maya Deren.

In response to requests for more women to be involved in this show Annabel Nicolson was invited to join the exhibition committee, which was responsible for deciding what would be shown and how it would be presented.

During this time the women 'officially' involved met regularly with a group of interested women to discuss developments. They felt themselves to be continually undermined by the lack of understanding and respect for their research by the Arts Council's committee.

For many reasons and with the support of women not officially involved in the 'Film as Film' committees they have decided to withhold their research and leave this gallery space empty.

This is Our Statement:
The gesture of withholding our work and the presentation in its stead of a statement of opposition is the only form of intervention open to us. It was impossible to allow the Arts Council to present our work as if there had been no struggle, as if it had been nurtured in the spirit of public patronage.

Informed by a feminist perspective it was our intention to begin a re-examination of the historicised past by introducing (welcoming) Alice Guy and re-presenting Germaine Dulac and Maya Deren.

Maya Deren and Germaine Dulac are both included in the 'Film as Film' historical survey but seen only in relation to the articulation of abstract/formal film. We were concerned that these women would be

186

inaccurately 'defined' by the concepts that they had been chosen to illustrate and we felt a necessity to re-locate their work within the context of their own concerns, giving it a complexity and fullness that the 'Film as Film' exhibition denied by excluding: Dulac's contribution to the feminist movement; her interviews with women artists expressing their struggle for recognition; her belief in a specifically feminine creativity; her political involvement in the unionisation of film workers and support for the popular front before World War II; Deren's (embarrassing) involvement with Voodoo; the relationship between her writing and her films; her interest in science, anthropology and religion; her attack on Surrealism.

Alice Guy is not represented in 'Film as Film' and has scarcely been recognised anywhere. She was actively involved in film-making at the turn of the century, experimenting with narrative structures and the use of sound with film, but has been forgotten by historians. Why are her films forgotten while those of Lumière and Méliès are used as standard texts?

We hoped to carry the historical research up to the present and open up the closed form of 'Film as Film' by creating an active space within the exhibition where contemporary women could show personal statements and histories, find their own continuity and share ideas for future shows.

In general: we object to the idea of a closed art exhibition which presents its subject anonymously, defining its truth in Letraset and four-foot display panels, denying the space within it to answer back, to add or disagree, denying the ideological implications inherent in the pursuit of an academic dream, the uncomplicated pattern where everything fits.

Specifically: we object to being invited, presumably on the strength of our skills and past work, to participate in the organisation and definition of an exhibition, yet not being left free to characterise our own contributions. We object to the subtle insinuations of intellectual woolliness and inefficiency, as if our perspectives were tolerated rather than considered seriously.

Months ago we made 'requests' for more representation by women on the committees, for recognition of our ideas for the exhibition, for a space within the gallery and for the freedom to exhibit our work, to determine what it would include and how it would look. These requests could have become demands. We might have 'won' by subversive personal methods or by insisting on a democratic vote. But how does one demand collectivity, support and a real working relationship which includes discussion of ideas and ideological positions, within the framework of meetings structured by an hierarchical institution?

We made the decision not to carry on, not to continue working in a situation that was hostile and ultimately fruitless for the individual women involved. It is better that the historical research be published elsewhere and the work of contemporary women film-makers, artists and critics be presented in a context where they are valued.

The Norwich Women's Film Weekend

CAROLINE MERZ

CINEWOMEN is a group of women based in Norwich, whose main function has been to organise the annual Norwich Women's Film Weekend as well as to run occasional courses in film and television study for women. The group normally consists of five or six people: four of us have been part of it throughout its existence, while others have come and gone. Some of us work in film-making or teaching while others are feminists working in other areas. Our activities in organising the Weekend have always been on voluntary basis; most of us have other, paid work.

How the Women's Film Weekend Began
The idea of mounting an event in Norwich devoted to the promotion of feminist film-making as well as an analysis of the way women are represented in the cinema began in 1979. During the previous year a permanent home for the Norfolk and Norwich Film Theatre had been created in the shape of Cinema City, a BFI-sponsored Regional Film Theatre. This meant that a space had been opened up in Norwich where reasoned programming and discussion about film generally could take place. It also coincided with a time when feminist debate about cinema was gathering momentum: in the summer of 1979 at the Edinburgh Film Festival heated arguments had taken place about feminist versus 'women's' cinema.

At that time Cinewomen as a group didn't yet exist, although in Norwich there were individuals interested in feminism and film. One of these women, Ginette Vincendeau – a member of Cinema City's Council of Management (the directors of the cinema) – proposed that a weekend event should take place aimed at an audience of mostly women, with screenings of films made by and about women as well as discussion groups to cover issues raised by the films. The idea didn't receive whole-hearted support from the Council of Management however. There were many objections, mainly on the grounds that the cinema's 'deficit budget' couldn't be expected to cope with what was seen to be a minority interest event. A women's event was seen to be very different from other events which could be incorporated 'naturally' into the cinema's programming policy. Ginette had to fight many battles on our behalf to get the event going, since at that time others weren't allowed to attend Council of Management meetings. Every requirement we had seemed to cause expressions of grave doubt from the (mostly male) members of the committee who were controlling the budget.

Things have changed greatly for us since that first Women's Film Weekend, and nowadays we have our own meetings with the cinema's management, who are generally happy to arrange the event as we want it, book the films we select, give us a large enough budget to pay for visiting speakers to attend, and so on. In fact we are positively encouraged to keep the event going, and if we show any signs of flagging we are soon reminded of our commitments. We are cynical enough to realise that this shift in attitude has not been brought about solely by our attempts at consciousness-raising: rather, it has been effected by a realisation that, firstly, there *is* an audience for the event, many of whom come from a long way outside our own area; and secondly, that the BFI requires that certain 'marginal' (or non-mainstream) areas of film practice be highlighted, one of which is women's cinema. The Women's Film Weekend has thus come to serve as a high-profile, showcase activity for the cinema when applying for renewed funding, while for us it has meant the freedom and finance to bring films to Norwich which would otherwise never be screened in a major venue, or seen by a local audience.

A Question of Men
The fact that we did decide to operate from within an existing, male-dominated, organisation – albeit with very good screening and other facilities – has inevitably attracted some criticism, particularly in the first two years of the event. But the opportunities afforded by the cinema seem to have outweighed the disadvantages, although we have risked alienating some of the potential audience who would rather attend a women-only festival. Film events are so expensive to run that it is extremely unlikely that we would still be in operation now if we had to rely on fund-raising activities and makeshift facilities. A contradiction which is unlikely to disappear.

The Women's Film Weekend, although aimed primarily at a female audience, has also always been open to men. This is another 'problem' we have had to negotiate – sometimes clumsily – with some of the audience. In fact, very few men have attended the Weekends, and in 1984 the proportion of men to women reached an all-time low – so perhaps the question has resolved itself without much positive intervention on our part. Or maybe it's the sad fact that men who were interested think they've 'done' feminism. Whatever the case, we would defend the ideas of keeping the Women's Film Weekend a mixed event: partly on the grounds that we don't want to alienate non-feminist women from it, and partly because we feel that it offers something for men to learn from too. There have always been women-only discussion groups which have provided a useful and necessary space for women to speak about the films they have seen and the questions that have been raised in a reasonably unthreatening atmosphere.

Programming the Weekends

One question which has never been fully resolved about the Women's Film Weekend is whether it is meant to be a festival or a conference. It has elements of both, but for us the importance of getting as many films as possible shown in a relatively short space of time has meant that formal discussions have tended to be fairly brief – although we would never sacrifice them for a continuous programme of screenings. And although generally we have several film-makers at the event to introduce and discuss their films, we have tried also to organise discussions where the film-maker is not present, so that criticism and analysis, as well as discussion of production details and careers, can take place.

As feminists we have had to confront a question which all similar groups must have come up against: how do we select films? Or, to put it another way: *should* we select them at all? Since our aim is to promote and encourage women's cinema in all forms which are neglected in mainstream media, do we have the right, as exhibitors, to make value-judgments which are perhaps not very far from the kind of judgments those critics themselves make? (Although our own criteria of 'good'/ 'bad'/interesting are probably vastly different from theirs). In practice we have always selected films rather than simply take a 'slice' of whatever is available and, after having decided on the theme or orientation of the Weekend, have never had much of a problem reaching a consensus within the group about what we would like to show. In the first year of the Women's Film Weekend the problem of selection was less acute than it is today, since in the last five years the growth of feminist film-making in the independent sector has been rapid, particularly in the UK.

While this is very encouraging, it means that we can't simply include everything that has been made (even if we knew of the existence of half the films that have been made, which is another difficulty), and raises the question of whether an event like ours can carry on indefinitely in its present form. In an ideal world the Norwich Women's Film Weekend should, by now, have become redundant – with the interest it generated in the early years, alongside the existence of feminist distributors such as Circles and Cinema of Women, making feminist films far more easily available to a non-metropolitan, non-specialist audience. But the fact is that despite the relative abundance of available material, those films are being given screen space in not many more venues than they were five years ago. So while we feel that our own small contribution is still valuable, it may come to appear increasingly token.

Within the group, we've always had (quite healthy and productive) arguments about how to focus the Weekend in terms of the films we show. Whether, for example, it is an act of positive encouragement to show mainly British independent films, as opposed to well-funded European 'art' films – or whether this is merely narrow parochialism. Over the years we have developed a policy which seems to be fairly successful, popular and 'balanced', consisting of showing a mixture of independent and relatively commercial films made by women from as many countries as possible, and devoting a good part of the weekend to women's films of the past – such as retrospectives of Dorothy Arzner's and Ida Lupino's work. Perhaps the most successful example of this archival aspect of the Weekend was in 1984 when we showed British films of the 1940s and 50s directed by Jill Craigie and Kay Mander – enhanced by Kay Mander's presence and contribution to discussions around her work.

What we show is inevitably determined by factors other than personal taste and theory. Being a Norwich-based voluntary group is very different from being in London and funded to attend world-wide festivals – the only chance of really getting to know what is going on in the film world. One lesson we've learned is never to show films that at least one of us hasn't seen in advance, since doing that has caused some major disasters in the past. But controls over distribution and exhibition mean that it can be extremely difficult, as well as time-consuming and expensive, to see what is available. Individual women film-makers and groups are often happy to send us a viewing print or video of their film in advance, but commercial distributors wouldn't consider it since, in their view, a non-profit-making, 'minority-interest' event in a backwater like Norwich isn't worth the trouble. We are lucky in that operating from Cinema City, the BFI in London is usually willing to hire in and put on a day's worth of screenings for us in advance of the Weekend. Also, we can sometimes contrive a preview of a new European feature film, for example, through personal contact with the film-makers or with an institution such as a foreign embassy. In this way a number of films such as *A Question of Silence* and Jutta Brückner's *The Hungry Years* have received their British premiere at the Women's Film Weekend, although this has gone totally un-recognised by the press! But while we have shown films from most European countries as well as North America and Australia, we have rarely had the opportunity to screen anything from third-world countries.

The Audience

Although our intention was always to provide an event mainly for local women – since there are rarely opportunities to see feminist films in the area – the number of local people coming to the event has, in fact, dropped over the years: in 1984, although the total audience reached an all-time high, the majority of its members came from well outside East Anglia. We can only speculate about why more local women don't tend to come, since there are a number of lively, existing feminist groups in Norwich. What are *we* doing wrong? Why are *they* diffident? There isn't space to go into all the soul-searching here, though one possible reason is that a whole weekend away from home watching and discussing films is more attractive and more fun than simply dropping in to a local cinema. In any case, the Norwich Women's Film Weekend does seem to have established itself as a national event, which some women have attended each year since 1979.

The big difference between a feminist event such as this and other types of conference or festival does lie in the fact that there is a far more easy-going, friendly atmosphere generated. The audience generally consists of a mixture of film-makers (mainly from the independent sector), women working in other areas of film such as distribution, exhibition, teaching and research, and feminists either interested in film *per se* or in particular subjects with which the films may be concerned. Despite the fact that film-makers are invited to talk about their work with the audience, there is rarely a sense of competition or hierarchy which is all too common in other kinds of event. We arrange spaces for formal discussions to take place, but probably the most fruitful discussions happen informally, between groups of women during coffee or lunch breaks, or after the event altogether. There always has been a very genuine sense of participation and co-operation of everyone involved in the Weekends: women running the creche, providing accommodation, making the food, etc., even if they don't get the chance to see many of the films.

The Future

Many changes in the funding and structure of independent film-making in the UK have come about since the first Norwich Women's Film Weekend, notably the intervention of Channel Four and the consolidation of the workshop movement. While this has meant that more realistic funding is available for some feminist film and video projects, it has meant also that larger sums are, in many cases, going to fewer groups or individuals. The Women's Film Weekend, while committed to exhibiting a wide range of internationally-made films, has always been most closely linked with the independent film sector. It has provided a meeting-place for film-makers and potential user-groups, a forum where women's film groups can learn something about each other's work. Without this kind of meeting-place (another example of which is the National Feminist Film and Video Conference, held for the first time in Cardiff in 1984), Women can easily find themselves working in complete isolation from one another, with little sense of what is emerging elsewhere in the country.

At the time of writing this article [1984], it seems that we are faced with a paradox. It is impossible not to feel that there is a loss of momentum in the small-scale independent film movement, an uncertainty about the future. This loss is, ironically, linked to an increase of resources – an increase which has been concentrated in a small number of 'prestige' productions such as *The Gold Diggers*: the first British, feature-length, feminist film funded by the BFI Production Board. And it has become increasingly noticeable over the five years of the Women's Film Weekend that the gap is widening between the majority of British feminist films, still made on shoestring budgets, and the relative plethora of full-scale, high-production-value European films where there is a commitment to proper state funding for film-makers (including many feminists) who work outside the mainstream. It would have been quite easy for us, for example, to programme the entire 1984 Weekend with German or French feature films but this would be alien to the nature and purpose of the Norwich Women's Film Weekend as it has evolved. It has always drawn its main impetus, and strength, from current feminist film and video activity close to home, and will continue to seek out and encourage this kind of work as long as it can obtain the resources to do so effectively.

(Since this article was commissioned and written, the 6th NWFWE has taken place.)

Her Image Fades
as Her Voice Rises

LIS RHODES and FELICITY SPARROW

Extracts from an Arts Council Film Programme, 1983.

SITTING with her at the table, talking, her hands poised over the typewriter. The words in our minds turning between description and analysis – to write the image, or to write about an image. This will be a subjective gathering of threads of meaning, drawing attention to the spaces between three films that are dense with connections and difference. Seen thus, the programme becomes a fiction in itself; a looking at – a listening to – the relationships between the film-makers – their stories – avoiding false isolation, the separations determined by history as it is written – as it has been read – to mean meanings other than HERS.

We shall try to make explicit the links and fractures between three films made by three women whose lives and work belong to different times and different places – different languages even – but whose voices are placed within similar constraints. We all experience these constraints but most women are allowed no time or space to reflect upon them. [. . .]

. . . The idea came from the experience of sharing a kitchen with two men. Through realising, over a period of time, specific things that they didn't notice, I was able to crystallise my own response to particular tasks, particular parts of this room . . . I discovered several areas (often very small) within the kitchen that I was very aware of becoming dirty and I enjoyed – or rather was urged – to clean. I developed a special relationship to these 'corners'; I enjoyed the materials that constituted them and felt the repetitive cycle of things becoming dirty – the way each part became dirty and the different methods of cleaning. I became more aware of this in myself as I realised that the men had no understanding for it. Why? Was it education? My conditioning as a woman? Was it to do with me in particular? Or is it just part of 'women's nature? . . .'

Traces made, traces removed; a woman is caught mid-sentence often during the day. The traces of sound from the radio, as a newscaster's voice surfaces and sinks in a burble of music, remain peripheral, outside and obscured by the unnaturally foregrounded sounds of tea being poured and bread being cut repeatedly throughout the film. *Often During the Day* opens with a series of still images of a kitchen, photographs that have been delicately hand-tinted by the film-maker. A woman's voice is heard describing a particular kitchen space, through its geography – every minute detail of which she is familiar with – and through the various activities taking place within it. The room is referred to as the centre of the house and the voice describes the traces left by the users of the kitchen (the spatterings of food left on the floor round the saucer after the cat has finished eating – the little pieces of hair washed from a razor after a man has finished shaving). She reflects on the tasks of cleaning and repair, the 'small unnecessary' tasks, the caring for a space:

> When we first constructed the sink there was a gap between the enamel part and the wooden drawers that support it. The gap worried me because I saw water trickled through on to the things in the drawers. The others didn't notice, or didn't mind, and it took me several months to do anything about it.[2]

The attention given to a domestic space that Joanna Davis speaks of seems to avoid a strict definition of housework – the unpaid servicing that that usually implies – and centres on her pleasure. It is a pleasure that is expressed in relation to certain surfaces and textures, 'the way each part became dirty', and the placings of things. A different pleasure – the satisfaction of a job being done – is described by another voice, a man's, reading extracts from the testimonies of women's reflections on housework as catalogued in *The Sociology of Housework*.[3] This conflict – can pleasure be pleasing if that pleasure is seen as oppressive? – is expressed by the film-maker through images showing the continual violation of her feelings for the space. In the final shot of the film, a long continuous take, the tea is poured; the bread is cut; an arm reaches across a woman's body to reach the butter. SHE refolds the paper carefully after he has used it. Their consumption leaves traces: a scattering of crumbs on the surface of the table, the stain of tealeaves on the draining board. Disturbed by the crumbs she interrupts her meal to wipe them up.

This sense of impingement is confirmed by the quotations from *The Sociology of Housework*, which rest within the film as uneasily as the news from Armagh and the song 'Dancing in the City' . . . The printed words emerge from a thin veil of tissue paper with an authority of which Joanna Davis is extremely wary. Perhaps it is to enforce this distance from her own experience that a man's voice reads the passages, just as the women quoted are defined by the men they are married to: carpenter's or lorry-driver's wife. The implication is that the male voice is placed outside of the experience of the female film-maker, within the parameters of sociological research.

196

In *Often During the Day* the woman is not socially placed by a particular man. Thus the issues of sexual and economic control are recognised, rather than suffered, and the historical determinants that underlie her feelings of pleasure and anxiety in relationship to domestic tasks can be analysed.

It is here that one of the central issues connecting the films is raised and can be clearly seen in the different positioning of the women in *Often During the Day* and the earlier film. For Mme Beudet it is not only the institution of marriage, but also the collusion of the Catholic Church in reinforcing that institution, which is questioned. [. . .]

Imprisoned in Dependency or the Violence of Meaning

> The cinema can certainly tell a story, but you have to remember that the story is nothing. The story is surface.
>
> The seventh art, that of the screen, is depth rendered perceptible, the depth that lies beneath the surface; it is the musical ungraspable . . . Plot film or abstract film, the problem is the same. To touch the feelings through the sight and, as I've already said, to give predominance to the image . . .
>
> The image can be as complex as an orchestration since it may be composed of combined movements of expression and light.[4]

Six years before writing these words Germaine Dulac made *The Smiling Madame Beudet*. Its plot, the surface, is simple as a reviewer was to say sixty years later: 'Madame Beudet is married to a bombastic idiot, refuses to go to the opera with him, dreams up the nearly perfect murder and, when it fails, gets away with it because of Monsieur Beudet's lack of imagination.'[5]

The film's intensity, its visual impact and depth of feeling, are achieved through an orchestration of emotive gestures and facial expressions. Often described as the first feminist film, we share Madame Beudet's (and Germaine Dulac's) point of view throughout – her 'voice,' although silent, can only be that of the first person singular as in *Often During the Day*.

'*In a quiet provincial town*' . . . Madame Beudet is isolated. '. . . *behind the peaceful façades* . . .' she is trapped. Her gaze through the window is blocked by the view of the prison opposite; inwardly she sees the reflection of that institution in her wedding ring. Locked within the niceties of a middle-class marriage she struggles to maintain her sanity. The interior space of her home is constantly reflective of Madame Beudet's mental restriction; her gestures and expressions, constantly juxtaposed with those of her husband, are reflective of her emotional suffocation. The placing of a vase of flowers becomes symbolic of conflicting sensibilities, the key to her piano the control of her means of expression. Her book of poetry provides a way for her to retreat into herself and her desires. Baudelaire, Debussy and the ghost-like apparition of a male tennis player stepping out from the pages of a magazine are her only cultural reference points. But even these are impinged upon by the distorted face of Monsieur Beudet. Escape is impossible. Outside, the institutions of justice and religion have sealed and sanctified her dependency. Inside 'it was in this accumulation of other men's thoughts and experiences that she looked for affirmation of identity . . .'[6] She is excluded; even the running of the house is in her husband's hands; she is held accountable. Monsieur Beudet's obstructive and destructive presence occupies both her physical and mental space. With the loss of space she cannot act. In the absence of action she remains without response. She is shown looking at herself – alone with her own reflection – framed in a triple mirror.

In case we need more clues, Germaine Dulac shows the completeness of Madame Beudet's mental decapitation: as Monsieur Beudet tears the head off her ornamental doll, an inter-title reads *'a doll is fragile . . . a bit like a woman . . .'*. And he puts the head in his pocket. A fine symbol of men's idea of femininity and how this can be manipulated and used against women – they can be handled, idolised and popped away . . . so the cigar smokers can spit in peace and continue to exclude women from the 'real' business and understanding of life.

Close-ups of Madame Beudet's face earlier in the film show her awareness of, and resignation to Monsieur Beudet's stupidity. He thinks she knows nothing about Faust, that women have no minds of their own (which is probably true when their heads are forcibly removed). Her expression shows that she knows the story and recognises it as one of male dominance and female dependency. The bitterest moment of the film – the centre of the argument – is when he thinks she is suicidal. He is incapable of considering the possibility that she intended the bullet for him: *'How could I ever live without you?'* She is caught in *his* emotional dependency. She knows but cannot act. The happy conclusion reflected in the mirror, 'theatre,' to her, is a façade which the priest and Monsieur Beudet accept; the film ends with Madame Beudet's back to the camera while the two men greet each other and indicate their collusion and her exclusion.

'In the quiet streets, without horizon, under a low sky . . . united by habit.'

The Smiling Madame Beudet ends where it begins, unsmilingly. The provincial town is the scene of her imprisonment; behind the façade of habit is the scene of her attempts to escape. But the escape, the analysis of her situation, remains private to her, voiced in her fantasies. She cannot change her situation however clearly she understands it.

in her own voice she cried
the end cannot be confused with the end that ended
somewhere – but not here
not here at the beginning . . .[7]

Light Reading could be picking up the thread of Madame Beudet's story, the voice could be hers after seeing herself on film sixty years later. She has in the meantime been granted the right to vote; film can now record her spoken words and we can hear them. As for her image . . . that has gone. Sixty years of film and television and advertising have much to answer for.

Who turned the light away
the light away from her
she will not be placed in darkness
she will be present in darkness only to be apparent
to appear without image
to be heard unseen . . .
her hands reach out
she could only glimpse the shadow
the faint reflection of the fading image
stumbling on the traces of her knowing
sinking in the ruts of her experience
slipping amongst the shadows of her story
she couldn't reach herself . . .[8]

The film begins in darkness as a woman's voice is heard over a black screen. 'She' is spoken of as multiple subject – third person singular and plural. Her voice continues until images appear on the screen and then is silent. In the final section of the film she begins again, looking at the images as these are moved and re-placed, describing the piecing together of the film as she tries to piece together the tangle of strands of her story.

The voice is questioning, searching. She will act. But how? Act against what? The bloodstained bed suggests a crime . . . Could it be *his* blood – was that the action denied to Madame Beudet? No answers are given, after the torrent of words at the beginning all the film offers are closed images and more questions . . . Is it even blood on the bed, what fracture is there between seeing and certainty? Could it be *her* blood – rape/murder of the mind, of the body, of both? Her image has gone. If there has been a crime, 'she' might still be victim . . . How can a crime of such complexity and continuity be 'solved'? The voice searches for clues, sifting through them, reading and re-reading until the words and letters (in themselves harmless enough) loom up nightmarishly, no longer hung on the structure of language.

the violence of sequence tears at the threads of her thoughts

the folds of light fade into deep shadows
the sense of her dreams is disturbed by the presence
of a past not past
a past that holds her with fingers sharpened on logic
nails hardened with rationality
cutting the flow of her thoughts
forcing her back within herself
damned by the rattle of words
words already sentenced
imprisoned in meaning . . .[9]

The clues suggest it is language that has trapped her, meanings that have excluded her and a past that has been constructed to control her. Do we have to delve into history and reappropriate it? Perhaps there are other ways, like examining the scene of the crime as we're told in detective fiction. But magnifying the stain on the bed only reveals a blur, measured with a ruler, but that doesn't add up to much. She's forced back within herself and her own thoughts; she begins again cautiously:

she watched herself being looked at
she looked at herself being watched
but she could not perceive herself
as the subject of the sentence . . .[10]

Madame Beudet's light reading can neither provide escape nor reflect her own thoughts and desires. In *Light Reading*, Lis Rhodes recognises that dead-end. She searches for other clues and other means of finding her own reflection. But she seems to be framed everywhere she looks: the cosmetic mirror gives her back only part of her image, photographing herself in a mirror gives her back another. There are fragmented images, multiple images and shadowy photographs but they remain enigmatic and implacable as the stain on the bed. The images (snapshots of a past) are torn up and rearranged leaving gaps which she tries to measure with letters and figures – fragments.

Where do we begin? There is the past, always, which we can re-read, re-frame, just as we can try and re-place Alice Guy and Germaine Dulac. But it's not just a question of balancing out the injustices: 'There is nothing connected with the staging of a motion picture that a woman cannot do as easily as a man', it goes deeper than these crimes of exclusion and unequal opportunities.

'*She stopped the action . . .*'
Gertrude Stein said:

And now she wrote
and now mountains do not cloud over
let us wash our hair and stare
stare at mountains . . .[11]

Her words, quoted, are like a light refrain running through the threads of meaning in *Light Reading*'s monologue; and the thought of her there, so solidly, in the past and now . . . *Light Reading* ends with no single solution. But there is a beginning. Of that she is positive. She will not be looked at but listened to:

'*She begins to re-read
aloud*'

She is not alone, in speech, she can begin to find reflections of herself outside of herself. Nobody can say anything unless someone is listening. And we can't act without response . . .

I read to you and you read to me and we both read intently. And I waited for you and you waited for me and we both waited attentively. I find knitting to be a continuous occupation and I am full of gratitude because I realise how much I am indebted to the hands that wield the needles.[12]

Lis: Do you think we've written what we meant to write?
         I mean is what we've written *fiction*?

Felicity: We've shifted the 'facts' . . . but they needed shifting – like my carpet they gather dust – and that begins to obscure the patterns that make facts mean . . .

Lis: Arguing all the way round to here . . . sitting with her at the table – still talking –
         We wrote this together   she wrote on light reading – and we both wrote on the other three.

(This article was cut to exclude references to Alice Guy's *A House Divided*.)

Notes

1. Joanna Davis (from a conversation with Lis Rhodes and Felicity Sparrow, 1978).
2. From *Often During the Day*.
3. *The Sociology of Housework* by Ann Oakley (Oxford: Martin Robertson, 1974).
4. 'Visual and Anti-Visual Films' by Germaine Dulac, from *Le Rouge et le Noir*, July 1928. Reprinted in P. Adams Sitney, ed., *The Avant-Garde Film* (New York: New York University Press 1978).
5. Helen Mackintosh from *City Limits*, 16–22 April 1982.
6. P. D. James, *Innocent Blood* (London: Sphere Books, 1981).
7–10. From *Light Reading*.
11. 'Sonatina Followed by Another', Gertrude Stein. The entire poem is reprinted in *Bee Time Vine* (New Haven: Yale University Press, 1953).
12. 'Sonatina Followed by Another', Gertrude Stein.

Black Women and Representation

MARTINA ATTILLE and MAUREEN BLACKWOOD

Notes from the Workshops held in London, 1984.

THESE notes (some of which appeared in *Undercut* 14/15, 1985) document some of the concerns of the *Black Women and Representation Workshops* organised by a group of women in Spring 1984. The workshops were held at Four Corners, a film workshop with a small screening and discussion area in Bethnal Green, and funded by the Greater London Arts Association. Publicity leaflets were sent to all black women's organisations, to women's centres, law centres, film and video workshops and centres, colleges, Arts centres and projects like Riverside Studios and the Albany, as well as to individuals. The workshops were also advertised in *Spare Rib*, *Outwrite*, the black press, *City Limits* and *Time Out*.

Introduction

We are involved in a struggle for liberation: liberation from the exploitative and dehumanising system of racism . . . liberation from the constrictive norms; of 'mainstream' culture, from the synthetic myths that encourage us to fashion ourselves rashly from without (reaction) rather than from within (creation).   Toni Cade

Black Women and Representation was a series of screenings/discussions, and practical VHS workshops structured to locate discussion about representation outside the strict arena of the academic.

We want the course to be open to black women only, because we feel that the pervasive nature of racism and sexism means that black women/women of colour have the least opportunity to use video equipment, and talk about our relationship to the media.

GLAA application

The series was developed, organised and coordinated by a group of black women working in various areas of media – print, radio, video, film. Some had worked already in the areas of literary criticism/ semiology, some had also worked with sections of the black communities on media related projects; we were all critical of the fragmentation of our lives and politics. There were of course cultural and class differences and we considered it important to talk them through towards finding a common ground on which to draw other black women into discussion, knowing that it would not necessarily be on our terms, and therefore structuring the series to accommodate that.

> As black women, we must be the ones who define the areas of importance in our lives: we need to work towards the breakdown of 'mainstream' conventions, and popular assumptions perpetuated by existing forms of cinema and television.　　　　　　　　Publicity

Coming together as black women was/is an easy first step; the process that keeps us together and facilitates discussion is far more complex. That is why Black Women and Representation never set out to be a definitive analysis of our experiences. The intention was always to establish an ongoing forum for discussion around the social and political implications of the fragmentation of black women in film/video/television as well as a forum to talk about the kinds of images we want to construct ourselves, in an attempt to offer a more complete picture of our lives/politics.

> We need everybody and all that we are. We need to know and make known the complete, constantly unfolding, complicated heritage that is our black experience.　　　　　　June Jordan, *Civil Wars*

Discussion is not concluded over two months; when we have further researched, developed and printed our seminar papers, discussion will still not be concluded. But it is important for us to document this complex process, especially to let other black women know that we exist and that the dialogue is full of commitment and vitality. This will no doubt have repercussions in the wider communities, sections of which are always keen to know/be informed – those eager for reports and explanations.

　8 April　The History of Stereotypes: Accepted Conventions – Beyond the 'Mammie'
　15 April　Who Controls the Image?: Reflections on Social Relations – The Power to Create
　29 April　Towards New Social Realities: Alternative Images – Access to and Control over our Images
　20 May　Course Overview/Open Discussion

It was the issues that brought the steering group together to develop Black Women and Representation; but because we are all involved in other full-time occupations, it has not developed as an organisation with regular funding. Women in Sync (a women's video resource collective) and Sankofa (a black, production-based film and video workshop involved in developing a dialogue with black communities/

building audiences, and acknowledging our accountability to those audiences by regular screenings/discussions around representation) were the two established groups who gave skills and resources.

The limited range of Media Studies programmes, and the very limited range of literature about women and film/film criticism, or black people and film, has not been able to sustain a critique of images of black women. The importance of such critical analysis is overdue, especially in the light of the body of work produced by black women writers, and the development of the black independent film and video sector. The experience of Black Women and Representation shows that there are black women in the UK with some resources, working in and around media, who can put forward some of our differing perspectives.

We need a theory that takes into account the economic history of our (mis)representation and ensuing stereotyping, as well as the inter-action between social realities (whole lives) and cinematic fictions (fragmentation), and we, black women, need to give that theory its direction.

> Not the photograph . . . But the meaning the spectator associates with the image. Progressive meanings can only come out of a society with progressive values . . . Until then we will continue to look at media images without fully seeing . . . without fully understanding.
>
> Black Women and Representation

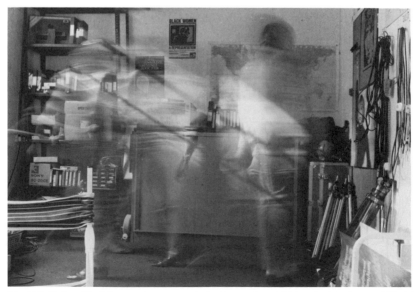

David A. Bailey, 'Black Women and Representation', from the exhibition, *Positive Images of Black People*

The following (edited) texts were originally spoken as introductions to the workshops and used to start discussion. They are offered here as part of the work in progress around black women and representation.

Stereotypes: Beyond the 'Mammie'
MAUREEN BLACKWOOD 8 *April 1984*
For me, 'Representation' refers to the presentation of an image which serves as a symbol for something else immediately, and then beyond that to the social, political and historical situations which have or have had a direct relationship to how an image is presented. The image or images which are used as symbols work in a sense by trying to conjure up in the viewer of the image certain thought processes which assume to a great extent that there is a shared or common set of assumptions/ concepts – that is to say 'general knowledge' – which both the viewer (you and me) and the creators of the image (film-makers, writers, media people, etc.) have. So the representation with which I'm concerned today refers to the portrayal – the presentation – of certain images of black women which serve as symbols for us, although we also have to bear in mind, perhaps for discussion in later sessions, the representation of black women within the actual processes of production. That is to say, in terms of access to training, equipment, finance and so on – and to think about how our situation in that field, the field of production, may affect our representation in terms of images.

If it is indeed the case that symbols work on the assumption of some kind of 'shared common knowledge' within specific cultures, the role of stereotypes in all this is very important, because essentially a stereotypical image is an imitation, a copy of something or someone which is, by means of the media machinery, held up firstly as THE symbol or symbols to the exclusion of others; and then repeatedly channelled out to viewers so often that in time it becomes a 'common' representation of something or someone in the minds of viewers. I'm using the word 'viewer' a lot because we're dealing primarily on this course with the visual image but stereotypes are reinforced through all media and artistic practices. The idea of repetition of the image is very important in terms of an analysis of stereotypes because essentially that is how they operate. We have to be aware of the fact that every stereotype on the market has, somewhere, a person to fit that image, but that's not what is important about them; what has to be remembered is that by the process of repetition those images which are repeated time and again to the viewer become internalised. So we actually start to take on board and accept some of the symbols we see. And at this point I just want to reference the fact that by and large media works on the idea that out there somewhere is a 'mass audience' with various shared knowledges for whom these programmes, etc. are being made and as far as most media workers are concerned, in the mainstream this mass audience is white, largely male and largely heterosexual; this also applies to the people making the material.

Every society or culture has its sets of stereotypes, not only in relation to people from different cultures but also in relation to each other. So what I'm trying to get at is the fact that images or symbols have roots in social, political, historical and ideological periods and spheres, and although I believe that this is the case I'm not trying to say that stereotypes are static, unchanging things; they are always being updated and new ones being created to a certain extent. So in the cartoons and excerpts which follow we can see how all these elements operate together to present various symbols and assumptions about black people and black women. In terms of the update of images we can see how the 'mammie' images in the cartoon *Lazy Town* change by the time we get to the 'mammie' as personified in Hattie McDaniels in *Gone with the Wind*; it changes again by the time we get to that image in *Imitation of Life*; but you also see that a radical break with the original image, and the various connotations which are tied up in it, is never made. Although I don't have an excerpt from it, some of you will remember the mother figure in *Pressure* and see that that is also another update of the 'mammie' symbol.

Who Controls the Image: Reflections on Social Relations?
MARTINA ATTILLE *15 April 1984*

When we look at the issue of representation, there is always something that lies beyond the picture on the screen: a social and political reality, contained in a whole series of conventions used in film and television, *conventions* that go hand-in-hand with ideas of *professionalism*. To change the reading of the image means at the same time to break down existing popular forms, and the social structures they maintain. We cannot create POSITIVE images (a concept that is in itself problematic) just by showing black bank managers. But to go back to the problem raised last week: where *do* we start? One of the reasons these workshops were set up was to find out what stage people in this room are at in challenging the images and the reality of our oppression in this society, in our communities. For film-makers, is the way forward to create images for the viewer/spectator to *aspire* to, or do we *document* our lives by taking up and confronting our everyday realities? Need the two be separated?

Who *controls* the image? Who *creates* it?

It would be too easy to hold white, middle-class men solely responsible; we know their intentions. But how do we explain *Mirror Mirror*, *Reassemblage*, *Pressure*, etc. that use the same currency of signs which have historically worked to limit understanding of our experiences? Although the intentions may be different, what work has been done to broaden the readings? The repetition of a very limited range of images goes towards building POPULAR MYTHS, commonsense assumptions about us.

VOYEURISM is one theory that has been put forward to explain the control of the image. *Voyeurism. To be able to look, without being part,* without participating, sets up a distance between the observer and the object of the look that puts the voyeur in a position of power. Looking is never a neutral activity. When we look at something we all have the power to decide the nature/existence of the object of our look. We have the power to define, to *limit the meaning* of objects. The stereotype is a limitation, a narrow sighted view of a person. But *whose* narrow view?

As we look, we make value judgments. Value judgments based on our 'personal' and cultural histories. When I look at a black woman, I see someone who *I think* must surely have suffered some of my oppression, because of the construction of race; but I see also an unknown quantity, a person that might turn out to be anything from an extremely wide range of possibilities. To me, another black person is not *just* a BLACK.

When a white person looks at me, behind that look is all the conditioning of a long history of colonisation, and 'civilisation'. They see: a DARK continent, something unknown, exciting, frightening, EXOTIC. DIFFERENT. Is it any wonder that British television as it stands finds it so difficult to locate black people in any context other than the ETHNIC? ETHNICITY has almost become a concept particular to black people, so intense is the concentration on *our* difference to them, rather than *their* difference to us.

The constant repetition of the stereotype outlined last week demonstrates very definitely that the dominant social/political group in this society still has the *same* fascination with all the things that make us appear peculiar to them: our customs, our families, what they define as our alienation; the clash of two cultures, the generation gaps – we can all think of examples.

The person who controls the image is the one who looks at it, creates it. And the reality is that the image created says more about the creator than about the people it is supposed to represent.

I have put together some clips using the commentary of *Reassemblage*. The film attempts to challenge the power of the voyeuristic look which is particular to ethnographic documentaries, where anthropologists go in and study an unknown culture. I like the film because some of the images are really beautiful, and as an ethnographic film it is progressive. Buy why the same fascination with our bodies? She questions her practice as a film-maker, but her words are not enough to challenge some of her more predictable images.

Black Women and Representation Steering Group:
Martina Attille (Sankofa Film and Video); Maureen Blackwood (Sankofa Film and Video); Nadine Marsh-Edwards (Sankofa Film and Video); Amina Patel (Mukti/Women in Sync); Ingrid Lewis (Black Womens Radio Workshop); Andrea Marsh (Islington Black Women); Lai Ngan Walsh; Gurrinder Chandha (Shakti); Evie Arup; Karen Alexander.

BLACK WOMEN

& REPRESENTATION

April 8—May 20 ● **Screenings & Discussions**

● at Four Corners
113 Roman Road, E1
● Tel: 981 6111

**For further information
tel: Women in Sync 278 2215**

Financially assisted
by
**Greater
London
Arts Association**

FOR BLACK WOMEN BY BLACK WOMEN

Feminism and Exhibition

SHEILA WHITAKER

From *Screen* vol. 23 no. 3/4, 1982, pp. 132–4.

THE FOLLOWING are my tentative thoughts about some questions raised by feminist politics and cinema exhibition in the UK. They are not a statement of policy.

The Tyneside Cinema in Newcastle upon Tyne, of which I am Director,* is a major regional exhibition centre, with two public auditoria, one housing 400 and the other 150 seats, and Club screenings which take place mainly in the smaller auditorium. Seasons, which feature 80 to 100 films every two months, are usually centred around a theme, with the specific aim of identifying different kinds of practices in cinema history, and the connections that can be made between individual films, cinema in general, and society. Past seasons have dealt with themes as varied as the genre of the musical, British Cinema, war films, the work of Italian director Luchino Visconti, and the representation of women. Programming is entirely my responsibility and there are no limitations on the work we do. An enviable position, perhaps, but I'd like to explore some of the contradictions involved.

The question of cinema exhibition is a difficult one for feminist politics. It could be argued, and often is, that any film which is ideologically anti-female or misogynist should not be screened, on the grounds that simply to do so furthers the dominant ideas about women and the economy which supports them, when the feminist task should be to resist those ideas. But that argument leaves us with perhaps a dozen films which provide acceptable images of women. This view of the non-availability of progressive films may seem unduly pessimistic, but it is really not surprising when we consider that our culture must represent (I use the term advisedly) a patriarchal society which places women in a subordinate role. Even a film which is not overtly anti-female must nevertheless be complicit in the reiteration of socially constructed gender roles. The choice is therefore between not screening anything other than progressive films which try to resist this process, or making the difficult decision to screen from a more 'liberal' perspective.

*Sheila Whitaker is now (1986) Head of Programming and Deputy Controller of the National Film Theatre, London.

The 'liberal feminist' perspective may result in the following decisions: 1) not to screen soft or hard-core pornography, except in a mixed or women-only forum specifically aimed at raising issues of sexual politics in connection with pornography; and 2) not to offer a high public profile (such as that afforded by our larger cinema) to those films which feminists consider to contain an unacceptable degree of anti-female elements: examples of these last would be *Dressed to Kill* (1980) and *Les Valseuses* (1974). This is *not* to suggest that they shouldn't be screened at all, but rather that the exhibition context must be such that questions of their ideology are raised, so that the process of undermining the pleasures they offer can begin. Misogynistic attitudes to women are not going to stop just because films are not shown, or are censored in certain exhibition contexts: in my view it will only stop when people confront the social processes which oppress women. Although picketing can draw issues to the public's attention, it is not enough for people to know that women want a film banned; they must understand why and how the films are working in order to become involved in the issues raised by feminist politics. It seems to me that it's important to consider the factors surrounding the screening of films, not just the films themselves, or their misogynist content, in isolation.

The question of gaining the attention of an audience is crucial. It can probably be assumed that in a screening of a popular mainstream film most of the audience (whether female or male) is not only not feminist, but either unaware of the issues of sexual politics or actively opposed to them. In order to draw them in, a feminist programmer has therefore to walk the fine line between alerting this audience to the issues and unsettling them in their pleasures (when the promise of satisfaction brought them to the cinema in the first place) while creating an environment which will not intensify their resistance to the project or to the exhibition context itself.

It has been argued that major centres of film exhibition cannot carry out any significant intervention into film culture in these or any other political terms, because they are economically tied to satisfying the demands of a large popular audience. The alternative seems to be a reliance on a cinema of social practice in which production, distribution and exhibition are closely linked, and which is directed at a specific, small audience. Fundamentally important though this cinema is, it cannot reach those individuals who are not engaged in any organised political activity, such as trade unionism, or those who have any other unorganised political awareness. The large, general audience is, for the most part, unlikely to engage automatically with cinema aimed at specific political interests, and will probably be inhibited by it. Indeed, they are likely to be inhibited from attending screenings of *Dressed to Kill* or *Les Valseuses* in a major exhibition centre under the controlled conditions described above.

The argument against the social effectivity of major exhibition centres suggests that their attempt to screen mainstream cinema in combination with educative and consciousness-raising activities cannot possibly achieve any significant success, particularly since they are to a large degree embedded in the traditional notions of film exhibition, and the maintenance of the industrial base of commercial cinema. Apparently, it is only in small-scale viewing situations that the desired results can be achieved. However, the increased tendency towards home-viewing, the one-way closed circuit of a production/ exhibition industry directly aimed at private consumption, will suppress public debate of social and political issues even more. It is precisely because of this tendency that the existence of major resource centres which combine a pleasurable social context for the screening of films and video with activities imaginatively designed to raise substantive issues becomes even more important. How else can we attract the interest of an audience of non-feminists? Moreover, the large-scale facilities of these centres do not necessarily prevent local political activist groups from working within them, but rather the opposite, since their resources and the access they offer to a large general audience could significantly support their work, and vice versa, giving them the opportunity to move out of a restricted, marginal social space.

To my mind, the cessation of all mainstream exhibition in favour of 'progressive' screenings is not an adequate answer to the problem of social change. It is a kind of censorship which can only make a very partial impact in the overall national situation, and is therefore ineffective in itself as a strategy for intervention at all levels of society. Clearly, however, 'open' exhibition as an end in itself does not meet the problem either. Surely it is not simply a question of banning certain ideologically suspect films in favour of those with a feminist stance, which would not seriously affect the overall socio-political structures, but of alerting a general audience to issues it may never otherwise consider – that is, the feminist issues of the pleasures of cinematic representation in relation to the social construction of gender and its repressive mechanisms. Although we may be justified in censoring extreme examples of these repressive mechanisms in cinema (such as pornography) in a high public profile exhibition forum, we must attempt to maintain a general audience with which certain consciousness-raising activities can be carried out, consolidated by parallel alternative screenings, activities and the provision of resources of information and knowledge, *in conjunction* with small-scale social practice activities.

It must be remembered that in our society feminist critiques of cinema and society, both in theory and in the practices of the Women's Movement, are still marginal and, more importantly, still resisted.

This resistance, conscious or not, will not be overcome by a policy of censorship on the one hand, and women-only and feminist screenings on the other, since, by definition, an audience outside committed feminists does not exist for them. A more productive project would recognise the different stages of awareness of each member of an audience, and allow that individual to insert her/himself into it at any point. Whatever else, this project must have the political aim of transforming the present cultural resistance to feminist issues and feminist films into opposition to anti-women and anti-feminist films, and therefore to the social context in which misogyny has its roots.

Distributing 'A Question of Silence' – A Cautionary Tale

JANE ROOT

THREE women, strangers to each other, are browsing in a boutique. One, a down-trodden housewife with a toddler in a pushchair, slips a blouse into her shopping bag. The male proprietor of the shop sees her and smugly replaces the garment. As he does so the other two women begin ostentatiously shop-lifting themselves. One slaps the manager round the face. The others move towards him armed with coathangers and heavy glass ashtrays. . . .

A Question of Silence (directed by Marleen Gorris, 1982) was a film which dramatically divided audiences. Some women stood up and cheered, while other (often male) viewers left enraged. Female viewers frequently described it as a celebration of gut-level female solidarity and an allegorical tragi-comedy about male society: men, meanwhile, tended to see it as a serious 'social problem' picture or a shocking and distrubing attack on them as individuals. I was told that the Pizza Hut restaurant next door to one of the cinemas was full, night after night, with couples engaged in deep and sometimes angry arguments about the film. Three years later, the film is still a *cause célèbre*, referred to in some reviews to lure audiences and mentioned disparagingly in others as an example of shockingly uncontrolled feminism.

The aim of this article is not to give another reading of this much-discussed film or to investigate why men and women responded to it so differently. Instead, I want to offer a personal, tentative account of how the strategies used by the feminist distribution company, Cinema of Women, might have influenced the way *A Question of Silence* was received.

The part distributors play in the circulation of films is usually hidden from view, their role rarely discussed outside the industry. In fact, they are a vital link in the chain between film production and audiences. It is distributors who decide what can be shown where and distributors who make crucial decisions about a film's public profile: decisions which irrevocably affect the way a film is seen. Distributors' ideas about marketing shape the expectations an audience has as it enters a cinema – expectations which, as we all know, directly affect the pleasure or irritation gained from a film. More abstractly, the range of interpretations easily available to the rowing couples in the Pizza Hut are also a result of the different elements that make up a film's 'opening' – from critical reviews to distributor's decisions about cinemas, poster images, interviews of directors and actors, festival entries, advertising budgets and slogans. But, perhaps most important of all from a feminist point of view, distribution strategies directly affect *who* makes up the audience for any particular film.

This article is therefore an investigation of the complicated web of institutionalised images, vested interests, good intentions and arguments which surrounded the commercial release of *A Question of Silence*. This, I hope, will reveal something of the part distribution plays in the circulation and reception of all films, and also indicate some of the issues associated with distribution which particularly affect feminist film: issues which need to be properly confronted if feminist films are to reach the audiences they deserve.

Cinema of Women

Cinema of Women, *A Question of Silence*'s British distributor, is a collectively-run feminist company. It was set up five years ago to promote and circulate films (and more recently videos) directed by women which, in the words of its rather all-embracing constitution, 'speak from or about the position of women'. The films and videos themselves range from direct campaign-oriented work such as *Bitter Wages* on workplace health hazards to more complex theoretical work such as *Thriller* and *Daughter Rite*. I have been involved with Cinema of Women for four years, originally as a paid employee, now as a voluntary collective member.

On first viewing, *A Question of Silence* excited the collective for the same reasons it made cinema audiences cheer: its fresh combination of provocative politics and knowing humour about the everyday substance of women's lives. We were warmed by its central theme of unspoken female solidarity, and enjoyed the way that it gave serious attention to a whole range of feminist concerns – marriage, sexuality, job opportunities, age, childcare – without ever feeling like a lecture. At the same time, as distributors, we were also impressed by it as a feminist film with the potential to touch women outside the inevitably limited festival/women's group circuit. Here was a feature which might conceivably run for an extended period at a 'proper' cinema, something which delighted us as women linked by a love of the experience of cinema as well as a commitment to feminism. In retrospect, it offered us our biggest chance to date to try for a goal we all silently shared: to tap the vast and subversive potential of providing pleasurable experiences for specifically female cinemagoers.

A Question of Silence also meant, however, investing financially on a level we were unused to, directly confronting the workings and requirements of the commercial film world (albeit its independent end) and dealing with agents, cinema-owners and critics, groups of people who (with a few notable exceptions, such as Liz Wren at London's Everyman Cinema) had not been overwhelmingly friendly towards Cinema of Women in the past. Although, for instance, Marleen Gorris, the Dutch director of *A Question of Silence*, wanted Cinema of Women to distribute her film, we had to negotiate for it with her producer, Matthijs van Heijningen, and his British agent, Don Getz, both men with generalised interests in many different sectors of the film industry. Their decision to give it to us was made by comparing our deal (a combination of advance money, 'opening' cinemas and publicity budget – the finance borrowed in part from the British Film Institute) with those offered by other distributors, rather than because of any interest in us as a feminist company. In retrospect we were undoubtedly walking on thin ice. If, at that early stage, we had taken a pessimistic view of the situation, the issue might have seemed whether we were going either to bankrupt the company or be trapped into compromising the principles which had brought us into film distribution in the first place.

Art Cinema
When the time came for British journalists to interview Marleen Gorris, several were surprised by her insistence that it had not been difficult to get the money to make the film, despite her politics and lack of experience as a director. Indeed, some writers were so bewildered by this that they disregarded her comments and wrote stories about her 'struggle' to make the film regardless.

In fact, like *Coup de foudre*, *Friends and Husbands* and so many other European women's films, *A Question of Silence* was the product of a highly government-subsidised film industry, in this case the Dutch. Although the historical circumstances in different 'subsidising' countries vary considerably, Steve Neale has suggested that they are linked by a common political need to maintain a local film culture capable of disrupting Hollywood's potential domination. Accordingly, the very diverse films funded by these subsidies are linked by their proud assertion of *difference* from mainstream American films: the trademarks of which often include a prioritisation of visual elements and interior life over Hollywood-style narrative and action. Most centrally these films are seen as *art* rather than entertainment, a definition underlined by the way they tend to circulate as the 'unique personal visions' of supremely inspired individuals, rather than as generic, industrial products.

If what is commonly described as 'art cinema' developed in opposition to Hollywood, then many British independent practices are *against* art cinema – in particular, the elitism which tends to go hand-in-hand with understandings of cinema as high art. While the Cinema of Women collective, for instance, rarely had time to discuss the future of feminist film in abstract terms, there was an implicit feeling that the cinema we were aiming for would somehow combine the politics of agit-prop with the popularist pleasures of Hollywood rather than self-consciously define itself as art.

Despite such qualms, political groups have had to acknowledge that the institution of 'art cinema' has allowed a whole range of political films from *Weekend* to *The German Sisters* to be completed and circulated (comparatively) widely. As Steve Neale points out, 'Art Cinema has, historically, provided real – if limited – spaces for genuinely radical work. . . .' It is a definition which clearly includes *A Question of Silence*, a film which despite its explicit political purpose, is nevertheless placed firmly within most definitions of 'art cinema' by its funding, acting, music, photography and narrative features such as the central, interior conflict of the psychiatrist. Neale continues his discussion by saying, however, that 'the impact of that (radical) work has often been blocked and nullified by the overall institutional contexts in which it has found itself'.[1] The problem for Cinema of Women was to find a way to distribute *A Question of Silence* that prevented this from happening.

Not Art Cinema

Only a distribution strategy which set out to single-mindedly mis-represent the content of the film could have obliterated the marks of art cinema from the public profile of *A Question of Silence*. Since Cinema of Women had been started partly in order to stop feminist films being marketed in an unrepresentative way we had little desire to do this. And, in any case, we knew such campaigns are almost always counter-productive. Unless you are a beleaguered major using the last-ditch strategy of swamping cinemas with a particularly hopeless film, advertising heavily and hoping to make money before the bad news gets around, there is no sense in making an audience think they are going to get something they will not.

Another, equally drastic, solution involves changing the film itself by dubbing the voices. A major characteristic of art cinema's 'difference from Hollywood' is the use of non-English languages. When screened in Britain, the subtitles key into a deep institutional-ised conflict about whether Britain is part of 'mass', 'entertainment-oriented' American society, or linked to older, more 'artistic' European traditions. Subtitles become seen as the mark of 'serious art' and the anathema of entertainment to the extent that the phrase 'subtitled film' operates almost as a genre-description. When these resonances are added to the fact that the skill of reading subtitles rapidly cannot be assumed to be possessed by all of the potential audience for women's films, dubbing begins to become a serious option. In dealing with *A Question of Silence* it was, however, far too expensive for us to contemplate. But, given more capital and the possibility of, say, a circuit release, we might have committed what is usually seen as the ultimate heresy in art cinema circles.

A more realistic way forward involved the construction of a marketing image which placed the art cinema elements in a context that suggested the subversive pleasures we perceived in the film. Our campaign therefore had to do two jobs: to sell enough tickets to cover our costs *and* to attract viewers, particularly women, who might have missed the special attractions of *A Question of Silence* if it had been marketed simply as art cinema. We would not have been happy if *A Question of Silence* had been received in the same way as *Coup de foudre*: that is to say if it had been a commercial success by disguising its particularly female pleasures under a cloak of art cinema respectability.

In detail, the components of our campaign were:

Cinema choice: The strongly metropolitan bias of British film culture makes a London opening central to any commercial film campaign. First-run cinemas have very distinct images attached to them, images which inevitably colour perceptions of the films that open there. In London the Camden Plaza, Curzon, Screen on the Hill and Academy all have the reputation of showing art cinema – the latter venue (where *Coup de foudre* opened) carefully underlining this by using posters with 'arty' woodcuts rather than photographic designs. Despite their potentially higher revenue, none of these was our first choice. Instead, we were keen to open *A Question of Silence* simultaneously at the north London Screen on the Green and the now defunct southwest London Paris Pullman. To us, the Screen on the Green seemed perfectly poised between definitions of art and entertainment, showing a combination of mainstream releases, especially those associated with the art cinema influenced 'movie brat' American directors, the occasional political film, music-related features and cult titles such as *Eraserhead*. Interestingly in this context, these last two categories represent the only genres other than the government-subsidised art cinema in which independent film-makers can get finance to make widely shown films.

The film's title: I have already commented on the defining nature of foreign language; the use of foreign titles is a further, and perhaps particularly pretentious way of categorising a film as art. Along with its US distributors, we changed the title from *De Stilte Rond Christina M.* to *A Question of Silence*.

Posters and Advertisements: It was important to us that we marketed *A Question of Silence* as an enjoyable experience for women viewers in general – both those who would describe themselves as feminists and those who might be more wary of the phrase. Early designer's drafts for the poster and advertising image based around themes of imprisonment and violence were rejected in favour of an image based on the cathartic moment at the end of the film were the male legal system is literally laughed out of court. Our 'laughing women' poster also contravened some of the rather po-faced conventions of marketing art cinema, which tend to downplay the humour in order to sell more intellectually 'important' activities. The poster places the women alongside the slogan 'They had never met before but they agreed to kill together', creating a series of enigmas which are a feature of the marketing of the majority of entertainment films. Were the women the killers? Why were they laughing if they had just done a murder? Why did they kill with strangers?[2] At the same time the slogan emphasises the generic themes of murder and detection, clearly suggesting that *A Question of Silence* can be seen in relation to other thrillers. Or, at least, that thrillers are one point of reference among many: the art cinema origins of the films and our own ambivalence are signalled by the amount of space allowed for the festival prizes the film has won, a classic indicator of art cinema 'quality'. We were, however, certain that we wanted *A Question of Silence* to be seen primarily in the context of *film*, and not more respectable literary forms which are frequently referenced by art cinema.

Feminism: Our keenness that *A Question of Silence* be perceived as a women's film, made by a woman particularly for women, meant that we made an effort to publicise it to specifically feminist audiences through a variety of channels not normally considered by (or available to) other distributors such as *Spare Rib*, the *London Women's*

A Question of Silence

218

Liberation Newsletter and the newsletter of the Women's Resource and Research Centre, now the Feminist Library. Part of this work involved publicising the feminist nature of the Cinema of Women collective, hoping that the resonances created by this would adhere to films which had our name on them. This strategy of trying to create a strong, recognisable image for the distributor has been tried by only a few other UK companies, notably Palace Pictures.

The Critics

Our certainty about the importance of *A Question of Silence*, the positive responses we gained when we showed it privately and the prizes that it continued to win made us feel reasonably confident about its release. In fact, by the end of the first week the audience figures were so low it looked in danger of sinking without trace.

Without doubt, we had drastically underestimated the extent to which male critics (who vastly outnumber women in the British press) would perceive the film as a threat. This was nowhere more evident than in Milton Shulman's *Standard* review, which claimed that the film's resolution 'is an argument that would have justified the Nazis' exterminating Jews, Herod's slaughter of babies and the lynching of blacks'. He continued: 'Genocide is a comparatively modest moral device compared to the ultimate logic of this film's message.'[3] Shulman's near-hysterical comments were the most virulently expressed, but the sentiments were not limited to the *Standard*. John Coleman of the *New Statesman*'s total review amounted to a comment that the film 'tries to catch my gender in a Catch-22. To hell with it',[4] while Philip French in the *Observer* maintained that the film was 'inherently stupid', the 'unacceptable face of feminism' and 'in no fruitful sense provocative'.[5]

Shulman and French seemed particularly angered by the way the film had been presented. French writes disparagingly of the 'fashionable cinemas' exhibiting the film, while Shulman begins his review by saying that *A Question of Silence* 'boasts of its feminist origins as if they were battle honours'. Since the film itself studiously avoids a feminist milieu, it is clear that he is referring to the advertising campaign. Would their responses have been different if the film had been distributed by an established art cinema distributor such as Artifical Eye and had been unambiguously marketed as an art movie?

Obviously, distributors never encourage critics to make vitriolic attacks, but the damage done by such reviews can be less than that inflicted by those who damn with faint praise. Particularly harmful were the reviews which dismissed the film in the few lines normally reserved for soft porn and children's fare, using terms which made it seem a rather peculiar little piece of art cinema. Tim Pulleine, writing in the *Guardian*, noted briefly that the film's 'insights are not fused by the structural design into a compelling whole' and that it 'fails to find a narrative convention capable of converting special pleading into polemic whole'.[6] And, for the *Financial Times* it was 'a pancake flat fable on feminism with a few interesting twitches early on'.[7]

It might almost be said that in a perverse way Shulman and French *had* appreciated *A Question of Silence*: their responses (primed, perhaps, by our publicity campaign) came from an alarmed reading of the potentially disturbing implications of the film for men. They did not review it in the context of art cinema: for them it was a political film through and through. The same was not true for a larger and (on this film) possibly more influential group of critics. Not only were comments on the substantial political issues raised in the film missing from their accounts, but they also failed to be either shocked or appreciative of the political daring suggested by film-making aimed so partisanly at women audiences. For them it wasn't a question of being appalled by humour which dared to use male behaviour as its butt: in classical patriarchal style, they simply failed to recognise that any joke had been made. Surprisingly, the most notable exception to this is offered by the review in the ultra-conservative *Daily Telegraph* by Patrick Gibbs. After repeating an earlier festival review where he described *A Question of Silence* as 'the fiercest feminist film I have ever seen', Gibbs goes on to comment that 'My original suggestion that some touches of Buñuel fantasy might have helped now seems inept, for it would have enabled us to laugh it off as black comedy, whereas it is so realistically chilling that few males, I imagine, will leave it without examining painfully their consciences and their conduct.'[8]

As distributors we were never impressed by the common illusion that newspaper critics are impartial arbiters of taste. We knew from bitter experience that critics are best understood as a part of an industry. The space and time they give to particular films usually reflects the agenda of mainstream film culture – some films and issues are seen as inherently important, while others fall so far outside these parameters that they can hardly be dealt with at all. There was simply no conceptual room for these critics to examine the questions outlined above or to look at the contribution *A Question of Silence* makes to the development of a new and more popular kind of political film-making. That job was left to *Time Out*,[9] *City Limits*,[10] *Marxism Today*,[11] *Spare Rib*,[12] and most recently *Feminist Review*,[13] who all published detailed examinations of the film, and, in some cases, its reception. Unfortunately for us, only the first two of these have a large enough place within the commercial market to be useful in combating the brickbats from the newspapers.

We felt, again probably far too optimistically, that the feminist audience referred to above would be sympathetic to these issues and would need little encouragement to attend. In fact, as *Spare Rib* readership surveys prove, feminists are not, in the main, in the habit of going to cinemas or even of thinking of it as a potential place to spend their time. This contrasts strongly with feminist theatre, music and literature, which have, over the years, built up large and committed audiences and readerships. In addition to this, some feminists and aficionados of independent film share a particular antipathy for 'proper' cinemas like the Screen on the Green and what might be seen as exploitative attempts to cash in on 'fashionable feminism'.

This protective attitude to 'independence' can be perceived between the lines of the *City Limits* review. Feminist poet and novelist Michèle Roberts, who had presumably been employed because of her understanding of feminist *literature* rather than cinema, ends a generally lukewarm review by saying that the film is 'glossy and accessible.'[14] In the context of *City Limits'* review-speak these words suggest an experience which *other people*, less politically correct than the readers of the magazine, might enjoy, but might be found trivial and 'obvious' by those already enlightened. Yet again, the questions of female pleasure, female audiences and widely available political film-making are pushed underground, as was suggested by a letter in the magazine the following week complaining that the review 'does little to encourage viewers to flock to what is surely a major event for women's film'.

Strategies in Response to the Critics
In order to prevent the Screen on the Green and the Paris Pullman from prematurely replacing the film, Cinema of Women launched a 'rescue mission' aimed at transforming the generally favourable 'word-of-mouth' publicity we knew was circulating into audiences. Feminist businesses, women's newsletters and personal contacts were mobilised to help the film. Over 25,000 leaflets bearing the new slogan 'The critics were shocked but the audiences are cheering' were personally handed out by the collective and various press-ganged friends, mainly to women attending cinemas, theatres, political meetings, demonstrations and music events. Originally, leaflet distribution was used because it was a cheap alternative to press advertising, but I believe that the visible presence of Cinema of Women was also helpful in linking us (and the film) into the feminist community, thereby dispelling lingering doubts about the Screen on the Green. Overall, it is impossible to underestimate the importance of the response of the women's community in making the film a success.

At the same time we tried to use Shulman and French's reviews to our own advantage, press releasing them to journalists accompanied by a reply in the hope that the film might be covered in the news sections of papers and magazines. Partly, we were trying to convince feminists that the film was under attack and needed their support, but we also hoped that the publicity hook of 'the film that shocked critics' might bring in a few viewers. In effect, we were making a last-ditch attempt to occupy one of the few 'mainstream' critical spaces still available to the film: the category marked 'controversy'. By this point in the saga of the film's distribution we could not afford to ignore any possibilities for publicising the film, but we were aware of the uncomfortably marginalised space we were being forced into. Indeed, a few years later we and other feminists complained when almost all the feminist films in the London Film Festival appeared under a controversy heading, rather than in the main body of the festival. Although the tag can be useful in problematising real issues surrounding a film, all too often the phrase is used by distributors either too lazy or unimaginative to publicise hybrids, oddities or failures. Just as calling *Heaven's Gate* 'the most talked about film of the year' did little to lure people to an expansive and political western, we knew an obsessional concentration on the arguments of Shulman et al. about violence would not underline the pleasures for women we saw in the film.

Later Thoughts and a Bitter Postscript
Despite all the early problems *A Question of Silence* became a considerable success, transferring, within London, to the Gate Cinema in Bloomsbury, the Ritzy in Brixton and the Everyman in Hampstead. Even now, three years later, it is still drawing large crowds on the repertory circuit in and outside London. It has also achieved a central place within writing on feminist cinema. Cinema of Women was able to use the image it had given us and the leassons about distribution we had learned to promote subsequent features, including *Born in Flames*, *Leila and the Wolves* and *Committed*. We did not, however, get the chance to deal with the cinema release of the next and far more difficult film directed by Marleen Gorris, *Broken Mirrors*. Following our record with *A Question of Silence*, the huge multinational Thorn-EMI bought the rights for a sum we could not contemplate matching. Cinema of Women got the 16mm distribution of the film and gained the dubious pleasure of watching *Broken Mirrors* disappear from London cinemas with indecent haste, having failed to gain either general audiences or feminist support.

(This article was commissioned for the book and subsequently appeared in *Screen* vol. 26 no. 6, November/December 1985, pp. 58–64.)

Notes

1. Steve Neale, 'Art Cinema as Institution', *Screen* vol. 22 no. 1, 1981, pp. 11–39.
2. See John Ellis' discussion of film slogans in *Visible Fictions* (London: Routledge and Kegan Paul, 1983), pp. 31–5.
3. *The Standard*, 17 February 1983, p. 23.
4. *New Statesman*, 25 February 1983, p. 28.
5. *Observer*, 20 February 1983, p. 30.
6. *Guardian*, 17 February 1983, p. 13.
7. *Financial Times*, 18 February 1983, p. 17.
8. *Daily Telegraph*, 18 February 1983, p. 13.
9. Sarah Lefanu, 'A Matter of Murder', *Time Out*, 18–24 February 1983.
10. Helen Mackintosh, 'Asking Why', *City Limits*, 18–24 February 1983.
11. Sarah Lefanu, 'A Question of Silence', *Marxism Today*, February 1983, p. 37.
12. Mandy Merck, 'Contempt of Court', *Spare Rib* 128, March 1983, p. 26.
13. Sarah Montgomery, 'Women's Women's Films', *Feminist Review* 18, Winter 1984, pp. 39–41.
14. Michèle Roberts, *City Limits*, 18–24 February 1983, p. 20.

Appendix

CINEMA OF WOMEN (COW)

Why a Feminist Distribution?

We see the following reasons for needing a feminist film and video distribution:

a) We need to control our own culture. If we don't, films and videos made by women can be co-opted by men. For example, *Not a Love Story* (a film about pornography which includes pornography), distributed by a non-feminist distribution, has been shown in a Soho cinema as part of a raunchy double bill with *Prostitutes*.

b) Feminist film and video needs to be named as such from within the women's movement, not by the distribution establishment. For example, *Girlfriends* was presented and advertised as feminist simply because it was about a woman, despite the fact that it was anti-lesbian and negative about women (and boring!).

c) We can use money which comes from more 'popular' feminist films and videos to subsidise other feminist films and videos which do not have such a wide audience, and also this prevents this money being used to support sexist and pornographic work.

d) It helps encourage the exchange of feminist film/video ideas in Britain and other countries.

e) We can try to get feminist films/videos into mainstream television and cinema (e.g. *A Question of Silence, Born in Flames, Leila and the Wolves*).

f) This kind of work is being done in other areas of our culture (e.g. music and publishing).

Films and Videos We Distribute

We are a collective of six women and we try to look at as many women's films and videos as we can with a view to distribution. We decide to distribute them (or not) bearing in mind the following major priorities, although particular films or videos might bring up other considerations:

a) Films/videos dealing with specific areas (e.g. health, work, abortion, lesbianism) are always good as discussion starters and certain areas have quite a few films/videos and others have very few. So we try and build up areas that are under-represented (e.g. lesbianism).

b) Whether a film/video is feminist as opposed to (just) being made about or by women. We often need to ask groups working in particular areas what they think. For example, we would ask Rape Crisis Centre what they felt about a film/video we were considering on rape.

c) Whether we can financially afford to buy a print of a film.

d) How difficult the film/video will be to distribute (though if a film or video is difficult that doesn't necessarily mean we won't distribute it). For example, if a film or video made for a school audience is too long to show in lesson time it will be difficult to encourage teachers to use it. This is one of the reasons it is essential to have a link between film/video-makers and distribution.

e) Which women are included in the films/videos. For example, we prefer all our films/videos to include working-class women and women of colour, not just those that address themselves to the specific issues of class and race. But as is shown in the selection available these films and videos are in a minority. This is another reason that it is essential to have a link between film/video-making and distribution. Films or videos, for example, which have no women of colour in them are not relevant to huge groups of women.

To Whom We Distribute

a) Publicity: we actively publicise as widely as possible and do particular mailings for specific films/videos. For example, we have produced a leaflet on women at work and mailed to all trade unions.

b) Certain films/videos we distribute only to women's groups, for example *Self Health*, showing women's self-examination.

c) A wide range of groups such as CR groups, community groups, trade unions, black women's groups, schools, film societies, etc.

d) Regional film theatres and independent cinemas, whenever possible. In the past we have arranged Cinema of Women showings at cinemas such as the Ritzy, Brixton and we hope to increase this as it means that the films get to a wider audience, and thus increase chances of wider distribution. We have also now opened five feature films at London first-run cinemas.

Finance

Our basic running costs come from the percentage of the hire fee we charge. We keep 40% of the fee if we have not paid for the print (usually British films) and 50% if we have paid for the print (usually foreign films).

Until two years ago we have had very little outside funding and are finding it increasingly difficult to manage without this. During the last two years we have received capital and revenue funding from the GLC which has enabled us to employ another worker with responsibility for screenings in London.

Relationship With Film/Video-makers

We have found that it has been impossible to keep up with our original aims in maintaining close contact with all of our film/video-makers because of the workload involved in keeping the mechanics of distribution (taking bookings, cleaning and checking films and videos, parcelling them up, publicity, etc. . . .) going. So it has worked out that we have closer contact with film/video-makers who maintain interest in distribution and less contact with those who don't, or who live abroad. But with all film/video-makers we send them a list of the screenings together with their royalty statement every six months.

Structure of Cinema of Women

There are six women on the collective (Jane Root, Penny Ashbrook, Eileen McNulty, Vida Kashizadeh, Jenny Wallace and Denise Vale) some of whom do paid work in the office: fourteen days between us in all. Two of us work full-time in the office and two work part-time.

We have at various times advertised for women interested in distribution to join our support group, and new collective members have joined from there.

The support group has arranged screenings at community and arts centres and some members have often dropped out after the project they were involved in has ended. We are keen for women interested in distribution to become involved.

Relationship to the Women's Movement

We see ourselves as part of the Women's Movement and therefore responsible to it. In the past we have withdrawn films from distribution because of negative feedback (e.g. *Susana*, a film about a lesbian), and we ask for feedback whenever possible. Individual collective members are involved with other aspects of the women's movement and reflect the priorities of the movement when we are choosing films.

We have tried to raise in this paper some of the major issues we think are involved in feminist distribution and hope it will be a starting point for discussion.

CIRCLES

Circles is a feminist distribution network, set up by and for women, to distribute women's film and video, and to promote women's work in other related media such as tape-slide presentations and performance art. Circles also encourages research into the history of women's work in these areas. In addition to distributing films and videotapes, Circles organises women-only screenings with the opportunity for discussion afterwards. In this way Circles hopes to encourage more women to make and show their work on their own terms.

Structure/Membership

Every woman who has a film or video distributed by Circles is a 'member' of Circles and has a say in our policy-making. Circles is a company limited by guarantee (without share capital); it is non-profit making and its legal constitution has been drawn up to comply with requirements for registering as a charity. At its Annual General Meetings, Circles' members delegate responsibility for day-to-day running to an Executive Committee which meets on a monthly basis. This Committee (sometimes in consultation with specialist women's groups) is also ultimately responsible for the viewing and selection of new work to be included in the Circles catalogue. The film/video-maker's decision to place work with Circles reflects her commitment to the principles of feminist distribution.

Research

Women have been making films for the past ninety years, but much of this work has been hidden, or overlooked by 'historians'. As well as promoting current productions, Circles is also concerned to bring back into distribution women's work which has been previously unknown in this country, or which has been unavailable for a long time. It is important that earlier films are presented alongside contemporary material so that women can see that they have a history in film-making, and can begin to discover the threads which run through and link much of the work. Circles wishes to encourage more research by women for women, and is slowly building up a collection of reference materials which are available for consultation on its premises.

Women-Only Screenings

Circles organises regular women-only screenings at 113 Roman Road and elsewhere. Programmes are usually around a particular theme or issue (e.g. Women and Mental Health, childbirth, sexual politics) followed by discussions with the film/video-makers. Sometimes guest speakers, perhaps women from specialist groups, are invited to co-ordinate discussion. It is important that the barriers between film-maker and audience are broken down, and that there is interaction and feedback between the two. We also feel it is important to create a public space for discussion and for all women to participate in the making and showing of their work.

Programming and Audience

Because of the continuing male domination of education, there is still a tendency to ignore women's work. It is, therefore, important to get this work included in the curricula of more schools and colleges, as well as to ensure its availability generally. Programme information is sent, not only to mainstream education institutions, but also to women's, trade union and community groups around the country. Groups who cannot (or who do not wish to) attend Circles' screenings are encouraged to hire these programmes to stimulate their own discussions. Circles' films, videotapes and programming advice are available to individuals and to organisations which may have mixed audiences, but, as we wish to promote the idea of women-only screenings, reduced hire fees are offered to women's (and some educational) groups.

Working Practice
Circles sees the making, showing and distribution of films and videotapes as part of a unified practice whereby film/video-makers can retain control of their work. This is particularly important for women who must also have the opportunity to question dominant modes of representation. It is important, too, that women's work is not mis-appropriated and that contexts for that work are created both in Circles' catalogue and in the women-only screenings and discussions that are organised. It is equally important that women receive proper financial recognition for their work. For this reason, more than 50% (and usually 60–75%) of all rentals and sales is paid to the film-maker; any profits go back into Circles to enable it to continue its activities.

SHEFFIELD FILM CO-OP
Sheffield Film Co-op is a group of socialist feminist film-makers working together with the following aims:
    a) to produce films around issues of concern to women
    b) to develop our skills as film-makers
    c) to use these skills with other women in the community to enable them to have access to and control over their representation in the medium.

What Does it Do?
Sheffield Film Co-op is an ACTT-enfranchised workshop working under the workshop declaration. This is an ACTT union agreement which allows for the continuity of funding to groups in the indepen-dent film-making sector who are concerned most of all with the cultural, social and political contribution of their work as an alternative to mainstream and commercial product.

As socialist feminist film-makers working in film production, distribution and exhibition we place a high priority on engaging with the current concerns of ordinary women in the local community and on sensitively representing their experience in film. Our work is intended to combine a challenge to the usual representation of women in the media with the depiction of their real activity in society in a useful and accessible form. Using the documentary or drama-documentary format in different ways we have produced films on the important themes of abortion, domestic violence, job opportunities for girls, low-paid women's work and women's history. Currently we are working on a fiction around the theme of health and birth control.

We also have a wide-ranging distribution service and our films are regularly screened locally and nationally at community centres, women's groups, union meetings, schools, colleges and film centres. We welcome invitations to be present at screenings of the films where discussions with the audience can take place. This relationship with our audience plays a vital role in the continuing development of our film practice.

Sheffield Film Co-op hopes to continue producing films that are enjoyable and that stimulate discussion in a way which furthers the understanding of women's experience, their representation in film and the possibilities for social change.

How Did it Develop?
Sheffield Film Co-op was established in 1975 and made its early films on grants to specific film projects received from sponsors and other interested institutions, such as the British Pregnancy Advisory Service, the National Women's Aid Federation, the Equal Opportunities Commission and the Yorkshire Arts Association, and used the equipment resources of the Sheffield Independent Film Group.

It was not until 1980 that wages became an element of our financial support. We were registered as a Workers Co-operative in 1980 and joined the Association of Cinematograph Television and Allied Technicians. We received funding from the Yorkshire Arts Association and Sheffield City Council to support some full-time waged work and a programme of film production, distribution and exhibition activity. Our distribution network developed extensively and films were being shown at a wide range of local venues. Continuity of funding for these activities became more vital as independent film-making was developing on a national scale and other groups like ours were emerging. In response to this the Workshop Declaration was formulated within the ACTT, and confirmed the union's acknowledgment of the cultural and social intervention of independent film-makers and established a precedent for the regular funding of workshops like Sheffield Film Co-op. We became an enfranchised ACTT workshop in 1982 and received funding from the British Film Institute and were able to establish a production office and editing room with equipment from Channel Four Television. Further financial support for our work into 1984 comes from the newly set up BFI Regional Production Fund.

Sheffield Film Co-op Productions
A Woman Like You 1976 18 mins; *That's No Lady* 1977 14 mins; *Jobs For the Girls* 1979 29 mins; *A Question of Choice* 1982 18 mins; *Red Skirts on Clydeside* 1984 40 mins; *Changing Our Lives* 1984 18 mins; *Women of Steel* 1984 27 mins.

CATALOGUES/DOCUMENTATION

Cinema of Women Catalogue, obtainable from 27 Clerkenwell Close, London EC1.

The Circles Catalogue, ed. Felicity Sparrow, obtainable from 113 Roman Road, London E2.

The Other Cinema Women's Movement Catalogue, obtainable from 79 Wardour Street, London W1V 3TH.

First National Feminist Film and Video Conference Report Back, ed. South Wales Women's Film Group, Chapter Arts Centre, Cardiff.

Felicity Oppé, 'Distribution and Exhibition: the Practices of the Women's Movement', in Rod Stoneman and Hilary Thompson, ed., *The New Social Function of Cinema* (London: British Film Institute, 1981), pp. 136–9.

Filmography

Burning an Illusion
BFI Production Board 1981; *d/sc*: Menelik Shabazz; *ph*: Roy Cornwall; *ed*: Judy Seymour. *l.p*: Cassie McFarlane (*Pat Williams*), Victor Romero (*Del Bennett*), Beverley Martin (*Sonia*), Angela Wynter (*Cynthia*). 111 mins.

Coma
MGM 1977; *p*: Martin Erlichman; *d/sc*: Michael Crichton; *ph*: Victor J. Kemper; *ed*: David Bretherton. *l.p.*: Geneviève Bujold (*Dr Susan Wheeler*), Michael Douglas (*Dr Mark Bellows*), Elizabeth Ashley (*Mrs Emerson*), Rip Torn (*Dr George*), Richard Widmark (*Dr George A. Harris*). 113 mins.

Comedy in Six Unnatural Acts, A
USA 1976; *p/d/sc/ph/ed*: Jan Oxenberg. *l.p*: Evan Paxton, Sue Talbot, Jan Oxenberg, Susan Gluck, Jacci Weller, Joy Franklin, Cheryl Swannack, Ellen Broidy, Alice Bloch. 26 mins.

Daughter Rite
Chicago 1978; *d/sc/ed*: Michelle Citron; *ph*: Sharon Bement, Barbara Roos. *l.p*: Penelope Victor (*Maggie*), Anne Wilford (*Stephanie*), Jerri Hancock (*Narrator*). 50 mins.

Epic Poem, An
Eastern Arts 1982; *d*: Lezli-An Barrett. *l.p*: Henriette Park, David Sanction, Kay Flack, Rex Barker, Steve Hurrel, Kathy Biggs, Plume Tarrant. 25 mins.

German Sisters, The (Marianne and Juliane/Die bleierne Zeit)
1981; *p*: Eberhard Junkersdorf; *d/sc*: Margarethe von Trotta; *ph*: Franz Rath; *ed*: Dagmar Hirtz. *l.p*: Jutta Lampe (*Juliane*), Barbara Sukowa (*Marianne*); Rüdiger Vogler (*Wolfgang*); Verenice Rudolph (*Sabine*); Luc Bondy (*Werner*). 109 mins.

Girlfriends
Claudia Weill/New York State Council on the Arts/The National Endowment for the Arts/The Creative Artist Public Service Program/American Film Institute 1978; *p*: Claudia Weill, Jan Saunders; *d*: Claudia Weill; *sc*: Vicki Polon; *story*: Claudia Weill, Vicki Polon; *ph*: Fred Murphy; *ed*: Suzanne Pettit. *l.p*: Melanie Mayron (*Susan Weinblatt*), Eli Wallach (*Rabbi Gold*), Anita Skinner (*Anne Munroe*). 88 mins.

Jeanne Dielman, 23 Quai de Commerce – 1080 Bruxelles
Paradise Films, United Trois 175; *d/sc*: Chantal Akerman; *ph*: Babette Mangolte. *l.p*: Delphine Seyrig, Jan Decorte, Henri Storek, J. Doniol-Valcroze. 198 mins.

Julia
Twentieth Century-Fox 1977; *p*: Richard Roth; *d*: Fred Zinnemann; *sc*: Alvin Sargent. Based on the story in the collection *Pentimento* by Lillian Hellman.*ph*: Douglas Slocombe; *ed*: Walter Murch, Marcel Durham. *l.p*: Jane Fonda (*Lillian Hellman*), Vanessa Redgrave (*Julia*), Jason Robards (*Dashiell Hammett*). 117 mins.

Lianna
Winwood Company 1982; *p*: Jeffrey Nelson, Maggie Renzi; *d/sc/ed*: John Sayles; *ph*: Austin de Besche. *l.p*: Linda Griffiths (*Lianna*), Jane Hallaren (*Ruth*), Jon DeVries (*Dick*), John Sayles (*Jerry*). 112 mins.

Light Reading
p.c/p/d/sc/ph/ed/sd: Lis Rhodes 1978. 19 mins.

Maeve
British Film Institute in association with Radio Telefís Eireann 1981; *d*: Pat Murphy, John Davies; *sc*: Pat Murphy; *ph*: Robert Smith; *ed*: John Davies; *m*: Molly Brambeld and the Country Four. *l.p*: Mary Jackson, Mark Mulholland, Brid Brennan, Trudy Kelly, John Keegan, Nuala McCann, George Shane, Aingeal Greghan. 110 mins.

Mahogany
Nikor Film Industries 1975; *p*: Rob Cohen, Jack Ballard; *d*: Berry Gordy; *sc*: John Byrum. Based on a story by Toni Amber. *ph*: David Watkin; *ed*: Peter Zinner; *m*: Michael Masser; *cost*: Diana Ross. *l.p*: Diana Ross (*Tracy Chambers, 'Mahogany'*), Billy Dee Williams (*Brian Walker*), Anthony Perkins (*Sean McAvoy*), Jean-Pierre Aumont (*Christiano Rosetti*). 109 mins.

Not a Love Story
National Film Board of Canada 1981; *p*: Dorothy Todd Hénaut; *d/sc*: Bonnie Sherr Klein; *ph*: Pierre Letarte; *ed*: Anne Henderson; *m*: Ginette Bellavance. *l.p*: Bonnie Sherr Klein, Linda Lee Tracey. 68 mins.

Often During the Day
Four Corner Films 1979; *d*: Joanna Davis; *ph*: Wilfrid Thun. 15 mins.

Personal Best
Geffen Company. For Warners 1983. *p/d/sc*: Robert Towne; *ph*: Michael Chapman; *ed*: Ned Humphreys, Jere Huggins, Jacqueline Cambas, Walt Mulconery. *l.p*: Mariel Hemingway (*Chris Cahill*), Scott Glenn (*Terry Tingloff*), Patrice Donnelly (*Tory Skinner*), Kenny Moore (*Denny Stites*). 127 mins.

Question of Silence, A
Sigma Films 1982; *p*: Matthijs van Heijningen; *d/sc*: Marleen Gorris; *ph*: Frans Bromet; *ed*: Hans van Dongen. *l.p*: Edda Barends (*Christine*), Nelly Frijda (*Annie*), Henriette Tol (*Andrea*), Cox Habbema (*Dr Janine van den Bos*), Eddy Brugman (*Janine's husband*). 96 mins.

Self-Health
Lighthouse Films 1974; *d*: Catherine Allen, Judy Irola, Allie Light, Joan Musante. 23 mins.

Smiling Madame Beudet, The (Souriante Madame Beudet, La)
Vandal-Delac-Aubert 1923; *d*: Germaine Dulac. From the play by André
Obey and Denys Amiel. *l.p*: Germaine Dermoz, Alexandre C. Arquillière,
Madeleine Guitty, Jean d'Yd. 30 mins.

Song of the Shirt, The
Film and History Project 1979; *d*: Susan Clayton, Jonathan Curling; *ph*:
Jonathan Collinson, Anne Cottringer, Ieuan Morris; *ed*: Fran McLean; *m*:
composed and arranged by Lindsay Cooper. *l.p*: Martha Gibson, Geraldine
Pilgrim, Anne McNiff, Jill Greenhalgh, Sally Cranfield, Paul Bental, Fraser
Cains, Edward Clayton. 135 mins.

Unmarried Woman, An
Twentieth Century-Fox 1977; *p/d/sc*: Paul Mazursky; *ph*: Arthur Ornitz; *ed*:
Stuart H. Pappé. *l.p*: Jill Clayburgh (*Erica Benton*), Alan Bates (*Saul Kaplan*),
Michael Murphy (*Martin Benton*), Cliff Gorman (*Charlie*), Pat Quinn (*Sue*),
Kelly Bishop (*Elaine*). 124 mins.

Index